The Nature and Limits of Standards-Based Reform and Assessment

The Nature and Limits of Standards-Based Reform and Assessment

Defending Public Schools

EDITED BY
SANDRA MATHISON AND E. WAYNE ROSS

Teachers College, Columbia University
New York and London

Library of Congress Cataloging-in-Publication Data

The nature and limits of standards-based reform and assessment : defending public schools
  / edited by Sandra Mathison and E. Wayne Ross.
      p. cm.
    Originally published in hard cover as v. 4 of Defending public schools: Praeger :
  Westport, CT, 2004.
    Includes bibliographical references and index.
    ISBN 978-0-8077-4901-2 (pbk. : alk. paper)
    1. Education—Standards—United States.   2. Educational tests and measurements—
  United States—Evaluation.   3. Educational change—United States.   4. Public
  schools—United States.   I. Mathison, Sandra.   II. Ross, E. Wayne, 1956–
  III. Defending public schools.
  LB3060.83.N38 2008
  379.73—dc22   2008017459

Defending Public Schools Vol. IV: The Nature and Limits of Standards-Based Reform and Assessment, edited by Sandra Mathison and E. Wayne Ross, was orignally published in hard cover by Praeger, www.greenwood.com/praeger an imprint of Greenwood Publishing Group, Inc., Westport, CT. Copyright © 2004 by Sandra Mathison and E. Wayne Ross. This paperback edition by arrangement with Greenwood Publishing Group, Inc. All rights reserved.

ISBN 978-0-8077-4901-2

Printed on acid-free paper

Manufactured in the United States of America

15 14 13 12 11 10 09 08   8 7 6 5 4 3 2 1

For Colin
and children everywhere
who deserve schools that live up to their promise
and for
all those who resist tyrannical accountability in education.

Contents

General Editor's Introduction: Defending Public Schools, Defending Democracy

E. Wayne Ross

WHY DO PUBLIC SCHOOLS NEED TO BE DEFENDED?

Why do public schools need to be defended? This may be the first question some readers have about this multivolume collection of essays, and it's a good one. Certainly, the title suggests schools are under attack, and they are. Public schools in the United States have always carried a heavy burden as one of the principal instruments in our efforts to create an ideal society. For example, public schools have been given great responsibility for equalizing gender and racial inequalities, providing the knowledge and skills that give everyone an equal opportunity to experience the "American Dream," producing a workforce with skills that enable U.S. corporations to compete effectively in the global marketplace, and preparing citizens to be effective participants in a democratic society, just to name a few.

Critics of public schools come from across the political spectrum, but it is important to understand the reasons behind the various criticisms of public schools. The diverse responsibilities of public schools present a huge challenge to educators, and even when schools are performing well, it is difficult, if not impossible, for them to deliver all the expected results when their mission necessarily entails contradictory purposes. For example:

- Should schools focus on increasing equity or increasing school performance (e.g., student test scores)?
- Should the school curriculum be limited to the development of students'

cognitive processes, or do schools have a responsibility for supporting the development of the whole person?

- Should public schools serve the interests of the state, or should they serve the interests of local school communities?
- Should schools prepare a workforce to meet economic needs identified by corporations, or should they prepare students to construct personally meaningful understandings of their world and the knowledge and skills to act on their world?
- Should schools be an instrument of cultural transmission with the goal of preparing students to adopt (and adapt to) the dominant culture, or should schools function as an engine for social and cultural change, reconstructing society based upon principles of progress aimed at amelioration of problems?

It is important not to view the contradictory goals of public education as merely "either/or" questions as presented above. The terrain of public schooling, as with all aspects of the human endeavor, is too complex to be reduced to dualisms.

PUBLIC SCHOOLS IN A DEMOCRACY[1]

In his magnum opus *Democracy and Education*, John Dewey—widely regarded as America's greatest philosopher—states that all societies use education as means of social control in which adults consciously shape the dispositions of children. He continues by arguing that "education" in and of itself has no definite meaning until people define the kind of society they want to have. In other words, there is no "objective" answer to the question of what the purposes and goals of public schools should be.

The implication of Dewey's position is that we—the people—must decide what we want our society to be and, with that vision in mind, decide what the purposes of public education should be. The challenge then is assuring that a pluralism of views on the nature and purposes of public schools is preserved in the process of defining what they should be. This is the problem of democracy. It also explains why public schools are the object of criticism from various points along the political spectrum (e.g., from liberals and conservatives) as schools become the context in which we work out, in part, our collective aims and desires and who we are as a people.

Our understanding of what happens (as well as what various people would like to see happen) in U.S. public schools can be enhanced by taking a closer look at our conceptions of democracy and how democracy functions in contemporary American society.

Democracy is most often understood as a system of government providing a set of rules that allow individuals wide latitude to do as they wish. The first principle of democracy, however, is providing means for giving power to the people, not to an individual or to a restricted class of people. "Democracy," Dewey said, is "a mode of associated living, of conjoint communicated experience."[2] In this conception, democratic life involves paying attention to the multiple implications of our actions on others. In fact, the primary responsibility of democratic citizens is concern with the development of shared interests that lead to sensitivity to the repercussions of their actions on others. Dewey further characterized democracy as a force that breaks down the barriers that separate people and creates community.

From a Deweyan perspective, democracy is not merely a form of government nor is it an end in itself; it is the means by which people discover, extend, and manifest human nature and human rights. For Dewey, democracy has three roots: (a) free individual existence, (b) solidarity with others, and (c) choice of work and other forms of participation in society. The aim of a democratic society is the production of free human beings associated with one another on terms of equality.

Dewey's conception of democracy contrasts sharply with the prevailing political economic paradigm—neoliberalism. Although the term *neoliberalism* is largely unused by the public in the United States, it references something everyone is familiar with—policies and processes that permit a relative handful of private interests to control as much as possible of social life in order to maximize their personal profit.[3] Neoliberalism is embraced by parties across the political spectrum, from right to left, and is characterized by social and economic policy that is shaped in the interests of wealthy investors and large corporations. The free market, private enterprise, consumer choice, entrepreneurial initiative, and government deregulation are some important principles of neoliberalism.

Neoliberalism is not new. It is merely the current version of the wealthy few's attempt to restrict the rights and powers of the many. Although democracy and capitalism are popularly understood (and often taught) as "birds of a feather," the conflict between protecting private wealth and creating a democratic society is conspicuous throughout U.S. history. The framers of the U.S. Constitution were keenly aware of the "threat" of democracy. According to James Madison, the primary responsibility of government was "to protect the minority of the opulent against the majority." Madison believed the threat to democracy was likely to increase over time as there was an increase in "the proportion of those who will labor under all the hardships of life and secretly sigh for a more equal distribution of its blessing."[4]

In crafting a system giving primacy to property over people, Madison and the framers were guarding against the increased influence of the unpropertied masses. The Federalists expected that the public would remain compliant and deferential to the politically active elite—and for the most part that has been true throughout U.S. history. Despite the Federalists' electoral defeat, their conception of democracy prevailed, though in a different form, as industrial capitalism emerged. Their view was most succinctly expressed by John Jay—president of the Continental Congress and first Chief Justice of the U.S.

Supreme Court—who said that "the people who own the country ought to govern it." Jay's maxim is a principle upon which the United States was founded and is one of the roots of neoliberalism.

For over two hundred years, politicians and political theorists have argued *against* a truly participatory democracy that engages the public in controlling their own affairs; for example, founding father Alexander Hamilton warned of the "great beast" that must be tamed. In the twentieth century, Walter Lippman warned of the "bewildered herd" that would trample itself without external control, and the eminent political scientist Harold Lasswell warned elites of the "ignorance and stupidity of the masses" and called for elites not to succumb to the "democratic dogmatisms" about people being the best judges of their own interests.

These perspectives have nurtured a neoliberal version of democracy that turns citizens into spectators, deters or prohibits the public from managing its own affairs, and controls the means of information.[5] This may seem an odd conception of democracy, but it is the prevailing conception of "liberal-democratic" thought—and it is the philosophical foundation for current mainstream approaches to educational reform (known collectively as "standards-based educational reform"). In spectator democracy, a specialized class of experts identifies what our common interests are and thinks and plans accordingly. The function of the rest of us is to be "spectators" rather than participants in action (for example, casting votes in elections or implementing educational reforms that are conceived by people who know little or nothing about our community, our desires, or our interests).

Although the Madisonian principle that the government should provide special protections for the rights of property owners is central to U.S. democracy, there is also a critique of inequality (and the principles of neoliberalism)—in a tradition of thought that includes Thomas Jefferson, Dewey, and many others—that argues that the root of human nature is the need for free creative work under one's control.[6] For example, Thomas Jefferson distinguished between the aristocrats, "who fear and distrust the people and wish to draw all powers from them into the hands of the higher classes," and democrats, who "identify with the people, have confidence in them, cherish and consider them as the most honest and safe . . . depository of the public interest."[7]

Dewey also warned of the antidemocratic effects of the concentration of private power in absolutist institutions, such as corporations. He was clear that as long as there was no democratic control of the workplace and economic systems, democracy would be limited, stunted. Dewey emphasized that democracy has little content when big business rules the life of the country through its control of "the means of production, exchange, publicity, transportation and communication, reinforced by command of the press, press agents and other means of publicity and propaganda." "Politics," Dewey said, "is the shadow cast on society by big business, the attenuation of the shadow will not change the substance." A free and democratic society, according to Dewey, is one where people are "masters of their own . . . fate."[8]

Therefore, when it comes to determining the purposes of public schools in a democracy, the key factor is how one conceives of what democracy is and, as illustrated earlier, there are longstanding contradictions about the nature of democracy in the United States. In the contemporary context, mainstream discourse on the problems and the solutions for public schools has been based upon the principles of neoliberalism and manifest in standards-based educational reform, the subject of many of the contributions to *Defending Public Schools.*

WHY ARE WE DEFENDING PUBLIC SCHOOLS?

The editors and authors of *Defending Public Schools* are not interested in defending the status quo. Each contributor is, however, very interested in preserving public schools as a key part of the two-centuries-old experiment that is American democracy. Public schools are in a centripetal position in our society and, as result, they always have been and will continue to be battle-grounds for conflicting visions of what our society should be.

We believe that public schools serve the public, "We, the people." We believe that schools should strengthen our democracy in the sense that our ability to meaningfully participate in the decision-making processes that impact our communities and our lives is enhanced, not constricted. Educational resources need to be directed toward increasing people's awareness of the relevant facts about their lives and increasing people's abilities to act upon these facts in their own true interests. Since the 1980s and even before, the purposes of public schools have been by the interests of the state and of concentrated private/corporate power, as follows from what I described earlier, as neoliberalism. We believe that public education ought to serve public interests, not the interests of private power and privilege.

At a time when our democracy and many of the liberties we hold dear are in crisis, we propose that the preservation of public schools is necessary to reverse antidemocratic trends that have accelerated under standards-based educational reforms, which intend to transform the nature and purposes of public schools and our society. Each of the volumes in *Defending Public Schools* takes on a different aspect of education, yet these volumes are bound together by the underlying assumption that preserving public schools is a necessary part of preserving democracy. The following ten points provide a synopsis of what defending public schools means to us:

1. The statist view of schools treats teachers as mere appendages to the machinery of the state and seeks to hold them accountable to serving the interests of state power. Linked as it is to the interests of private wealth, this view defines children's value in life as human resources and future consumers. Education

should foster critical citizenship skills to advance a more viable and vibrant democratic society. Schools should be organized around preparing for democratic citizenship through engagement with real-world issues, problem solving, and critical thinking, and through active participation in civic and political processes. Informed citizenship in a broad-based, grassroots democracy must be based on principles of cooperation with others, nonviolent conflict resolution, dialogue, inquiry and rational debate, environmental activism, and the preservation and expansion of human rights. These skills, capacities, and dispositions need to be taught and practiced.

2. The current system uses "carrots and sticks" to coerce compliance with an alienating system of schooling aimed at inducing conformity among teachers and students through high-stakes testing and accountability. This system alienates teachers from their work by stripping it of all creative endeavors and reduces it to following scripted lesson plans. We believe that teaching is a matter of the heart, that place where intellect meets up with emotion and spirit in constant dialogue with the world around us. We call for the elimination of high-stakes standardized tests and the institution of more fair, equitable, and meaningful systems of accountability and assessment of both students and schools.

3. Current federal educational policy, embodied in the No Child Left Behind Act, sets impossible standards for a reason. Public access to institutions of learning helps promote the levels of critical civic activism witnessed during the 1960s and 1970s that challenged the power of the state and the corporations that it primarily serves. The current reform environment creates conditions in which public schools can only fail, thus providing "statistical evidence" for an alleged need to turn education over to private companies in the name of "freedom of choice." In combination with the growing corporate monopolization of the media, these reforms are part of a longer-range plan to consolidate private power's control over the total information system, thus eliminating avenues for the articulation of honest inquiry and dissent.

4. The current system of public schooling alienates students by stripping learning from its engagement with the world in all of its complexity. It reduces learning to test preparation as part of a larger rat race where students are situated within an economic competition for dwindling numbers of jobs. We believe that educational excellence needs to be defined in terms of teachers' abilities to inspire children to engage the world, for it is through such critical engagement that true learning (as opposed to rote memorization) actually occurs. Students living in the twenty-first century are going to have to deal with a host of problems created by their predecessors: global warming and other ecological disasters, global conflicts, human rights abuses, loss of civil liberties, and other inequities. The curriculum needs to address what students need to know and be able to do in the twenty-first century to tackle these problems—and it needs to be relevant to students' current interests and concerns.

5. Teachers matter. Teaching is a public act that bears directly on our collective future. We must ensure the quality of the profession by providing meaningful forms of preparation, induction, mentoring, professional development, career advancement, and improved working conditions. High learning standards should serve as guidelines, not curricular mandates, for teachers. Restore teacher control, in collaboration with students and communities, over decision mak-

ing about issues of curriculum and instruction in the classroom—no more scripted teaching, no more mandated outcomes, no more "teacher-proof" curricula. Local control of education is at the heart of democracy; state and nationally mandated curriculum and assessment are a prescription for totalitarianism.

6. In the past two decades, the corporate sector has become increasingly involved with education in terms of supplementing public spending in exchange for school-based marketing (including advertising space in schools and textbooks, junk fast-food and vending machines, and commercial-laden "free" TV). We believe that students should not be thought of as a potential market or as consumers, but as future citizens.

7. All schools should be funded equally and fully, eliminating the dependence on private corporate funds and on property taxes, which create a two-tiered educational system by distributing educational monies inequitably. Include universal prekindergarten and tuition-free higher education for all qualified students in state universities.

8. Children of immigrants make up approximately 20 percent of the children in the United States, bringing linguistic and cultural differences to many classrooms. Added to this are 2.4 million children who speak a language other than English at home. Ensure that the learning needs of English language learners are met through caring, multicultural, multilingual education.

9. Citizens in a pluralistic democracy need to value difference and interact with people of differing abilities, orientations, ethnicities, cultures, and dispositions. Discard outmoded notions of a hypothetical norm, and describe either *all* students as different, or none of them. All classrooms should be *inclusive*, meeting the needs of all students together, in a way that is just, caring, challenging, and meaningful.

10. All students should have opportunities to learn and excel in the fine and performing arts, physical education and sports, and extracurricular clubs and activities in order to develop the skills of interaction and responsibility necessary for participation in a robust civil society.

In the end, whether the savage inequalities of neoliberalism—which define current social and national relations as well as approaches to school reform—will be overcome depends on how people organize, respond, learn, and teach in schools. Teachers and educational leaders need to link their own interests in the improvement of teaching and learning to a broad-based movement for social, political, and economic justice, and work together for the democratic renewal of public life and public education in America.

***

I would like to acknowledge the many people who have contributed to the creation of *Defending Public Schools*.

Each of my coeditors—David Gabbard, Kathleen Kesson, Sandra Mathison and Kevin D. Vinson—are first-rate scholars, without whom this project could never have been completed. They have spent untold hours conceiving of, writing for, and editing their respective volumes. I have learned much from them as educators, researchers, and as advocates for more just and democratic schools and society.

I would also like to acknowledge the truly remarkable contributions of the chapter authors who have provided *Defending Public Schools* with cutting-edge analysis of the most recent educational research and practice. I know of no other work on issues of public schooling that brings together a comparable collection of highly respected scholars, researchers, and practitioners.

I would be terribly remiss not to acknowledge the tremendous support and invaluable advice I have received from my editor, Marie Ellen Larcada. *Defending Public Schools* was initially envisioned by Marie Ellen, and she has been an essential part of its successful completion. Additionally, I would like to thank Shana Grob who, as our editorial assistant, was always attentive to the crucial details and made editing these four volumes a much more manageable and enjoyable job.

Thanks also to the folks who inspire and support me on a daily basis, comrades who are exemplary scholars, teachers, and activists: Perry Marker, Kevin Vinson, Steve Fleury, David Hursh, Rich Gibson, Jeff Cornett, Marc Bousquet, Heather Julien, Marc Pruyn, Valerie Pang, Larry Stedman, Ken Teitelbaum, Ceola Ross Baber, Lisa Cary, John Welsh, Chris Carter, Curry Malott, Richard Brosio, and Dave Hill.

Lastly, words cannot express my love for Sandra, Rachel, and Colin.

Introduction:
The Nature and Limits
of Standards-Based Reform
and Assessment

SANDRA MATHISON AND E. WAYNE ROSS

The second half of the twentieth century witnessed two major and distinct educational reform movements in the United States. It seems *de rigueur* for any article on educational reform in the United States to mention the launching of the Soviet satellite *Sputnik* in 1957 and the U.S. Department of Education's National Commission on Excellence in Education report *A Nation at Risk*, published in 1983. While these events produced dramatically different consequences, they both illustrate how the nature of educational reform efforts cannot be separated from the social, political, and economic circumstances of the times.

The launch of *Sputnik I* has been described as a "technological Pearl Harbor." The success of the world's first artificial satellite, which was the size of a basketball and weighed only 183 pounds, produced a massive response. In the context of the Cold War, *Sputnik* not only jump-started the "space race" between the United States and the USSR, but also ushered in new military, political, scientific, technical, as well as educational developments. The month following the *Sputnik* launch, President Dwight Eisenhower addressed the nation from the Oval Office on the topic of "Science in National Security." Eisenhower declared that "one of our greatest, most glaring deficiencies is the failure of us in this country to give high enough priority to scientific education and to the place of science in our national life." He also called the shortage of highly skilled workers "the most critical problem of all."[1]

The following year, Congress passed The National Defense Education Act, which was a turning point in educational policymaking, providing an enormous level of new federal spending on education, including money for university scholarships and loans as well as resources for the development of new curriculum materials for public schools in all areas, but particularly in mathematics and science. Well-funded teams of disciplinary knowledge specialists, psychologists, and educators produced a wide variety of curriculum projects.[2] Although the development and dissemination of these projects were well funded, they failed to have a major or lasting effect on teaching practices or the curricular focus of classrooms. Some have argued that the failure of these projects was attributable to technical problems, such as inadequate training of teachers to use the packages or lack of formative evaluation. In contrast, proponents of grassroots democracy in curriculum argue the failure was due to the blatant disregard of teachers and students in the curriculum development process. This point is ironic inasmuch as the authors of these curriculum projects, who promoted "discovery" and "inquiry" approaches to learning, neglected to allow inquiry by teachers, students, and other stakeholders about matters most fundamental to their lives, that is, inquiry about what is most worthwhile to know and experience.[3]

The post-*Sputnik* era of educational reform left little residue in public schools; however, the most recent reform efforts have produced a sea change in public schools, but, as the chapters that follow argue, this dramatic shift has not necessarily produced improved teaching and learning. *A Nation at Risk* must also be understood in the context of the Cold War. By 1983, the circumstances were vastly different from the post-*Sputnik* reform era, the Cold War was waning, and within five years the Berlin Wall would fall. The military and political concerns of the Cold War, which had previously provided the impetus for educational reform, gave way to more explicit economic concerns.

A Nation at Risk linked—dubiously[4]—American education performance with the decline in the "once unchallenged preeminence [of the United States] in commerce, industry, science and technological innovation." The report's recommendations focused attention on raising expectations for student learning. The National Commission on Excellence in Education encouraged states and local schools to adopt tougher graduation requirements (for example, requiring students to take more of the basic subjects), extend the school year, and administer standardized achievement tests as a part of nationwide, but not federal, system of examinations. Concern for student performance standards (what students should know and be able to do) was transformed into specific content standards and, with the passage of the No Child Left Behind Act (NCLB) in 2001, federally mandated testing was linked with financial sanctions for schools not meeting specific test score goals.

The fundamental assumption of the standards-based educational reform (SBER) movement, of which NCLB is the crowning achievement, is that uniform, externally formulated goals along with content standards and a strict accountability system (that relies upon high-stakes tests) can improve curriculum and instruction. The history of educational reform illustrates, however, that changing educational polices is much easier than changing the conditions and operation of schools. Despite many efforts to reform schools in the past century, the major features remain largely unchanged.[5] A number a factors account for the stability of schools in the face of repeated reform efforts:

1. Schools are structured and teaching roles defined in ways that make improved teaching performance difficult to achieve. Schools are fragmented with artificial barriers between disciplines and between teachers (e.g., distinct subject matters, narrow time blocks for teaching, teaching in isolation and teachers working in isolation).
2. The inadequacies of in-service education, which generally asks teachers to leave their classrooms so that they can travel to distant locations in order to get general advice from people who have never seen them teaching.
3. Rigid and enduring norms define what teachers are supposed to be, how children are supposed to act, and what constitutes an appropriate set of expectations for a subject.
4. Conservative expectations for the function of schools. It is difficult for the schools to exceed in aim, form, and content what the public is willing to accept.
5. Reformers typically view teachers as the conduit for the delivery of curriculum. Reformers usually strive to create a uniform program for students regardless of who they are or where they live, which requires centralized decision making. This marginalizes teachers in the curriculum development process.
6. Changes that require new content and new repertoires are likely to be met with resistance by teachers who have not participated in the development of an initiative and have defined for themselves an array of routines (regarding what and how to teach) they can efficiently employ.
7. Fragmented efforts to change schools that fail to account for the multiple dimensions of the ecology of schools (e.g., purposes, structures, curriculum, pedagogy, and evaluation).[6]

NCLB, the progeny of *A Nation at Risk*, is creating important changes in schools, in part because the advocates of SBER have been successful in reconfiguring the *discourse* of educational reform, that is, establishing the boundaries of what should be the appropriate or legitimate function of schools in our society. For example, the primary goal of schooling, student learning, has been redefined as "test scores" rather than authentic knowledge, skills, or abilities. As a result, the school curriculum has also been narrowed to focus merely on what is tested; and a further implication is that teachers' have been de-skilled (e.g., their professional autonomy is eroded) by requirements to teach from scripted lesson plans that are keyed to test content. The discourse of standards then has reshaped the way we think about students as learners, teachers as professionals, the nature of the curriculum, as well as the appropriate indicators of "educational progress."

The factors that have accounted for previous stability of schools have been challenged, indeed trumped, in many instances by SBER. Unlike previous educational reform efforts, SBER is not a fragmented approach to educational change but rather a systematic—even totalizing—approach that has standardized the goals of schools, redefined the work of educators (and students), and passed into law a system of rewards and sanctions to ensure compliance.

Our goal in this collection of essays is to present readers with an overview of the origins and development of standards-based educational reform and assessment; a description of SBER's essential elements; and a critical analysis of the means and ends of what is perhaps the most important reform effort U.S. schools have ever experienced.

OVERVIEW OF THE BOOK

Sandra Mathison opens our examination of standards and assessment in education with a historical overview of the mental measurement and curriculum standards movements in schools. She traces the use of standardized tests in schools back to the mid-nineteenth century and Horace Mann's concern for a lack of quality and consistency in Massachusetts public schools, and follows the development of the field of educational measurement from its infancy (at the turn of the twentieth century) to the present, emphasizing the importance of both technical developments as well as the social, political, and economic nature of measurement. She also traces the development of the curriculum standards movement and how it set the stage for the currently dominant approach to educational accountability, embodied in NCLB. The chapters that follow in this volume discuss the nature, limits, and alternatives to the typical testing strategies that are the accountability mechanism inherent in the standards-based educational reform movement.

In chapter 2, James Popham argues that SBER is a good idea gone bad as a result of two fundamental implementation mistakes. First, he argues that state-level curriculum standards identify too many outcomes. As a result, there is not enough time in the school year to teach (and test) all the specified material. The second mistake stems from the selection of the wrong kinds of tests to find out what students have learned. Too often states employ tests that are instructionally insensitive. And, as Popham says, "to use students' performances on instructionally insensitive tests to identify instructionally effective (or ineffective) schools is every bit as silly as it sounds."

Alfie Kohn outlines "The Costs of Overemphasizing Achievement" in chapter 3. Kohn argues that assessment should be the servant of teaching and learning, rather than the reverse. Assessment that aims to motivate students (through rewards or punishment) or to sort students (e.g., to figure out who is better than whom) is wrongheaded and actually undermines excellence in learning. Kohn describes the disturbing consequences that result from encouraging students to focus on how well they are doing something (test scores) rather than focusing on what they are doing (authentic learning): valuing ability over effort, shallow thinking, avoiding challenging tasks, perceiving learning as a "chore"—all are conditions that undermine genuine excellence in education.

International comparisons of student achievement have dominated headlines in recent years and as a result, educators, politicians, and the public are attuned to how U.S. students stack up against other students from around the world. But as Gerald Bracey illustrates in chapter 4, while procedures for conducting international comparisons have gotten much better, that does not mean these comparisons are without problems. Unfortunately, there has been little critical scrutiny of the international comparisons in this country. In this chapter, Bracey pays particular attention to the meanings constructed from the results of international comparisons, particular the Third International Mathematics and Science Study and connections that are often made between U.S. global economic competitiveness and international student achievement rankings.

The No Child Left Behind Act, passed in 2001, is one of the most important pieces of federal education legislation ever passed. In chapter 5, "Assessment, Accountability, and the Impossible Dream," Linda Mabry examines the rhetoric and reality of NCLB. The rhetoric is attractive—who wants to leave any child behind? But, as Mabry illustrates, it is a matter of contention whether NCLB articulates a "wonderful dream" for inspiring new accomplishments or if it is a nightmare of unintended consequences. Her detailed analysis of NCLB and the research on educational reform concludes that "Perseverance even toward laudable goals becomes perseveration when mounting negative evidence is ignored or when taken too far. The benefits of universal education do not make universal education *standards* beneficial. The benefits of compulsory education do not make compulsory *achievement targets* beneficial. History, recent experience, and research offer critical cautions."

"To say that we want to hold schools accountable only for test scores is saying that nothing else matters—not what a school offers to students in terms of opportunities and challenges, not the quality of relationships that exists to sustain children and adults in the work that they do, not what capacities students demonstrate outside of the narrow curriculum that is tested, not how responsive a school is to its parents and community." In chapter 6, Ken Jones argues that schools should be held accountable to change and improve to better serve the needs of all students but that the present accountability system, which relies on high-stakes testing, does not help schools improve. Jones offers us an approach to accountability that is based on the premises that schools should be accountable to students, parents, and the local community for the physical and emotional well-being of students; for student learning; for teacher learning; for equity and access; and for overall improvement as learning organizations. In short, he describes a new model for school accountability that redefines the discourse of educational reform.

It is apparent how assessment mechanisms embedded within current school reform efforts affect what happens in classrooms. However, there are areas of practice more hidden but equally affected. Mathison and Muñoz believe that evaluation practice, done well, can contribute to the democratization of schools; however, state-mandated assessments have stripped the practice of evaluation of much of this potential for inclusiveness and improvement, and redirected resources to creating and maintaining student assessment systems including test administration, analysis, and reporting activities. In a chapter written in part as a play, they present research that shows how state-mandated assessments have contributed to bad evaluation practice and limited our knowledge of the impact of current educational reforms.

Accountability strategies of school reform that rely heavily on measuring outcomes with accompanying consequences, either positive or negative, affect everyone and every aspect of schools. Chapter 8, by Sandra Mathison and Melissa Freeman, examines the ways state curriculum standards and mandated student testing, the primary vehicle of accountability, affect teachers' work. Drawing on their studies of the impact of standards-based reform efforts in elementary and middle schools, Mathison and Freeman describe the dilemmas and difficulties teachers face in maintaining professionalism and in helping all children to succeed in a school climate dominated by concern for increasing test scores. State-mandated curriculum and testing places teachers in a "lose–lose" situation where they often act in ways inconsistent with what they believe to be the best teaching practices in order to increase the likelihood that students will succeed on state tests. As a result, "Teachers must often do the wrong thing in order to do the right thing, sort of." Mathison and Freeman present a portrait of teachers who are more angry and frustrated than better as a result of standards-based reforms and assessment.

Teachers and students are not the only stakeholders affected by standards-based reform and assessments. Melissa Freeman examines the issue of parental involvement in chapter 9. Freeman brings the voices of two different groups of parents to the forefront in her effort to answer two questions: (1) To what extent are parents really partners in the standards-based accountability movement? and (2) When government officials speak of parents, what kind of parent are they talking about? Freeman's work is "based on the idea that listening to parents talk about their experiences with testing can foster an understanding of how the culture of accountability affects different parents' understandings of their role as partners in their children's education and what those understandings reveal about their expectations of a public school system."

She concludes that the vision of good schooling that depends on students passing high-stakes tests is a vision that favors "the privileged over the underprivileged and is not a view that seeks a strong education system for all." Developing and sustaining relationships between parents and schools requires educators, policymakers, and parents to work toward public educational systems that improve schooling for everyone.

Margaret J. McLaughlin and Katherine M. Nagle explore the ambiguities and implications of the concepts of "individual rights" and "equity" in their examination of the issues surrounding students with disabilities within a standards-driven system. In "Leaving No Child Left Behind: Accountability Reform and Students with Disabilities," they lead us through the complex maze of public laws and educational policy that affect the education of students with disabilities. Standards-based reform policies have shifted the meaning of individual rights and equity and thus redefined the meaning of special education and the core legal entitlements. McLaughlin and Nagle fear that this new vision will bring serious unintended consequences and describe the factors that will determine whether students with disabilities will have truly equal opportunities to participate in schools driven by standards-based reforms, including existing beliefs about the abilities and potential of this group of students, and they highlight the importance of keeping the promise of meaningful and equitable educational opportunities for all students at the forefront in all considerations of school reform.

In chapter 11, Sandra Mathison investigates the ways in which standardized testing puts children of color and children in poverty at a disadvantage. She illustrates how education, when driven by standardized testing, is not the great equalizer it is often portrayed to be. Mathison illustrates the ways in which inequities that exist when students arrive at schools are compounded across their educational careers as a result of standardized tests, resulting in increased retention and dropout rates and diminishing quality of education for all children, but especially for minority students, as manifest in the "achievement gap" rhetoric. She concludes that "there is every reason to believe that access and quality of schooling is differentiated in this country and that differentiation is along race and class lines." Mathison suggests there is little reason to believe that current test-based reforms in precollegiate,

collegiate, and professional education will redress the inequities between white and minority students and between those living in poverty and those not. She closes this chapter with an examination of K–16 alliances that have combined the knowledge and resources of educators, researchers, and parents to respond to the disadvantage created by standardized tests.

Educational leaders—including, superintendents, central office specialists, and principals, among others—greatly influence how standards and assessments are interpreted and how curriculum and instruction change as a result. William Firestone's chapter makes three observations on how educational leaders contribute to this interpretation process. First, standards and assessments must compete with other accountability demands for leaders' attention. These include political accountability (pressures from school boards and parents), professional accountability (ideas from national associations like the National Council of Teachers of Mathematics), and moral accountability (the individual leader's sense of right and wrong). Secondly, the process of interpreting and acting on demands from state assessments and other accountability demands is fragmented. Leaders in different roles get different information and interpret it through different lenses so that it is difficult to reach consensus on a course of action. Moreover, central office and district leaders influence instruction in different ways. Finally, it appears that real improvement in teaching and learning does not come about in response to external pressure from standards or anything else. It occurs in response to a collective internal and moral sense of accountability. Firestone concludes that the reform problem for educational leaders is not so much how to cope with testing as how to ensure that all children receive a high-quality education.

William Cala concludes this volume with a passionate argument for why school officials must resist state and national standardized testing reforms. Cala, an upstate New York school superintendent, examines the reasons for "administrative paralysis" and the importance of resistance by school leaders to the "mismeasure and abuse" of children as a result of reforms driven by high-stakes standardized tests. Cala calls on school administrators to engage their role as leaders by joining an ever-growing movement of resistance, rather than continuing as accomplices and mere managers of the status quo. He describes "the power of one" in successful resistance strategies that have been used in New York State, which have produced historic results for communities working to preserve control over their schools.

Educational standards and assessment practices are the engine driving the historic changes public schools are experiencing today. It is our hope that the chapters that follow will provide readers with the foundation for a more holistic understanding of the nature and limits of standards-based educational reforms and, in particular, the ways in which current assessment practices influence the quotidian experiences of students, teachers, administrators, and parents in public schools. Moreover, we are hopeful that this effort enhances the ability of the primary stakeholders in public schools—the local school community, students, parents, and teachers—to create and sustain the schools they want and deserve.

— I —

History, Context, and the Future of Educational Standards and Assessment

— 1 —

A Short History of Educational Assessment and Standards-Based Educational Reform

SANDRA MATHISON

MENTAL MEASUREMENT GOES TO SCHOOL

The use of standardized student achievement testing in American schools dates back to 1845 with the administration of the Boston Survey. Horace Mann, then secretary of the Massachusetts State Board of Education, over-saw the development of a written examination that covered various topics including arithmetic, geography, history, grammar, science, and so on. The test battery, 154 questions in all, was given to 530 pupils sampled from the more than 7,000 students attending the Boston schools. Mann was moved to create these tests because of what he perceived to be a lack of consistency and quality in the Boston schools.

This was followed not long after by Joseph Rice's work, also in Boston.

In the decade beginning in 1895, Rice organized assessment programs in areas such as spelling and mathematics in a number of large school systems. Much as Horace Mann wanted to see more consistency in what was taught in schools, Rice was motivated by a perceived need to standardize curriculum.

About this same time, in 1904, E. L. Thorndike, known as the father of educational testing, published the first book on educational measurement, *An Introduction to the Theory of Mental and Social Measurement*.[1] He and his students developed many of the first achievement tests emphasizing controlled and uniform test administration and scoring.

But the real impetus for the growth of testing in schools grew out of the then developing emphasis on intelligence tests, particularly those that could be administered to groups rather than individuals, work that built on the basics of Thorndike's achievement tests. Between 1914 and 1918, the Army Alpha (for literate test takers) and the Army Beta (for illiterates) intelligence tests were developed. Lewis Terman, who took up the challenge during World War I of helping the military to distinguish between those recruits who were officer material and those who were better suited to the trenches, developed these tests. Within a year and a half, Terman and his student Arthur S. Otis had tested more than 1.5 million recruits.

Terman also created the Stanford Achievement Test, which he used in his longitudinal study of gifted children and from which came the term "intelligence quotient," or IQ. So taken with Terman's work, the Rockefeller Foundation supported his recommendation that every child be administered a "mental test" and in 1919 gave Terman a grant to develop a national intelligence test. Within the year, tests were made available to public elementary schools.

Test publishers quickly recognized the potential of testing in schools and began developing and selling intelligence tests. Houghton Mifflin published the Stanford-Binet Intelligence test in 1916. The commercial publication of tests is critical since many of the efficiencies of the testing industry, such as machine scanning, resulted from efforts to gain market share. In turn, the ability to process large quantities of data permitted ever more sophisticated statistical analyses of test scores, certainly with the intention of making the data more useful to schools, teachers, and counselors.

Until the onset of the current high-stakes testing movement associated with the standards-based reform of schools, achievement and ability tests served a number of purposes, but in 1966, David Goslin summarized what were at the time the typical uses of standardized tests in schools:

- To promote better adjustment, motivation, and progress of the individual student through a better understanding of his abilities and weaknesses, both on his own part and on the part of his teachers and parents;
- To aid in decisions about the readiness of the pupil for exposure to new subject matter;
- To measure the progress of pupils;
- To aid in the grade placement of individuals and the special grouping of children for instructional purposes within classes or grades;
- To aid in the identification of children with special problem or abilities;
- To provide objective measures of the relative effectiveness of alternative teaching techniques, curriculum content, and the like;
- To aid in the identification of special needs from the standpoint of the efficiency of the school relative to other schools.[2]

While Goslin's list represents the emphasis on local uses of testing, at this same time, during the administration of John F. Kennedy there was a growing interest in national assessment. During this period, Ralph Tyler was called upon to oversee the development of a national testing system, which would become the National Assessment of Educational Progress (NAEP) first administered in 1969 by the Education Commission of the States.[3] The creation of NAEP allowed for the possibility of state-by-state comparisons and a common metric for all American students and, indeed, participation by all states is now required in spite of its beginnings as a voluntary strategy.

Eugenics and Testing

This early American work on mental measurement was deeply informed by a presumed genetic basis for intelligence and differences. In 1905, the French psychologist Alfred Binet developed a scale for measuring intelligence that was translated into English by the American psychologist Henry H. Goddard, who was keenly interested in the inheritability of intelligence. Although Binet did not hold the view that intelligence was heritable and he thought that tests were a means for identifying ways to help children having difficulty, Goddard and other American hereditarians disregarded his principles. Goddard was influenced by Mendelian genetics and believed that "feeble-mindedness" was the result of a single recessive gene. He became a pioneer of the American eugenicist movement.

"Morons" were Goddard's primary interest, and he defined morons as "high grade defectives" who possess low intelligence but appear normal to casual observers. In addition to their learning difficulties, Goddard characterized morons as lacking self-control and susceptible to sexual immorality and vulnerable to other individuals who might exploit them for use in criminal activity.[4]

Lewis Terman was also a eugenicist and popularized Binet's work (that is, Goddard's translation of it) with the creation of the Stanford-Binet Test. A critical development, and one that still sets the parameters for standardized testing, was Terman's standardizing the scale of test scores—100 was the average score and the standard deviation was set at 15. Terman (along with others, including E. L. Thorndike and R. M. Yerkes) promoted group testing for the purpose of classifying children in grades three through eight, tests that were published by the World Book Company (the current-day Harcourt Brace). The intent of these tests was clear: to identify the feeble-minded and curtail their opportunity to reproduce, thus saving America from "crime, pauperism, and industrial inefficiency." Although lively discussion (most especially with Walter Lippman),[5] about the value of and justifiability of Terman's claims was waged in the popular press, this eugenicist perspective persisted.

In addition, Terman's classifying of student ability coincided with ideas emerging among Progressive educators in the 1910s. Progressives believed curriculum and instructional methods should be scientifically determined, and Terman's tests and interpretations fit the bill. Few seriously questioned his assumptions about the hereditary nature of intelligence or that IQ was indeed a valid measurement of intelligence. By "scientifically" proving that recent immigrants and blacks scored lower than whites due to an inferior mental endowment, he catered strongly to the nativism and prejudice of many Americans.

While most contemporary experts in mental measurement eschew these eugenicist beginnings, the debate lives on, manifest more recently in the work of Herrnstein and Murray in the much-debated book *The Bell Curve*.[6] The authors of this treatise have used intelligence testing to claim that African-Americans are intellectually genetically inferior. But their arguments are connected to class as well, and herein may lie the most obvious connections to the advocacy of testing by powerful politicians and corporate CEOs. Questions and answers they pose are:

> How much good would it do to encourage education for the people earning low wages? If somehow government can cajole or entice youths to stay in school for a few extra years, will their economic disadvantage in the new labor market go away? We doubt it. Their disadvantage might be diminished, but only modestly. There is reason to think that the job market has been rewarding not just education but intelligence.[7]

Race and class, which are inextricably linked in contemporary society, remain important considerations in measurement and assessment. There is ample evidence that suggests achievement tests are better predicators of parental income than anything else. Peter Sacks, in his critique of the SAT, suggests, "Those born into less privileged social and economic circumstances are punished at least twice: first, when they start life already behind their more privileged peers; and second, when the testing game's sorting, labeling, and screening of children begins."[8]

The Technical and Sociopolitical Nature of Measurement

The development of standardized means for measuring intelligence, ability, and achievement coincided with a remarkable explosion of scientific knowledge and technological advance across a wide range of domains. The industrial growth of most of the twentieth century and the information technology growth of the late twentieth century are the context for the use and development of assessments that differentiate individuals for the allocation of scarce resources such as jobs, postsecondary education, and scholarships.

Without the power of more and more advanced and complex technology, both in terms of data management and statistical analysis, it is doubtful that student assessment would be the driving force of the accountability demanded in the current standards-based reform movement. George Madaus describes the development of testing technology as a series of changes, each responding to a contemporary constraint on testing, and each of which enhanced the efficiency of testing, that is, the ability to test more people at less cost and in less time.[9] Charles Pearson's invention of factor analysis in 1904, Lindquist's invention of the optical scanner in 1955, the development of item response theory in the early 1950s by Fred Lord and Darrell Bock, as well as the variant developed by Georg Rasch in 1960 and the development of matrix sampling by Darrell Bock and Robert Mislevy in the 1960s and 1970s, are examples of these technological enhancements. A number of areas in student assessment remain astonishingly unsophisticated, such as, for example, strategies for standard setting. In many ways, the educational measurement community has operated on the assumption that appropriate uses of assessment in schools is a matter of making good tests and being able to manipulate the scores in sophisticated ways. However, testing is also a sociopolitical activity and even technically sound measures and procedures are transformed when they are thrown into the educational policy and practice arena.

There is and has been great optimism about what testing and measurement in schools can accomplish. Robert Linn, contemporary father of educational measurement, suggests we are overly optimistic about the promises of what can be delivered:

> I am led to conclude that in most cases the instruments and technology have not been up to the demands that have been placed on them by high-stakes accountability. Assessment systems that are useful monitors lose much of their dependability and credibility for that purpose when high stakes are attached to them. The unintended negative effects of high-stakes accountability uses often outweigh the intended positive effects.[10]

THE CURRICULUM STANDARDS MOVEMENT

Standards-based education refers to the setting of content standards for what students should know and be able to do, grade by grade, in each subject area, assessing students' progress toward achieving the standards, and holding schools accountable for results. Standards are meant to be the threads tying curriculum, instruction, and assessment together. There are three principal reasons for the development of standards. Standards serve to: (1) clarify expectations, (2) raise expectations, and (3) establish a common set of expectations. The standards-based reform initiatives also entail a rhetoric of equality and are presumed to establish not only clear and measurable expectations but ones that are equally high for all students.

The push for standards is based on a number of premises, typically without the support of evidence: (1) today's students do not "know enough" (no matter how "knowing enough" is defined); (2) curriculum and assessment standards will lead to higher achievement (although arguably many students achieve highly now—they just do so differently or in ways not easily quantified); (3) national and state standards are crucial in terms of successful U.S.-corporate-global economic competition; (4) standards-based reform should occur with federal guidance yet be implemented under local control (thus keeping both big government liberals and New Federalist conservatives happy); and (5) "higher" standards and standardization will promote equal educational and, thus, economic and political opportunity.

The idea of establishing high standards for education is intuitively appealing, and frequent comparisons to certification of professionals are made—you would want your doctor to meet high standards or the city engineer building the bridge you cross each day to meet high standards—as well as comparisons to public control over the environment—you would want the food you eat and the air you breathe to be safe. High standards are presumed to provide public safety and an improved quality of life. Unfortunately, the connection between issues of public safety and quality of life and the content and pedagogy in schools is quite tenuous.

When we speak of standards (and, indeed, the term is frequently misused[11]), we are referring to one or more of the following: (1) academic content, (2) levels or types of performance (or how much learning and how it is demonstrated), and (3) opportunity to learn standards.

How We Got to Where We Are

A Nation at Risk[12] is generally seen as the initiating event of the modern standards movement. The apocalyptic predictions mixed with military metaphors in the report became a clarion call for educational reform: "The educational foundations of our society are presently being eroded by a rising tide of mediocrity that threatens our very future as a nation and a people. . . . We have, in effect, been committing an act of unthinking, unilateral educational disarmament."[13]

Although it took a few years, in 1989 President Bush and the state governors called an Education Summit in Charlottesville. That summit established six broad educational goals to be reached by the year 2000.[14] *Goals 2000* was signed into law in 1994 by President Clinton. Goals 3 and 4 were related specifically to academic achievement:

Goal 3: By the year 2000, American students will leave grades 4, 8, and 12 having demonstrated competency in challenging subject matter including English, mathematics, science, history, and geography; and every school in America will ensure that all students learn to use their minds well, so they may be prepared for responsible citizenship, further learning, and productive employment in our modern economy.

Goal 4: By the year 2000, U.S. students will be first in the world in science and mathematics achievement.

In 1990, the federally funded procedures for moving the country toward accomplishment of these goals were established. The National Education Goals Panel (NEGP) and the National Council on Education Standards and Testing (NCEST) were created and charged with answering a number of questions: What is the subject matter to be addressed? What types of assessments should be used? What standards of performance should be set?

Subject-matter professional associations primarily handled the work of standard setting. The National Council for Teachers of Mathematics set the "standard" for establishing standards as they developed the *Curriculum and Evaluation Standards for School Mathematics* in 1989, prior to the federally directed mandates. Then U.S. Secretary of Education Lamar Alexander bankrolled many of the professional associations to development subject-matter curriculum standards, although others, such as the American Association for the Advancement of Science, worked on projects independent of federal funding. During the 1990s, virtually every subject area in schools was codified in a set of standards promulgated by a professional association. Table 5.1 summarizes this period of development.

The contemporary standards-based reform movement is characterized by a new level of federal intervention in education and a consistent and ongoing partnership between politicians and corporations. The following chronology of events in standards-based education reform highlights these relationships.[15]

1983: *A Nation at Risk* is published, calling for reform of the U.S. education system.

1983: Bill Honig, elected state superintendent of California public schools, begins a decade-long revision of the state public school system, developing content standards and curriculum frameworks.

1989: Charlottesville, VA: The nation's fifty governors and President Bush adopt National Education Goals for the year 2000. Five school subjects (English, mathematics, science, history, and geography) are identified for which challenging national achievement standards should be established.

1989: The National Council of Teachers of Mathematics publishes *Curriculum and Evaluation Standards for School Mathematics*.

1990: In his State of the Union address, President Bush announces the National Education Goals for the year 2000, and Congress establishes a National Education Goals Panel (NEGP).

1994, March: President Clinton signs into law *Goals 2000: Educate America Act*. This legislation creates the National Education Standards and Improvement Coun-

Table 5.1
Summary of Professional Curriculum Standards[16]

Content Area	Author/Sponsor	Title	Publication Date
Mathematics	National Council of Teachers of Mathematics	Curriculum and Evaluation Standards for School Mathematics	1989
		Principles and Standards for School Mathematics	2000
Science	American Association for the Advancement of Science	Science for All Americans	1992
	National Science Teachers	Scope, Sequence and Coordination of National Science Education Content Standards	1995
	National Research Council	National Science Education Standards	1996
History	National Center for History in the Schools	National Standards for History for Grades K–4, National Standards for United States History, National Standards for World History	1995
English language arts	National Council of Teachers of English	Standards for the English Language Arts	1996
	National Communication Association	Competent Communicators: K–12 Speaking, Listening, and Media Literacy Standards and Competency Statements	1998
Arts	Consortium of National Arts Education Associations	What Every Young American Should Know and Be Able to Do in the Arts	1994
Civics	Center for Civic Education	National Standards for Civics and Government	1994
Economics	National Council on Economic Education	Voluntary National Content Standards in Economics	1997

Subject	Organization	Title	Year
Foreign language	American Council on the Teaching of Foreign Languages	*Foreign Language Learning in the 21st Century*	1999
	Teachers of English to Speakers of Other Languages, Inc.	*ESL Standards for PreK–12 Students*	1998
Geography	Geography Education Standards Project	*Geography for Life: National Geography Standards*	1994
Health	Joint Committee on National Health Education Standards	*National Health Education Standards: Achieving Health Literacy*	1995
Physical education	National Association for Sport and Physical Education	*Moving into the Future: National Standards for Physical Education: A Guide to Content and Assessment*	1995
Social studies	National Council for the Social Studies	*Expectations of Excellence: Curriculum Standards for Social Studies*	1994
Technology	International Technology Education Association	*Standards for Technological Literacy: Content for the Study of Technology*	2000
	International Society for Technology in Education	*National Educational Technology Standards for Students: Connecting Curriculum and Technology*	2000
Work	American Society for Training and Development	*Workplace Basics: The Essential Skills Employers Want*	1990
	National Business Education Association	*National Standards for Business Education: What America's Students Should Know and Be Able to Do in Business*	1995

cil (NESIC) to certify national and state content and performance standards, opportunity-to-learn standards, and state assessments; adds two new goals to the national education goals; and brings to nine the number of areas for which students should demonstrate "competency over challenging subject matters." The subject areas now covered include foreign languages, the arts, economics, and civics and government.

1996, March: The National Education Summit is held. Forty state governors and more than forty-five business leaders convene. They support efforts to set clear academic standards in the core subject areas at the state and local levels. Business leaders pledge to consider the existence of state standards when locating facilities.

1997, February: President Clinton, in his State of the Union Address, calls for every state to adopt high national standards and declares that "by 1999, every state should test every 4th grader in reading and every 8th grader in math to make sure these standards are met."

1999, fall: The National Education Summit is held. Governors, educators, and business leaders identify three key challenges facing U.S. schools—improving educator quality, helping all students reach high standards, and strengthening accountability—and agree to specify how each of their states would address these challenges.

1999: The District of Columbia, Puerto Rico, and every state except Iowa have set or are setting common academic standards for students.

2001: Governors and business leaders met at the IBM Conference Center in Palisades, New York, to provide guidance to states in creating and using tests, including the development of a national testing plan.

2001: The private and politically conservative Achieve, Inc., The Education Trust, The Thomas B. Fordham Foundation, and The National Alliance of Business joined forces to establish The American Diploma Project, an effort to further influence standards-based reform at the state level.

2002: Reauthorization of the *Elementary and Secondary School Act* (aka No Child Left Behind) and unprecedented federal involvement in education.

Where We Are Now—Political Conservatism, State Curriculum Standards, and No Child Left Behind

While professional associations got the content-standards-setting ball rolling, they have little real authority, although sometimes much influence, at getting schools to adopt their standards. Most of these documents have, however, been influential at the state level, where mandates that establish what will be taught can and do occur. This process of local state development of standards is described in other chapters in this volume,[17] and it is this shift in locus of the standards that makes the movement more than a consensus building within a discipline area taught in schools.

The preceding chronology hints at the interests behind the current manifestation of the standards-based reform movement and, indeed, No Child Left Behind (NCLB) is a critical element supporting the connection between standards and accountability. NCLB, legislation supported equally by Democrats and Republicans and endorsed by corporate leaders, requires states to adhere to federal mandates in exchange for federal funding, primarily in the form of Title I money designated for educational services to poor children. The demands and problems with NCLB are serious—the impossibility for schools to make annual yearly progress, the serious technical flaws with establishing acceptable levels of performance, the impossibility of hiring only "highly qualified" teachers are just some of the issues.[18]

Although professional associations were key players in creating the initial statements of curriculum standards, other groups—ones that are often described as "independent, bipartisan, not-for-profit" but that nonetheless represent the special interests of politicians and big business—now champion the standards-based reform movement. For example, Achieve, Inc., was created at the 1996 National Education Summit, and the Board of Directors is composed of six governors (three Democrats and three Republicans) and six CEOs. Achieve, Inc., has partnered with government-funded research laboratories (McREL) to promote the use of standards through the "Align to Achieve" standards database project.[19] Many of the initiatives that sustain and drive the standards-based reform movement are driven by a small number of such groups; in addition to Achieve, Inc., major players are the Thomas B. Fordham Foundation, The Education Trust, and the for-profit curriculum and test publishers.

As indicated earlier in this chapter, publishers seized the opportunity for profit making around standards and testing in schools. The same companies, such as Houghton Mifflin, Harcourt Brace, CTB/McGraw-Hill, K–12 Works, and ETS Pulliam, the newly created and acquired for-profit divisions of the Educational Testing Service, are realizing huge profits as a consequence of the standards-based reform movement. That they do so often by marketing off-the-shelf norm-referenced tests as appropriate and aligned with state curriculum standards is questionable.[20] Standards and assessment are good for business at more than one level.

STANDARDS AND ACCOUNTABILITY

It should be clear from the preceding discussion that the specification of standards is accompanied by accountability strategies—it does no good to establish high expectations if one does not ensure they are met and, if they are not met, that there is a planned remedy. The dominant approach to educational accountability is an outcomes-based bureaucratic one. Almost universally, this is the approach adopted by individual states (one notable exception being Nebraska) and supported by the federal government, especially through NCLB. Indeed, the U.S. Department of Education has adopted the rhetoric of "stronger accountability" in promoting NCLB's regulatory requirements. Whether the stakes are high or low and whether the locus of control is local, state, or national, this strategy is one where a distant authority sets performance goals for students, schools or school systems; holds individuals and units directly accountable for meeting the goals; and consequences are applied, including rewards for meeting performance goals and sanctions for not meeting them.

While there is discussion and exploration of alternative approaches to accountability,[21] such as a teacher professionalism model or community involvement model, these alternatives are not compelling in the current political climate. Kenneth Sortnik has called for "responsible accountability" that recognizes "the importance of individualization and classroom-based information that ought to be naturally accumulated for each student during the formative processes of teaching, learning, and assessment. Each child, adolescent, and young adult needs to be cared for in terms of intellectual, social, personal, and career-oriented educational needs—not to meet some arbitrary level of performance on an on-demand test, but to develop the ability and likelihood 'to become.'"[22] The chapters in this volume discuss the nature, limits, and alternatives to the typical testing strategies that are the accountability mechanism inherent in the standards-based educational reform movement.

Standards-Based Education: Two Wrongs Don't Make a Right

W. James Popham

Standards-based education (SBE) represents a splendid strategy to improve our schools. Unfortunately, because of two monumental mistakes in the way educators are currently implementing SBE, this fine reform strategy is falling flat on its well-founded fanny.

Mistake number one occurs when the architects of a given state's SBE have allowed that state's curriculum specialists to identify the educational outcomes on which the state's SBE program will be based. Almost without exception, those curriculum specialists have identified far too many educational outcomes for the state's students to deal with—too many to be taught in the time available and too many to be tested in the time available. In most instances, the isolation of excessive curricular aims is well intentioned. It is also understandable. Nonetheless, it represents a colossal curricular blunder.

Mistake number two stems from the selection of the wrong types of tests to find out if students have, in fact, learned what they were supposed to learn. More often than not, the state-level tests being employed to implement SBE are *instructionally insensitive*, that is, incapable of detecting effective instruction even it were present. To use students' performances on instructionally insensitive tests to identify instructionally effective (or ineffective) schools is every bit as silly as it sounds. Yet that is precisely what is going on in most parts of our nation.

The ultimate goal of SBE, of course, is to improve the quality of the education programs we provide for children. Indeed, it is reasonable to conclude that the original reason for SBE's birth was to stimulate improved instructional practices when it was believed a state's education programs weren't working well. But an SBE program based on the wrong curricular aims, and relying on the wrong sorts of assessments, has no chance to spur instructional improvement. That hoped-for "right" result has been undermined by two significant "wrongs," namely, inappropriate curricular targets and instructionally insensitive assessments. This is a genuine shame, because SBE, if implemented properly, makes all sorts of educational sense. Indeed, it was most likely the inherently appealing qualities of SBE that inclined congressional lawmakers to install what is, in essence, a national SBE program when the No Child Left Behind Act (NCLB) was hammered out as a federal law in 2001. Even a hurried reading of NCLB will reveal it sits on top of an SBE foundation.

A STRATEGY IN SEARCH OF SOUND INSTALLATION

What's in a Name?

Let's take a quick peek at standards-based education and why it makes so much sense. First off, I ought to explain where the term *standards* comes from. I wish I could! Actually, when I was growing up, a *standard* referred to a *level* of performance or, as my dictionary puts it, something considered "as a basis of comparison." When I took my first teaching job in an eastern Oregon high school, we used the term *standard* in that very same way. If one of the teachers on my school's faculty was thought to have "low standards," all of the school's teachers understood instantly that the level of the teacher's aspirations for students was not sufficiently high. "Standards" had nothing to do with the nature of the curricular aspirations we had for our students.

Also, in those days, we described our curricular aims as educational *goals* (if the aims were stated somewhat broadly) or as educational *objectives* (if the aims were stated more specifically). For educators of that era, then, educational intentions were represented by curricular goals and objectives. Putting it in less lofty language, those goals and objectives represented the stuff we wanted our students to learn.

But somewhat over a decade ago, American educators began to refer to their curricular aims as *content standards*. I'm not sure who it was that first ascribed a brand-new meaning to the term *standard*, but that innovative usage has gained great popularity among educators. I have always assumed that the near-universal acceptance of *standards* as a descriptor for one's curricular aims was attributable to the positive perceptions that invariably ensue when educators tell the world that they are pursuing "high standards." Who could ever criticize a plucky band of poorly paid public schoolteachers who conduct their classes in unrelenting pursuit of *high standards*?

So, for well over a decade now, we find educators using the phrase *content standards* to refer to the knowledge and skills that students are supposed to learn in school. *Performance standards*, on the other hand, refer to the *levels* at which those content standards are supposed to be mastered by students.

I have no serious problem with using the phrase *content standards* to describe the things educators want students to learn. I also find the use of the phrase *performance standards* to be a helpful way to identify the desired level of excellence at which we want students to have mastered content standards. However, because there are two species of standards now roaming the educational landscape, a person needs to be sure that the right kind of standards are being considered. Anytime you hear the term *standards* being used, try to solicit a bit of clarification. Is the focus on standards that are thought of as curricular aims or is the focus on standards that are thought of as desired levels of student proficiency? *Standards* is a lovesick noun desperately pining for a modifying adjective.

Attempting to follow the commonsense guideline I just supplied about adjectival clarification, I want to assert that the *standards* I see implied by SBE are definitely *content* standards. Putting it another way, I believe any sensible educational reform strategy ought to be *based* on intended curricular outcomes, that is, the skills and knowledge we want our students to master. Performance standards, of course, are surely important. However, in my mind, the S in SBE definitely stands for content standards.

The Essence of Good Sense

SBE lays out an eminently sensible three-step strategy to improve the caliber of schooling. Step one calls for the isolation of appropriate curricular aims. Step two requires teachers to provide instruction in order for students to achieve the skills and knowledge set forth in the aforementioned curricular aims. And step three involves the assessment of students to see if they have, in fact, mastered the curricular aims that their teachers were seeking to accomplish.

If students' assessed performances reveal that the curricular aims (content standards) have been achieved by sufficient numbers of students, then teachers' instruction should be regarded as successful. If, on the other hand, students' test scores reveal that the curricular aims have not been mastered by enough students, then teachers need to revise their instruction so that their future students will be better able to master the content standards those students are supposed to master.

SBE is nothing more than a posh *ends-means* model wherein content standards represent intended ends, teaching constitutes the means for achieving those ends, and test results supply the evidence regarding whether the means did, in fact, achieve the intended ends. Humankind has been employing this sort of ends-means since well before historians first undertook their recording chores. A person first identifies a goal (end), tries to accomplish that goal via some procedure (means), then determines whether the means actually accomplished the intended end. SBE is, at bottom, fundamentally nothing more than the educational application of a traditional ends-means paradigm.

SBE makes a great deal of sense, therefore, as a way of improving the quality of education. But, if implemented unwisely, SBE will turn out to be altogether feckless. And that's what I want to deal with now, namely, the two monster mistakes being made when misguided educators attempt to implement SBE.

MISTAKE NO. 1: A PROFUSION OF CONTENT STANDARDS

If SBE is based on an ends-means model, then for educators to get that educational pot percolating, it is obviously necessary for those educators to first stake out the ends they hope to accomplish. And that's precisely where most state-level educational policymakers have initiated their SBE endeavors, namely, by calling for an identification of a state's curricular aims (that is, its content standards). Typically, twenty to thirty of the state's most formidable curriculum-savvy folks (in a particular area) are assembled to help determine the state's content standards. The purpose of such a standards-determination committee is to identify the content standards (in their subject area, for instance, mathematics) that, thereafter, would guide state-level instruction in a particular subject.

Typically, this group of subject matter specialists will hold multiple meetings, sometimes over a period of weeks, to reach agreement regarding what specific skills and bodies of knowledge should constitute the state-approved content standards for their field. And that, unfortunately, is where SBE first goes awry.

You see, a standards-determination committee's curriculum specialists are typically allowed to carve up their subject area into identifiable skills and knowledge without almost any significant constraints. Almost literally, these state-level teams of curriculum specialists are told to whip up a curricular wish list in which every suitable curricular target is set forth. Rarely, if ever, are the *assessment implications* of these curriculum carnivals trotted out. Rarely, if ever, are the educators who are carving out the content standards for their field warned that "too many targets invariably turn out to be no targets at all." In short, the educators who identify content standards for their state are rarely, if ever, directed to isolate a sensible "grain size" for their curricular aspirations. As a result, far too many curricular targets are almost always chosen.

How can a busy elementary teacher plan sensibly for the teacher's students to accomplish several hundred content standards? And in one school year! Yet, that's exactly the sort of curricular thinking that has gone on in many states. Literally hundreds of content standards have been staked out as the sought-for *ends* of an SBE program. The huge numbers of content standards could have been predicted, of course, because whenever you ask a subject matter *specialist* to identify what students should master in that subject matter specialist's field, the predictable answer will almost always be *everything*. Subject specialists groove on their subjects. That's only natural. Thus, when you tell a group of subject matter specialists to lay out the things in their field that students should learn, this is akin to what happens if one releases kittens in a catnip store. Everything looks so wonderful.

These excessively ambitious curricular yearnings are usually understandable. All of us think our own specialty area is worthwhile. Curricular whizbangs are no exception. But, understandable or not, most SBE programs rest perilously on far too many curricular aims. Those aims constitute a shortsighted, excessive array of the curricular ends that ought to guide instruction.

In recent months, I have come to believe there's another, less excusable reason that a small number of curriculum specialists have shoveled so much curricular content into their state's content standards. That less excusable reason is based on a person's desire for *self-esteem enhancement*. I don't want to wander down a psychological trail I'm ill equipped to travel, but I am certain that almost all of us not only want to feel good about ourselves, we also want others to regard us positively. The desire to enhance one's self-concept, therefore, is a powerful motivator for just about everyone.

Well, when a state's curricular specialists load so much content into their particular subject specialty, they are clearly making that content-loaded specialty more important. They aggrandize that specialty by decreeing that students ought to learn an immense number of things in that specialty. Yet, perhaps subconsciously, when some individuals aggrandize a subject area with which *they are identified*, they indirectly aggrandize themselves. Self-esteem enhancement, though psychologically understandable, should still not lead to patently excessive curricular aspirations.

Regardless of whether curricular specialists overload their state's content standards because of self-interest or student-interest, however, the curricular consequences are the same. That is, there are just too many content standards now forming the bases of state-level SBE programs.

In recognition that their state-level curricular deliberations were leading toward too many content standards, in some states we saw standards-determination committees attempt to mask their folly by labeling very broad curricular outcomes as their content standards. Thus, in certain states we find only a handful of so-called content standards, such as "measurement" or "geometry." But these are merely *labels*, not content standards. Beneath these general labels, the standards determiners then list a bevy of "benchmarks," "expectancies," "learning outcomes," or some synonymous labels to describe the many skills and bodies of knowledge they had up their curricular sleeves.

To make matters worse, in most states there has been little, if any, coordination among the standards-determination committees who were operating in different subject arenas. Thus, the content standards identified by a reading committee or by a mathematics committee might appear to be an altogether different curricular species. For example, whereas the standards-determination committee for writing might have carved out only a small number of rather broad composition skills to be taught, the standards-determination committee in reading might have put forward a whole galaxy of far more specific reading skills. The state's educators, encountering such grain-size inconsistency, are invariably confused—and with good reason! SBE, of course, soon sputters when its curricular ends have been botched. In most states, unfortunately, curricular botching has been the rule, not the exception. And, as a result, SBE-sputtering is the rule, not the exception.

The reality is that most states' SBE programs rest squarely on too many content standards—too many to be taught in the available instructional time and too many to be tested in the available assessment time. In short, the *ends* of an ends-means educational improvement strategy have been inadequately conceived. This is Mistake Number 1, and it would be fatal in and of itself. Yet, in the nation's SBE programs, a second serious error has been made that, at least partially, is linked to the initial mistake of identifying too many curricular targets. That second mistake is associated with the tests that are used to determine if the ends represented by an SBE program's content standards have, in fact, been attained.

MISTAKE NO. 2: INSTRUCTIONALLY INSENSITIVE TESTS

The second wrong turn taken by almost all of today's SBE programs hinges on the tests being used to find out whether an instructional intervention (the means) has promoted students' mastery of designated content standards (the ends). Clearly, if the wrong tests are employed to tell whether an instructional program has worked, it will be impossible to discern whether a given set of instructional activities succeeded. Sadly, today's SBE programs, with few exceptions, employ *instructionally insensitive tests.*

An instructionally insensitive test is one that is incapable of detecting improved learning on the part of students even if such improved learning has taken place. Clearly, the use of tests that are impervious to the impact of effective instruction renders an SBE ends-means model senseless. If you can't tell whether a set of curricular ends has been achieved, how can you tell if the instructional means aimed at those ends have actually worked?

We currently see two types of instructionally insensitive tests being employed in the state-level SBE programs decreed when President Bush signed the NCLB Act in early 2002. The first type of instructionally insensitive test is one that relies on a traditional approach to standardized achievement testing. The second kind of instructionally insensitive test consists of the so-called standards-based test, that is, a test pretending to assess the outlandish collection of state-sanctioned content standards currently encountered in almost every state. Both of these instructionally insensitive tests, though their insensitivity stems from different sources, will doom an SBE program to failure.

Traditionally Constructed Standard Achievement Tests

Many states are currently attempting to satisfy NCLB-imposed assessment requirements by using one of the nationally standardized achievement exams, such as the Stanford Achievement Tests. More often than not, these "off-the-shelf" tests have been supplemented with a sprinkling of additional items so that they are in better *alignment* with a given state's content standards. ("Alignment," incidentally, is a nine-letter word that, in the field of education, really ought to be used like a four-letter word.) Frequently, the item augmentation of existing standardized tests provides only the appearance of an improved match between the state's curricular emphases and the tests' assessment emphases. Any kind of rigorous appraisal of the alignment between a state's curriculum and what these "augmented" achievement tests measure will reveal an alignment that is, at best, debatable.

The difficulty with traditionally constructed achievement tests is that their underlying mission is to permit one test taker's score to be contrasted with the scores of previous test takers who constitute the test's norm group. Such norm-referenced comparisons, indeed, are at the heart of how a traditionally constructed standardized achievement test is supposed to work. However, to permit the fine-grained contrasts that are so necessary for these comparatively oriented assessment devices, such tests contain too many items that measure student attributes unrelated to the effectiveness of instruction. That's because, for these sorts of tests to do a really good comparative job, they must produce a considerable amount of *score spread*, that is, students' scores that are well spread out so there are plenty of high scores, low scores, and medium scores. To attain suitable score spread in the relatively brief time during which students are to be tested, certain kinds of items are employed that turn out to be inherently insensitive to instruction.

For example, because students' socioeconomic status (SES) is a delightfully spread-out variable, and a variable that doesn't change all that rapidly, items linked to SES will invariably yield plenty of score spread on a standardized achievement test. To illustrate, if the content of an item is likely to be better known by children from higher SES families than by children from lower SES families, you can be assured that such an item will contribute substantially to score spread.

Similarly, items linked to children's *inherited* academic aptitudes (such as their innate verbal, quantitative, or spatial aptitudes) will also do a good job in producing score spread. Let's be honest, some children get luckier than others in the gene pool lottery. Some children, from birth, have more quantitative potential than other children. And because these inherited aptitudes (just like SES) are nicely spread out and aren't readily altered, items linked to inherited aptitudes will also produce the sorts of score spread that the builders of traditional achievement tests strive to attain.

But SES-linked items and aptitude-linked items tend to measure what students bring to school, not what they are taught at school. The creators of traditional standardized achievement tests, even those that have been augmented for purposes of increased curricular alignment, are *not* thinking about measuring students' mastery of content standards. On the contrary, those test developers are thinking about the creation of sufficient score spread so that norm-referenced comparisons based on a test will be accurate. There are far too many items in traditionally constructed achievement tests that are flat out unable to detect decent instruction. It is for this reason that such tests are far too instructionally sensitive to make SBE programs work properly.

Customized "Standards-Based" Tests

A second variety of instructionally insensitive test is the so-called *standards-based* test that has been purportedly built to determine whether students have mastered a set of state-approved content standards. These tests are also instructionally insensitive but for different reasons. Let's see what those reasons are.

Remember, the wish list arrays of content standards now seen in almost all our states contain too many skills and bodies of knowledge to be assessed meaningfully during the hour or two typically allotted for testing that is now required by NCLB. And because there are so very many content standards to be taught, and to be tested, sensible teachers realize that they simply can't teach everything set forth in their state's overwhelming array of wish list content standards. Moreover, they know that not all of those content standards will even be assessed in any sort of meaningful manner. Accordingly, even sensible teachers are forced to *guess which* content standards will be assessed each year. This is because many states randomly rotate the content standards being "measured" by each year's accountability tests. As a result of such teacher-guessing, increased instructional attention is given to the content standards that the teacher guessed will be assessed in the upcoming accountability test. But, sadly, given the huge numbers of content standards serving as potential contenders for assessment, teachers often guess wrong!

A teacher might have put substantial instructional effort into promoting students' mastery of certain content standards that, in a given year, are tested by few, if any, items. The teacher may have done a marvelously effective job with respect to a set of selected (guessed) content standards but because the wrong content standards have been selected, students' test scores won't show how effective that instruction really was. These standards-based tests, even if custom-built for a particular state, are instructionally insensitive because much of the time they end up measuring stuff that teachers haven't taught or at least haven't taught with any thoroughness.

It would be easy to assign guilt once more to the curriculum crowd that ended up identifying far too many content standards. But the real culprits in this scenario are the measurement specialists who sit back and accept this sort of assessment nonsense. Many assessment personnel have actually promoted the image that their customized standards-based test are, in fact, capable of informing a state's citizenry about the degree to which the state's content standards have been successfully taught. This is blatant assessment hypocrisy. Such assessment personnel have failed to pass their own personal-honesty tests.

An important corollary problem seen in almost all of standards-based tests is that those tests fail to report results in a fashion that permits teachers to determine *which* curricular aims have been mastered by a teacher's students. As a consequence, teachers can't tell which parts of their instructional activities have worked and which ones haven't.

Because there are far too many curricular aims to assess, it is impossible for designers of standards-based tests to include enough items per assessed curricular aim so that a student's mastery of a particular curricular aim can be determined. For instance, suppose that it takes a student's responses to ten or more items to tell if that student had mastered a particular skill. Yet, the standards-based test might only have room for one or two items related to that skill. That's because, of course, there are too many curricular aims to be assessed.

So what usually happens is that a student's test results are reported (to teachers, students, and student's parents) at a very general level. For instance, a reading test's results might be reported only as the student's overall performances with respect to "literal comprehension" or "inferential comprehension." What kind of instructional decisions can a teacher make on the basis of such gunky reporting? How can teachers improve their instruction over time if those teachers can't tell which parts of their instruction actually worked?

Most of today's standards-based tests, and *all* of the standards-based tests that attempt to measure myriad content standards, are instructionally insensitive. They are insensitive because there are profound mismatches between what a state's teachers teach and what a state's tests measure. A test can't be sensitive to the detection of effective instruction if it's measuring stuff that hasn't been taught. Moreover, from the too-global reports provided by today's standards-based tests, teachers simply can't improve what they do in the classroom.

A FIX, QUICK BUT CORRECT

To make SBE attain its considerable potential, two quick fixes must be made without delay. Not surprisingly, both of those remedies relate to the two mistakes I've just identified.

First, a dramatic reconceptualization of a state's content standards must be undertaken so that rather than asking the state's teachers to pursue hundreds of curricular aims, a given teacher might need to promote (in a particular subject) students' mastery of only a handful of content standards. These few content standards, however, must obviously reflect genuinely significant student skills. A good example can be seen in the way the nation's teachers currently assess their students' composition skills. In most states these days, teachers are asked to prepare their students to generate an original essay (for example, a persuasive, narrative, or expository essay) that satisfies a number of important evaluative criteria (such as mechanics or organization). This powerful essay-writing skill, of course, embraces a number of lesser subskills, such as students' mastery of spelling, punctuation, and grammar. Yet, because of the manner in which the skill has been conceptualized, it offers teachers the clarity they need to devise *effective and efficient* instruction. Because only a few super-significant content standards would then be slated for state assessment, it is imperative that students master those standards *efficiently*—thereby allowing instructional time for teachers to pursue other curricular aims that, although worthwhile, are not assessed on such accountability tests as a state's NCLB exams.

The second fix, not surprisingly, calls for the installation of instructionally sensitive tests to measure students' mastery of the far more limited number of content standards sought in an SBE program. Those tests, happily focused on a smaller number of assessment targets, will be able to provide evidence about the particular content standards that have or haven't been mastered by students. Instructionally sensitive tests, therefore, need to contain a sufficient number of items so that a student's mastery of each assessed curricular aim can be ascertained. If instructionally sensitive tests are not only going to do an accurate job of measuring instructional effectiveness but are also going to stimulate improved instruction, those tests need to be accompanied by relatively brief, teacher-palatable descriptions of what's going to be assessed. The more clearly that teachers understand the nature of a skill they are promoting, the better job of instructional planning they can do.

In late 2001, an independent group of assessment specialists, the Commission on Instructionally Supportive Assessment, offered a series of suggestions regarding how accountability tests (such as those needed for NCLB) could be built to both provide accurate accountability evidence yet also nurture more effective instruction. Reports of the commission's recommendations are available on the websites of a number of national education associations.[1] The kinds of instructionally supportive accountability tests recommended by the commission could make SBE succeed.

If SBE programs are organized around a modest number of properly assessed curricular aims, then this eminently sensible strategy will be a boon to the students who are fortunate enough to be on its receiving end. If SBE programs make *either* of the two mistakes described here, then SBE will not only be a sham, it will deflect educators from doing the things that might educate students properly.

— 3 —

The Costs of Overemphasizing Achievement[1]

Alfie Kohn

> Only extraordinary education is concerned with learning; most is concerned with achieving: and for young minds, these two are very nearly opposite.
> — Marilyn French

Common sense suggests we should figure out what our educational goals are, then check in periodically to see how successful we have been at meeting them. Assessment thus would be an unobtrusive servant of teaching and learning. Unfortunately, common sense is in short supply today because assessment has come to dominate the whole educational process. Worse, the purposes and design of the most common forms of assessment—both within classrooms and across schools—often lead to disastrous consequences.

Part of the problem is that we shy away from asking the right questions and from following the data where they lead. Instead, we fiddle with relatively trivial details, fine-tuning the techniques of measurement while missing the bigger picture. Take grading, for example. Much of the current discussion focuses on how often to prepare grade reports or what mark should be given for a specified level of achievement (e.g., what constitutes "B" work). Some educators have become preoccupied with the possibility that too many students are ending up with A's.

[1]Copyright © 1999 by Alfie Kohn. Reprinted from *School Administrator* with the author's permission. For more infomation, please see www.alfiekohn.org

From another perspective, though, the real problem isn't grade inflation—it's grades, which by their very nature undermine learning. The proper occasion for outrage is not that too many students are getting A's, but that too many students have been led to believe that getting A's is the point of going to school. Specifically, research indicates that the use of traditional letter or number grades is reliably associated with three consequences.

First, students tend to lose interest in whatever they're learning. As motivation to get good grades goes up, motivation to explore ideas tends to go down. Second, students try to avoid challenging tasks whenever possible. More difficult assignments, after all, would be seen as an impediment to getting a top grade. Finally, the quality of students' thinking is less impressive. One study after another shows that creativity and even long-term recall of facts are adversely affected by the use of traditional grades.

A SOLVABLE TASK

The data to support these findings are available to anyone who cares to look, and the practical problems of eliminating grades—including the challenge of helping parents understand the benefit to their children of doing so—are solvable for anyone who is committed to the task. That commitment, however, entails some serious reflection about why we are assessing students in the first place.

If we are primarily interested in collecting information that will enhance the quality of learning, then traditional report cards are clearly inferior to more authentic models. Unhappily, assessment is sometimes driven by entirely different objectives—for example, to motivate students (with grades used as carrots and sticks to coerce them into working harder) or to sort students (the point being not to help everyone learn but to figure out who is better than whom). In either case, the project is doomed from the outset, not because we haven't found the right technique but because there is something fundamentally wrong with our goals.

The practice of sorting children is accomplished not only by grades (the most egregious example being grading on a curve) but also by standardized testing. So-called norm-referenced tests, like the Iowa Test of Basic Skills (ITBS) and Comprehensive Tests of Basic Skills (CTBS), are not intended to tell us whether teaching and learning have been successful. They are designed not to rate but to rank, to artificially spread out students' scores. Not only are the results reported in relative terms (rather than assessing how well each did according to a fixed standard), but the questions on the tests have been selected with that purpose in mind. The test designers will probably toss out an item that most students manage to answer correctly. Whether it is reasonable for students to know the answer is irrelevant. Thus, to use a test like the ITBS to gauge educational quality, as assessment expert W. James

Popham recently remarked, "is like measuring temperature with a table-spoon."

Standardized tests often have the additional disadvantages of being: (a) produced and scored far away from the classroom, (b) multiple choice in design (so students can't generate answers or explain their thinking), (c) timed (so speed matters more than thoughtfulness) and (d) administered on a one-shot, high-anxiety basis.

All of these features represent the very opposite of meaningful assessment. But that doesn't mean these tests are irrelevant to what goes on in class-rooms. To the contrary, they have a very powerful impact on instruction, almost always for the worse. Teachers feel increasingly pressured to take time away from real learning in order to prepare students to take these dreadful tests.

Some of this pressure originates from state capitals, of course. However, school district administrators often compound the harm by adding additional tests, sometimes those that are least informative (by virtue of being norm-referenced) and most destructive (by virtue of how teachers end up creating a dumbed-down, test-driven curriculum). All of this is done, of course, in the name of tougher standards and accountability, but, as any good teacher could tell you, the practical result is that the intellectual life is squeezed out of classrooms.

In fact, researchers could tell you this, too. In a study conducted in Colorado, some 4th-grade teachers were asked to teach a specific task. About half were told that when they were finished, their students must "perform up to standards" and do well on a test. The other teachers, given the identical task, were invited simply to "facilitate the children's learning." At the end, all the students were tested. The result: Students in the standards classrooms did not learn the task as well.

Why? For one thing, when teachers feel pressured to produce results, they tend to pressure their students in turn. That is exactly what was found in a second study, conducted in New York. Teachers became more controlling, removing virtually any opportunity for students to direct their own learn-ing. Since people rarely do their best when they feel controlled, the find-ings of the Colorado experiment make perfect sense: The more teachers are thinking about test results and "raising the bar," the less well the students actually perform—to say nothing of how their enthusiasm for learning is apt to wane.

A DISTURBING SITUATION

The implications of taking seriously these concerns about grades and tests obviously would be enormous. But even this critique doesn't get to the bottom of what's wrong with the current approach to assessment. The underlying problem concerns a fundamental distinction that has been at the center of some work in educational psychology for a couple of decades now. It is the difference between focusing on how well you're doing something and focusing on what you're doing.

Consider a school that constantly emphasizes the importance of performance! results! achievement! success! A student who has absorbed that message may find it difficult to get swept away with the process of creating a poem or trying to build a working telescope. He may be so concerned about the results that he's not all that engaged in the activity that produces those results. The two orientations aren't mutually exclusive, of course, but in practice they feel different and lead to different behaviors. Without even knowing how well a student actually did at a task or how smart she is supposed to be, we can tell a lot just from knowing whether she has been led to be more concerned about layers of learning or levels of achievement.

Doesn't it matter how effectively students are learning? Of course it does. It makes sense to sit down with them every so often to figure out how successful they (and we) have been. But when we get carried away with results, we wind up, paradoxically, with results that are less than ideal. Specifically, the evidence suggests that five disturbing consequences are likely to accompany an obsession with standards and achievement:

1. Students come to regard learning as a chore. When kids are encouraged constantly to think about how well they're doing in school, the first casualty is their attitude toward learning. They may come to view the tasks themselves—the stories and science projects and math problems—as material that must be gotten through. It's stuff they're supposed to do better at, not stuff they're excited about exploring. The kind of student who is mostly concerned with being a top performer may persevere at a task, but genuine interest in it or excitement about the whole idea of learning often begins to evaporate as soon as achievement becomes the main point.

This is related to the discovery by psychologists that intrinsic motivation and extrinsic motivation tend to be inversely related: The more people are rewarded for doing something, the more they tend to lose interest in whatever they had to do to get the reward. Thus, it shouldn't be surprising that when students are told they'll need to know something for a test—or, more generally, that something they're about to do will count for a grade—they are likely to find that task (or book or idea) less appealing in its own right.

2. Students try to avoid challenging tasks. If the point is to succeed rather than to stretch one's thinking or discover new ideas, then it is completely logical for a student to want to do whatever is easiest. That, after all, will maximize the probability of success—or at least minimize the probability of failure.

A number of researchers have tested this hypothesis. Typically, in such an experiment, kids are told they're going to be given a task. Some are informed that their performance will be evaluated while others are encouraged to think of this as an opportunity to learn rather than to do well. Then each student is given a chance to choose how hard a version of the task he or she wants to try. The result is always the same: Those who had been told it's "an opportunity to learn" are more willing to challenge themselves than are those who had been led to think about how well they'll do.

It's convenient for us to assume that kids who cut corners are just being lazy because then it's the kids who have to be fixed. But perhaps they're just being rational. They have adapted to an environment where results, not intellectual exploration, are what count. When school systems use traditional grading systems—or, worse, when they add honor rolls and other incentives to enhance the significance of grades—they are unwittingly discouraging students from stretching themselves to see what they're capable of doing. It's almost painfully ironic: School officials and reformers complain bitterly about how kids today just want to take the easy way out . . . while simultaneously creating an emphasis on performance and results that leads predictably to that very outcome.

3. Students tend to think less deeply. The goal of some students is to acquire new skills, to find out about the world, to understand what they're doing. When they pick up a book, they're thinking about what they're reading, not about how well they're reading it. Paradoxically, these students who have put success out of their minds are likely to be successful. They process information more deeply, review things they didn't understand the first time, make connections between what they're doing now and what they learned earlier, and use more strategies to make sense of the ideas they're encountering. All of this has been demonstrated empirically.

By contrast, students who have been led to focus on producing the right answer or scoring well on a test tend to think more superficially. Consider just one of dozens of studies on this question, which concerns the ability to transfer understanding—that is, to take something learned over here and apply it to a new task or question over there. As a group of 8th graders were about to begin a week-long unit in science class, researchers gauged whether each student was more interested in understanding or in being successful. When the unit was over, the students were tested on their ability to transfer their new knowledge. Regardless of whether their earlier test scores had been high or low, the success-oriented students simply did not do as well as those who were more learning-oriented.

4. Students may fall apart when they fail. No one succeeds all the time, and no one can learn very effectively without making mistakes and bumping up against his or her limits. It's important, therefore, to encourage a healthy and resilient attitude toward failure. As a rule, that is exactly what students tend to have if their main goal is to learn: When they do something incorrectly, they see the result as useful information. They figure out what went wrong and how to fix it.

Not so for the kids who believe (often because they have been explicitly told) that the point is to succeed—or even to do better than everyone else. They seem to be fine as long as they are succeeding, but as soon as they hit a bump they may regard themselves as failures and act as though they're helpless to do anything about it. Even a momentary stumble can seem to cancel out all their past successes. When the point isn't to figure things out but to prove how good you are, it's often hard to cope with being less than good.

Consider the student who becomes frantic when he gets a 92 instead of his usual 100. We usually see this as a problem with the individual and conclude that such students are just too hard on themselves. But the "what I'm doing" versus "how well I'm doing" distinction can give us a new lens through which to see what is going on here. It may be the systemic demand for high achievement that led him to become debilitated when he failed, even if the failure is only relative.

The important point isn't what level of performance qualifies as failure (a 92 versus a 40, say). It's the perceived pressure not to fail, which can have a particularly harmful impact on high-achieving and high-ability students. Thus, to reassure such a student that "a 92 is still very good" or that we're sure he'll "do better next time" doesn't just miss the point; it makes things worse by underscoring yet again that the point of school isn't to explore ideas, it's to triumph.

5. Students value ability more than effort. How do we react when a student receives a score of 100 on a quiz? Most teachers and parents treat that as news worth celebrating. Those who are more thoughtful, by contrast, are not necessarily pleased. First of all, they will be concerned about the "bunch o' facts" approach to instruction and assessment that may be reflected by the use of traditional quizzes. Even successful students are not well-served by such teaching.

But even when better forms of assessment are used, perceptive observers realize that a student's score is less important than why she thinks she got that score. Let's ask how a student might explain doing especially well on a test. One possibility is effort: She tried hard, studied, did all she could to learn the material. A second possibility is ability: If you asked her how she got a hundred, she might reply (or think), "Well, I guess I'm just smart." Yet another answer is luck: She believes she guessed correctly or was just having a good day. Finally, she might explain the result in terms of the level of task difficulty—in this case, the fact that the test was easy. (Notice that these same four reasons could be used by another student to make sense of his grade of 23 on the same quiz: I didn't try hard; I'm just stupid; it was bad luck; or the test was difficult.)

Which of these four explanations for doing well (or poorly) do you favor? Which would you like to see students using to account for their performance in school? Almost everyone would vote for effort. It bodes well for the future when kids attribute a good score to how carefully they prepared for the test. Likewise, those who attribute a low score to not preparing for the test tend to perceive failure as something they can prevent next time. So here's the punch line: When students are led to focus on how well they are performing in school, they tend to explain their performance not by how hard they tried but by how smart they are.

Researchers have demonstrated that a student with a performance focus— How am I doing? Are my grades high enough? Do I know the right answer?—is likely to interpret these questions "in terms of how much ability [he or she has] and whether or not this ability is adequate to achieve success," as educational psychologist Carol Dweck and a colleague have explained. In their study of academically advanced students, for example, the more that teachers emphasized getting good grades, avoiding mistakes and keeping up with everyone else, the more the students tended to attribute poor performance to factors they thought were outside their control, such as a lack of ability. When students are made to think constantly about how well they are doing, they are apt to explain the outcome in terms of who they are rather than how hard they tried.

Research also demonstrates that adolescents who explain their achievement in terms of their intelligence tend to think less deeply and carefully about what they're learning than do those who appeal to the idea of effort. Similarly, elementary school students who attribute failure to ability are likely to be poorer readers. And if children are encouraged to think of themselves as "smart" when they succeed, doing poorly on a subsequent task will bring down their achievement even though it doesn't have that effect on other kids.

The upshot of all this is that beliefs about intelligence and about the causes of one's own success and failure matter a lot. They often make more of a difference than how confident students are or what they're truly capable of doing or how they did on last week's exam. If, like the cheerleaders for tougher standards, we look only at the bottom line, only at the test scores and grades, we'll end up overlooking the ways that students make sense of those results. And if we get kids thinking too much about how to improve the bottom line, they may end up making sense of those results in the least constructive way.

UNDERMINING EXCELLENCE

If all of this seems radical, it is—in the original, Latin sense of the word radical, which means "of the root." Indeed, cutting-edge research raises root questions, including the possibility that the problem with tests is not limited to their content. Rather, the harm comes from paying too much attention to the results. Even the most unbiased, carefully constructed, "authentic" measure of what students know is likely to be worrisome, psychologically speaking, if too big a deal is made about how students did, thus leading them (and their teachers) to think less about learning and more about test outcomes. As Martin Maehr and Carol Midgley at the University of Michigan have concluded, "An overemphasis on assessment can actually undermine the pursuit of excellence." That's true regardless of the quality of the assessment. Bad tests just multiply the damage.

Most of the time students are in school, particularly younger students but arguably older ones too, they should be able to think and write and explore without worrying about how good they are. Only now and then does it make sense for the teacher to help them attend to how successful they've been and how they can improve. On those occasions, the assessment can and should be done without the use of traditional grades and standardized tests. But most of the time, students should be immersed in learning.

— 4 —

International Comparisons: Worth the Cost?

Gerald W. Bracey

When one considers international comparisons of academic achievement, a question that early arises is, Why should anyone care? Different cultures, after all, have different goals for their educational systems. Why try to put in place some kind of "one-size-fits-all" assessment?

One answer to this question, at least insofar as the United States goes, has to do with our being such a normative and competitive nation. In any endeavor, be it sports, business, or television ratings, we want to know who's Number 1. And, in the case of the United States in relationship to other countries, we always want to know what is our position among the ranks, and if it is not Number 1, why not?

Another reason has to do with globalization and some misplaced perceptions about the importance of schools vis-à-vis global competitiveness. As first airplanes and then information technology increased the links among countries, people became more and more curious about how other nations were faring and about what one nation might learn from another. Julia Child ascribed the extraordinary improvements in American cooking since the early 1960s simply to the flow of people across the Atlantic after the arrival of jet-powered passenger airplanes made trans-Atlantic crossings rapid enough and cheap enough for many people to go abroad.

The flow of curriculum materials and instructional practices has been somewhat less than that seen in the area of the culinary arts. After all, few people go abroad with the idea of studying other nations' educational systems (this is a fairly small field known as comparative education). But everyone who goes abroad does eat. In addition, the qualities of a fine bouillabaisse make themselves known more quickly and concretely than do, say, the intricacies of Singapore math.

Interest in other nations' educational systems is more likely to arise from results of formal international studies. For instance, some of the researchers who directed the Third International Mathematics and Science Study examined the five highest scoring countries in mathematics for common qualities. Among the commonalities was that all five had highly centralized educational systems directed by the federal government. This was in stark contrast to the state and locally controlled systems in this country, and the researchers wondered if we might do better if we had a system with a uniform curriculum.

People lost some interest in the issue when it was noted that while eight of the top ten countries had centralized systems, so did eight of the ten lowest-scoring countries. The first group of researchers had erred in not checking both high- and low-scoring nations.

Similar, the PISA study (Program of International Student Assessment) of 2001 resulted in hundreds of educators in Europe flocking to Finland, which ranked first in Europe in reading, mathematics, and science (more about PISA later). Many of the educators heading north were Germans. Germany had not fared well among the thirty-two countries in PISA. German media carried headlines such as "Dumbkopf!" and "Are German Students Stupid?" German educators sought to find out what the Finns were doing right in hopes of importing best practices back to Germany.[1]

In a narrow sense, concern about the international competitiveness reached a crisis level when the Soviet Union launched *Sputnik*, the first man-made satellite, in 1957. The worries that *Sputnik* aroused were limited to the space and weapons race between Russia and the United States.

A more general concern about economic competitiveness became intense in the 1970s and crystallized with the publication of *A Nation at Risk* in 1983. *Risk* presented the argument that the biggest threat to our well-being was not that the Soviets would bomb the United States off the planet but that our friends, especially Germany, Japan, and South Korea, would outsmart the United States and take away our number one position in the global economic system. The commissioners who put *Risk* together wrote, "If only to keep and improve on the slim competitive edge we still retain in world markets, we must dedicate ourselves to the reform of our educational system."

The commissioners who wrote *A Nation at Risk* presented no real evidence for the contention that it was the *schools* that were causing us to lose our competitive edge. Generally, people looked to Japan and saw the "Japanese economic miracle," saw that Japanese students scored high on the international comparisons, and put the two together in an illogical inference that high test scores *caused* economic prosperity. The theory that high test scores equal economic well-being became quite popular after *A Nation at Risk*, as the United States slid into recession. Many variations were heard on "Lousy schools are producing a lousy workforce and that is killing us in the global marketplace."

However, by the early 1990s, the country's economy had rebounded. "The American Economy: Back on Top," proclaimed *The New York Times* in February 1994. "Rising Sun Meets Rising Sam," echoed *The Washington Post*. No one credited the schools for the turnaround. Indeed, critics claimed the school hadn't improved. A mere three months after *The New York Times* declared that the U.S. economy had been restored to first place, Louis Gerstner, CEO at IBM, penned an op-ed essay for the *Times*, "Our Schools Are Failing." Why were they failing? Because, said Gerstner, the products of our high schools can't compete with the graduates of other developed nations.

This sequence of events reflects a common occurrence in America. When something goes wrong in society, people blame the schools. When the wrong is righted, schools are not credited. That the schools are not credited is fair, since blaming them in the first places was silly.

Not only did the American economy again surge ahead, the Japanese realized the lunacy of a widespread cliché in that country: that the Emperor's palace and grounds were worth more than the entire state of California. "It was crazy," said a Japanese commentator on National Public Radio's "All Things Considered." Japan went into an economic swoon from which it has yet, now thirteen years later, to emerge.

As Japan slumped, the so-called "Asian Tiger" economies went into free fall in the mid-1990's, while America continued to enjoy the longest sustained boom in history. This is likely why the "lousy schools" theory of recessions and competitiveness died away. In the most recent recession of 2001–2002, no one blamed the schools, and that is a good thing.

In fact, global competitiveness is a tremendously complex affair and certainly could not be controlled or much influenced by schools. To determine a nation's global competitiveness requires knowledge of its roads, water system, power system, the relative value of its currency, the access citizens have to computers and cell phones, its "corruption index," and literally hundreds of other variables. The World Economic Forum (WEF) produces annual ratings for global competitiveness and projections for global competitiveness growth over the next five years. In 2001–2002, the United States was ranked first in both among the seventy-five nations ranked.

As noted earlier, *A Nation at Risk* had no real evidence to link test scores to competitiveness, nor has anyone else brought such evidence forward since that document appeared in 1983. I decided to collect some empirical evidence on whether these rankings were related to rankings on test scores. From the seventy-five nations ranked by the WEF, and the forty-one nations that took part in the Third International Mathematics and Science Study (TIMSS), I was able to find thirty-five nations that had rankings on both variables, competitiveness and test scores. If test scores are important to competitiveness, we should see a strong correlation coefficient, a statistic that measures the relationship of two variables, say in the vicinity of +0.40. The correlation was +0.19. That is a tiny correlation. If the five nations that were low on both were removed from the analysis, the correlation actually became *negative,* although the correlation coefficient was so small one would say that it was really zero. That means that some countries with high test scores were not competitive and some countries with low test scores were highly competitive.

This should not be surprising because, as noted, the WEF uses hundreds of indicators in its calculations of competitiveness. In the 2002–2003 rankings, the United States "fell" to second place behind Finland (which had been number two the previous year). The reasons given had nothing to do with schools. The WEF looked at the weak dollar, the Bush administration tax cuts, the ever-increasing trade deficit with other nations, and the myriad scandals from the corporate world and Wall Street and did not like what it saw.

International comparisons have also gotten more attention lately simply because they have gotten so much better. The studies from the 1960s, 1970s, and 1980s were afflicted with many methodological problems. Countries were asked to participate and allowed to choose whom to test. Most countries do not have a culture of public self-criticism that one sees in the United States. The United States could always be counted on to pick a representative sample of students to test. Some countries tended to test students the countries felt would make them look good.

The organizations that conduct international studies have improved the sampling situation either by developing in-house expertise or by turning to organizations that specialize in sampling (it's a tricky issue) and setting conditions on countries for participation in the studies. For example, in the TIMSS, all participating countries were required to send a list of every school in the country, as well as a set of demographic characteristics for that school (percent in poverty, percent of immigrants, location, etc.) to Statistics Canada, Inc., in Ottawa. StatCan, as it is known, specializes in drawing samples.

Of course, in many countries, one cannot force the selected schools to participate, and that remains a problem in some nations. Schools that elect not to participate tend to be those with characteristics that would lead one to expect the schools might not score well. When a school opts out of a study, it is replaced with another school, but there is a question of whether the replacement schools are truly equivalent to the schools that opted out. Indeed, as we shall see in the following paragraphs, one researcher in England has argued that England's high scores in PISA occurred because so many potentially low-scoring schools opted out.

Even without the sampling problems, there were problems of comparability in the early studies. For instance, many European nations tracked students from an early age, meaning that different groups of children received different curricula. Early tracking is now seen only in Germany, and it might well end there soon, too. When Germany did not do well in PISA, early tracking was brought forth as the principal culprit.

Tracking is still a problem at the high school level. Most students in the United States leave eighth grade for a comprehensive high school, although there is tracking within these high schools. In many other countries, the schools themselves are tracked. Some provide a college preparatory curriculum, some provide vocational or technical courses, some are oriented to science and technology, and some to arts and humanities. The most recent attempt to test students at the end of secondary school, 1995's Third International Mathematics and Science Study, did not, in my opinion, succeed. Worse, it gave the world a devastating cliché about American schools. Former Secretary of Education William J. Bennett, in a speech to the Heritage Foundation, declared, "In America today, the longer you stay in school, the dumber you get relative to your peers in other industrialized nations." We will deal with Bennett's contention later and present evidence about the true performance of American students in the three grades tested: fourth, eighth, and twelfth.

Beyond tracking, until recently, many European nations had low rates of high school completion, again making comparability difficult or next to impossible at the secondary level. For instance, in the Second International Mathematics Study, 100 percent of high school seniors in Hungary were still taking math courses. But only 50 percent of the age group was still in school. How does one compare performance in Hungary with performance in countries that have smaller percentages studying math but much higher percentages still in school?

The historic low completion rates in Europe might well have affected the curriculum at lower grades. Students left in large numbers after eighth grade. That meant if educators in a particular country felt that a subject were important for everyone to study, they had to introduce it before the end of eighth grade. These middle school years are more intense with new material than they are in the United States. For example, seventh graders in Japan receive considerable amounts of algebra, and eighth graders spend a fair amount of time on plane geometry. America, by contrast, could safely wait until ninth grade for algebra and tenth grade for geometry, knowing that almost everyone would still be in school in these grades. Whether we *should* wait until these later years is another question.

The fact that international comparisons have gotten much better does not mean that they are without problems. These are enormously complex operations to manage, requiring the cooperation of many people in each country. Unfortunately, there has been little critical scrutiny of the comparisons in this country. Elsewhere, results that looked anomalous to those familiar with results of earlier studies have received critical review.

For instance, S. J. Prais of the National Institute of Economic and Social Research in London noticed that the PISA scores for students in the United Kingdom looked suspiciously high when compared with earlier results. In the 1999 version of TIMSS, English youth had finished about forty points behind such nations as Switzerland, France, Belgium, the Czech Republic, and Hungary. Yet on PISA, they finished about twenty points ahead. The cumulative difference of sixty points is quite large.[2] (Although the test questions in PISA and TIMSS were different, the results of both studies were placed on the same scale, meaning that a 500 in PISA has the same meaning as a 500 in TIMSS.)

Either English students had experienced a tremendous growth spurt in math skills or something was amiss with the scores. Prais was skeptical of the growth spurt hypothesis when he noted that it would have occurred in a single year, between the TIMSS testing of 1999 and PISA's testing in 2000. In fact, since TIMSS tested fourteen-year-olds and PISA fifteen-year-olds, the students would all have come from the same age cohort, namely children born in 1984.

As fuller reports on PISA emerged, Prais and his colleagues found four problematic areas of the PISA assessment: the nature of the questions asked, the difference in the age group covered, the representativeness of the schools participating in PISA, and the representativeness of the students actually taking the tests in those schools that did take part.

From the outset, PISA officials made it clear that, unlike TIMSS, PISA's goals were not to determine how well the students had mastered school subjects but how well students could function in "everyday life." Says the PISA website, "Previous international assessments have concentrated on 'school' knowledge. PISA aims at measuring how well students perform beyond the school curriculum" (http://www.pisa-oecd.org/pisa/skills.htm).

Limiting himself to math items, Prais is fairly dismissive of the idea that PISA items have something to do with everyday life. He presents one of the released items as an example:

> A graph shows the fluctuating "speed of a racing car along a flat 3 km racing track (second lap)" against the distance covered along the track. Pupils were assumed to know that the track was some form of a closed loop; they were also assumed to know that normally there are various bends along the track, and that speed had to be reduced before entering each bend. Pupils were required to read from the graph the "approximate distance from the starting time to the beginning of the longest straight section of the track," and similar matters; they then had to match the speed-distance graph with five possible track-circuit diagrams.

Prais comments: "Perhaps these are perfectly reasonable assumptions and reasonable questions in relation to Austrian or German boys—but for girls in rural Greece or Portugal? Answering such questions correctly may be more a test of 'common sense' or of 'IQ' than the results of mathematical schooling at this age." Indeed, overall, the item favored boys a lot. In the case of Austrian and German boys, 43 percent and 38 percent, respectively, got it right. For Portuguese and Greek girls, the figures were 10 percent and 8 percent, respectively. (This question would not have survived a gender-bias review committee in this country.)

Choosing an age rather than a grade always introduces complications in any assessment. TIMSS stopped at age fourteen, when virtually everyone is still in school. PISA, by moving up to fifteen, picked an age by which almost half of the students have left school in a few of the developing countries. Even within developed countries, the age choice caused problems. For instance, in Belgium, the fifteen-year-olds in tenth grade scored 564, while those in ninth grade scored 455, and those in eighth grade a mere 364. The fifteen-year-olds in eighth grade would have had little impact on the overall Belgian average because there were so few of them, but almost one-fourth of Belgium's fifteen-year-olds were in ninth grade.

As noted, in contemporary international comparisons, usually some external agency draws the sample of schools to be included in the study. It remains to the country to convince those schools to actually participate. In most nations, around 90 percent of those schools selected for participation actually took part, but in the United Kingdom the figure was a mere 61 percent. Usually, those schools that opt out of a study have demographic characteristics that would lead one to predict low scores, and Prais feels that this was the case in PISA: "The missing schools on the whole were probably low-attaining schools; and there must be grave suspicions of upward bias in the average score of responding schools as a results of such a low response rate."

The United Kingdom also had the lowest participation rate among its students of any nation in the study. The participation rates for individual schools seem to be clouded in obscurity. Says Prais, "The *true* proportion of pupils participating, including all schools contributing to each country's published average score, has so far not been revealed. The shenanigans of the Official Minds at work here raise wider worries."

Virtually throwing his hands up in frustration, Prais observes that although English students were listed as scoring higher than Swiss students on twenty-one of thirty-one released items, the Swiss outperformed the English. He expresses dismay that the papers concerning these findings are "not easy reading even for professional mathematicians, and make no concessions to those who are not fully adept research-psychometricians." You and me, in other words.

I present Prais's analysis at some length to emphasize that international comparisons, although presented in the media as no more complicated than an end-of-course study in high school, are in fact extremely complicated. Apparently, some of the items in PISA were not reviewed for gender bias. Even if they were, one must ask if a test can be built that is fair to children in thirty-five different countries (PISA) or forty-one countries (TIMSS). These kinds of problems have been sloughed over. Little attention has been paid to some of the problems in the official documents and how some of these documents are themselves masterpieces of obscurantism ("an exercise for the student of Kafkaism," Prais puts it).

THE DUMBER YOU GET

With all these reservations in mind, let us consider Bennett's assertion that "In America today, the longer you stay in school the dumber you get in relation to peers in other developed nations."

This contention comes out of TIMSS. In TIMSS, American fourth graders were above average in mathematics and near the top in science among the twenty-six participating countries. As eighth graders, they were average in both subjects among forty-one nations. As twelfth graders, they were apparently at or near the bottom among twenty-one countries.

I believe that the decline between fourth and eighth grade is real but that the apparent decline from eighth grade to twelfth is just that, apparent. I consider each decline in turn. There are two factors that can be brought to bear on the decline between fourth and eighth grade—the size of U.S. textbooks and the historical treatment of the middle grades in this country.

In recent years, a number of cartoons have turned on the size and weight of backpacks on children's backs, and pediatricians report increasing rates of scoliosis and other spine-related illnesses. American textbooks are about three times as thick as those in other nations. In other countries, the state determines the books' contents. Here, giant for-profit publishers compete for lucrative textbook contracts from states, especially Texas and California, the two most populous states in the nation. Aiming for the broadest possible market, publishers take a "kitchen sink" approach to inclusion.[3]

American teachers attempt to cover it all. A TIMSS curriculum study found that American teachers cover far more topics per year than teachers in other countries. Other nations spend more time on fewer topics. It is thus quite possible that the desire for "coverage" results in coverage that is too brief and shallow to "take."

Secondly, American educators have historically regarded the middle school years as a time of consolidation and review of material covered in the elementary grades, a time to prepare for the more intense study of high school. Some middle school specialists contend that these grades should *not* concentrate on intellectual development but rather on the emerging sexuality and search for identity among students in this age range. Other countries are more inclined to see those middle grades as the start of high school and to introduce new material.

The part of TIMSS that tested American twelfth graders was known as the Final Year of Secondary School Assessment in recognition of the fact that the "Final Year" of secondary school means different things in different countries. In some countries, the final year would be the thirteenth or fourteenth grade in the United States. Attempts to render such comparisons as apples to apples comparison is virtually impossible.

In addition to the structural differences in secondary schooling across countries, the Final Year study was afflicted with a number of methodological flaws and what might be considered "quirky" occurrences. I have detailed the flaws in the March 2000 issue of *Educational Researcher*.[4]

The TIMSS Final Year study administered a math-science literacy test to what was to have been a representative sample of final-year students. In fact, a number of countries failed to produce such samples. In addition, countries were permitted to choose which students should be tested on the other two areas assessed, Advanced Mathematics and Physics. This was a reasonable idea but led to quirky selections.

For instance, for the Advanced Mathematics test, the United States tested all students taking precalculus or calculus courses. When I inquired of a TIMSS official why we had included precalculus students, the answer was, "Just to see how they'd do."

Well, they did awful. And not surprisingly. Fully 23 percent of the items on the advanced mathematics test *presumed* that the test taker had already taken a calculus course. American students who actually had calculus under their belts score right at the international average—the same position as eighth graders.

Students in precalculus courses scored 100 points lower. This is an enormous difference. If we consider the American students with calculus to be at the 50th percentile, then the students without calculus scored at the 16th percentile. It is a truism that students do not test well on material they have not been taught.

Those of us who have lived abroad will always hold suspicions about the validity of international comparisons because of differences in cultures that would be hard to quantify and measure but which affect test scores nonetheless. For instance, I have friends with grandchildren in French schools, and they are appalled at the common use of shame as a motivational technique. A teacher might take the worst paper from an assignment, post it on a bulletin board, and make fun of it. What does this do to children? Is it responsible for the rapier-like wit and repartee the French are so noted for? Do the kids sit there and think of sharp-tongued responses they could make to the teacher if they dared?

One such cultural variable that TIMSS did manage to quantify was hours worked at a paid job. In most nations, one is either a student or a worker, not both. But the American vision of the adolescent years includes jobs. The research on how jobs affect school performance generally shows that students who work up to twenty hours a week actually do better in school than students who work longer hours or who don't work at all. A sense of responsibility and a development of time management skills are the usual reasons given.

In TIMSS, fully 55 percent of American high school seniors reported that they worked more than twenty-one hours a week at a job. Fully 28 percent said they worked more than thirty-five hours a week. Their scores reflected their working hours. While American students who worked up to twenty hours a week were again right at the international average, those who worked more were well below it (a more typical national profile would be of, say, Sweden, where 84 percent of students worked zero to fourteen hours a week and only 1 percent reported working more than thirty-five hours a week).

Finally, among the potential culturally idiosyncratic factors, do other nations have a "senior slump?" High schools in this country report great difficulties in getting seniors to perform academic work. Most of them know what they will be doing after high school. In at least some other countries—Germany, France, and England, for instance—at least some students will spend their senior year gearing up for important end-of-year exams. In any case, in an attempt to have TIMSS Final Year come as close to the end of the final year as possible, we administered the tests to seniors in May.

When we turn to PISA, we find little to take from it except perhaps confirmation of America's standing as average among developed nations. Because PISA attempted to measure "everyday" problem solving skills it has little to say about the school system itself (TIMSS, by contrast, was supposed to reflect what happened in courses). PISA tested reading, math, and science skills in fifteen-year-olds in thirty-two mostly developed nations. The United States was average in all three subjects.

PIRLS OF WISDOM

The most recent international study is PIRLS, Progress in International Reading Literacy Study, which measures reading skills among ten-year-olds in thirty-five countries. This study is interesting for what it, taken with TIMSS, says about the way media in this country treat international comparisons, as well as what it says about reading skills in this country.

Although TIMSS tested students in grades four, eight, and twelve, the results were released in order of eight, four, and twelve over a two-year period from 1996 to 1998. The media tended to give the eighth-grade results the "if it bleeds it leads" treatment. Virtually all reports called the average finish of American students "mediocre." But "average" is a statistic, "mediocre" is a judgment. The people who finish fourth and fifth in the final heat of the 100-meter dash at the Olympics are average but hardly mediocre.

The fourth-grade results received very little attention at all. The report of the Final Year Study makes it clear that comparisons across countries are difficult: "It was no small task for many countries to describe the final year. In most TIMSS countries, students' final year of school depends on their course of study (e.g., academic, technical, or apprenticeship)." The press conference held by the U.S. Department of Education revealed no such subtlety. The results came out as an apples-to-apples comparison in which American seniors were among the worst performing. The media pounced:

> American high school seniors have scored far below their peers from many other countries (*Washington Post*).

> American high school seniors—even the best and brightest among them—score well below the average for their peers participating in TIMSS (*Education Week*).

> US twelfth graders rank poorly in math and science (*New York Times*).

Virtually every paper in the country covered TIMSS and virtually all of them took a "woe is us" tack on the results.

In contrast, the appearance of PIRLS in April 2003 was accompanied by virtually no press coverage. Only three newspapers, the *Boston Globe, Boston Herald,* and *Washington Times* had bylined stories. PIRLS was released through Boston College, which would account for the coverage in that city, but where was everyone else?

The Associated Press put out a non-bylined wire story. This was picked up by *The Washington Post,* which filled one-twelfth of the back page of section A with it. The rest of the back page contained ads for a department store. About fifteen papers around the nation used some or all of the AP story, among them only the *San Francisco Chronicle* and *Seattle Times,* being large-market papers. *The New York Times* never printed a word, nor did any papers in Philadelphia, Atlanta, Miami, Dallas, Houston, Chicago, St. Louis, Denver, or Los Angeles. If it bleeds, it leads, but good news is no news.

The essential facts of PIRLS are these: U.S. ten-year-olds finished ninth among students in thirty-five countries. Only three countries, though, had significantly higher scores.

What is more significant about PIRLS than the basic result, though, are what those results look like analyzed by poverty level. The United States has a much higher proportion of its children living in poverty than do other developed nations. The most recent international study of poverty found 22 percent of America children in poverty (it has since fallen to 20 percent). The next highest nation was Australia at 14 percent, and no other nation even had double-digits.

Some reformers have argued that poverty is "no excuse," that poor children can learn as well as other children. I agree that poverty is not an excuse. It is a condition. Gravity is a condition; so is poverty. Gravity affects every aspect of life; so does poverty. Poor kids are far more likely to come from mothers who did not receive adequate prenatal care. They are far more likely to be malnourished, to suffer injury or death, to be physically or mentally abused. It makes a difference on how they fare in school.

The U.S. Department of Education analyzed the PISA results by poverty level and the results are stunning:

Top nation, among 35: Sweden, scoring at 561
U.S. overall score, 543
International average, 500

Thus, even the overall results show American students well above the international average, but consider the results analyzed by the poverty levels of the schools, poverty being defined in terms of the proportion of students eligible for free or reduced price meals:

Percent of students	Percent in Poverty	Score
13	<10	589
17	10–25	567
28	25–50	551
22	50–75	518
20	75+	485

From this table, we see that the 13 percent of American students who attend schools where fewer than 10 percent of the children live in poverty score much higher than the highest scoring nation. The 17 percent of the students in schools with 10 to 25 percent poverty also outscore the top nation, although not by much. If the 28 percent of American students who attend schools where 25 to 50 percent of the students live in poverty constituted a nation, that nation, by scoring 551, would rank fourth in the world. It is only the 20 percent of the students whose schools contain more than 75 percent of the students in poverty whose average score falls below the international average of all thirty-five nations.

OTHER ASPECTS OF INTERNATIONAL STUDIES

This chapter has focused largely on the test results of international studies. These are the aspects of the studies that have received the most attention, but the reader should be aware that there were other aspects of some of them as well. Most recent studies have gathered background information on students, but these have produced little new knowledge. For instance, in all of the studies within each country, students from higher income families or students whose homes contained more books scored higher.

The curriculum studies part of TIMSS found that different countries have many different aims for their curricula. It also found that American teachers teach many more topics per year than do teachers in other countries— confronted with those huge textbooks, they try to get through it all.

Another part of TIMSS made videotapes of teachers in six high-scoring countries plus the United States teaching eighth-grade mathematics. Getting representatives from these countries to agree on what they were seeing proved nearly impossible. There was even some suggestion that in order to get the seven nations to agree on what categories to use and what behaviors meant, some important aspects of teaching might have been overlooked. In any case, the video study concluded that the nations did not share any one thing in common that accounted for their high test scores.

The international studies have become a regular aspect of globalization. They are not likely to disappear, because they have become something of a growth industry and a number of people have fashioned their careers around them. They do seem to me to be rather expensive—TIMSS cost U.S. taxpayers over $53 million dollars. It was designed largely by psychometricians and researchers, people who are remote from the daily life of classrooms. One wonders what the studies might have looked like had they received significant input from schoolteachers and building administrators.[5]

— 5 —

Assessment, Accountability, and the Impossible Dream

Linda Mabry

MABRY: "Do you personally believe that 100 percent of third through eighth grade students in the United States will reach proficiency in reading and math by the year 2014?"

STEVENSON: "Yes."

MABRY: "I'm not sure you can get 100 percent of students out of bed on time in the morning by 2014."

STEVENSON: "You asked me my opinion, and that's my opinion."

This interchange opened a question-and-answer period with Zollie Stevenson of the U.S. Department of Education Office of Compensatory Education, after his presentation at the 2003 annual meeting of the National Council of Measurement in Education regarding the Annual Yearly Progress (AYP) provision of the No Child Left Behind Act (2001).[1] The problem is that it is not merely Stevenson's opinion that all these students will reach proficiency by the year 2014—it is the law of the land.

The rhetoric of the law is attractive. Who would want to leave a child behind? Who would not want universal literacy and numeracy? But it is a matter of contention whether NCLB articulates a wonderful dream for inspiring public education to admirable new accomplishments or a nightmare of unintended—perhaps not entirely unforeseeable—consequences. With the intent to contribute to an educational assessment and accountability policy that is awake to historical lessons and current realities, this chapter will critique the current standards, assessment, and accountability dream.

ASSESSMENT AND ACCOUNTABILITY POLICY

National Policy

Although its far-ranging provisions mandate such things as teacher qualifications and federal preference in funding research methods,[2] at its core, NCLB is an assessment and accountability policy. It is the latest of the periodic reauthorizations of the federal Elementary and Secondary Education Act of 1965. The last reauthorization prior to NCLB, "Goals 2000,"[3] identified six national goals, still unmet:

- All children to be ready to learn
- A 90 percent high school graduation rate
- All children to be competent in core subjects, including fine arts and foreign languages
- The United States to be first in the world in math and science
- Every adult to be literate and competitive in the workforce
- Safe, disciplined, drug-free schools

Seven years later when NCLB became law, Goals 2000's more explicit state requirements had been fully met by only nineteen states.[4]

Goals 2000 envisioned a system of national testing, including performance assessments, aligned to *content standards* to be developed in each academic subject area, and *opportunity-to-learn standards* to ensure adequate resources for all schools. This vision of national testing was modified in NCLB to a requirement that each state use its own standards-based tests. For credibility and comparability, each state's scores must be considered against its scores on the National Assessment of Educational Progress (NAEP), designed in 1969 as a long-term trend instrument, a completely different purpose from accountability. NCLB requires states to participate in biennial NAEP testing whereas, previously, participation had been voluntary.

State Trends

NCLB might be considered the next step in the trend toward alarmingly strict assessment and accountability.[5] By the time NCLB became law, the movement toward content standards and standards-based testing had overtaken all states but one, Iowa.[6] NCLB required an increase in testing for two-thirds of the states.

NCLB also ratcheted up the states' already high stakes. As NCLB was enacted, eighteen states rewarded high-performing or improved schools, and twenty states threatened low-performing schools with closure or reconstitution, student transfers, or loss of funding. Seventeen states denied high school diplomas to students who failed exit or end-of-course exams. NCLB additionally required proficiency in reading and math by all students in grades three through eight within twelve years, by 2014, and proportional annual yearly progress (AYP) toward 100 percent proficiency. In January 2003, states were required to submit AYP plans for federal approval. Failure to meet their AYP targets will result, over the first five years, in successive penalties: requirements to offer school choice, to provide tutoring, to replace curricula and/or staff, to reconstitute schools. The first year of reporting AYP results, 2003, saw massive proportions of schools classified as "needing improvement."

NCLB represents the most profound incursion to date of the federal government into the U.S. Constitution's reservation to the states of the obligation to provide for public education. States *could* choose to ignore the statute. The incentive to comply is that NCLB empowers the federal government to withhold Title I funding, intended to assist struggling students with remedial services. As yet, no state has chosen to forego these funds, although Vermont initially considered doing so. In some states, legislation is being designed to permit opting out of NCLB and foregoing Title I funds.[7] Parents and other groups are developing opt-out plans.[8] In Pennsylvania, the Reading School District is suing the state on the grounds that sanctioning six of its schools for failure to make AYP and putting seven schools on a warning list is illegal.[9] Such contentiousness might be characterized as the predictable collision between the federal dream and local realities.

THE STANDARDS DREAM

On its face, the idea of having educational standards (or, as it is often phrased, high standards for all) is as attractive as the idea of leaving no child behind. Would we want pilots who failed to meet airline standards or surgeons who failed to meet medical standards? The frequent analogies of this type are flawed because professionals meeting standards for specific licensure are categorically different from high school students meeting general graduation standards or from schools meeting state standards while working with vastly different student populations and resources. But the rhetoric is compelling, and it sustains policy based on the dream of all students achieving universal educational standards.

Issues

Uniform expectations directly contradict not only our romantic collective self-concept as a nation of rugged individualists but also the best current learning theory. That theory is constructivism, the idea that each person constructs an individual knowledge base from his or her experiences and values.[10] Uniformity of standards is also at odds with the popular notion of multiple intelligences,[11] the idea that people have different intelligence profiles, again readily apparent, some of us better at logical reasoning and others at interpersonal relationships, for example. Individuality means differences in students' academic interests, choices, and performances.

There is no evidence that society is better served by teaching students the same content standards, expecting them to meet the same performance standards, or testing them with the same tests than it is by students coached individually to define and to perform their best on educative, authentic tasks.[12] Rather, common is the experience that teams function best where members have distinct skills to contribute, different interests and performance capacities, and the capability to consider a variety of thoughts and perspectives on addressing ill-defined real-world problems.[13]

It is not at all clear how comprehensive or how specific content standards should be. Teachers report that vague general standards can be used to justify any teaching,[14] even poor teaching. Conversely, they report that excruciatingly specific standards prevent them from exercising their professional obligation to design and adapt instruction for the particular children in their classrooms. Their concerns about test-driven curricula[15] compound into concerns about test developers controlling the content of education.[16]

It is not at all clear that state performance standards are set at appropriate levels or even that they can be.[17] All the standard-setting procedures in current use have been judged technically flawed,[18] and they vary widely from state to state. It is because state performance standards vary so widely that, partly to discourage states from using easy tests that might distort achievement and might lower expectations, NCLB requires scores on state tests to be confirmed against NAEP scores. But the NAEP standards and standard setting have also been judged flawed in repeated evaluations.[19]

Implications

Even if content standards and performance standards were satisfactory, NCLB's requirement of full proficiency by 2014 is unattainable. Total compliance by a huge, diverse population is unrealistic on its face. Even if it were not, AYP targets are about double the best NAEP score increases that have been documented. Analysis of NAEP trends has suggested it would take more than 100 years, not twelve years, to have all students in grades three through eight proficient in reading and math.[20] Those schools and districts escaping labels as failures in early years are unlikely to continue to do so.

It is not clear whether *opportunity-to-learn standards* could level the proverbial playing field for resource-poor schools and students. Opportunity-to-learn standards were an early Goals 2000 casualty, declared unworkable[21] until recently revived for scrutiny.[22] Inequitable school finance remains an intractable problem. Because high test scores are known to correlate with high socioeconomic status, a clear implication of test-driven accountability is inequitable educational consequences—impoverished students and the schools that serve them being allocated the fewest resources and facing low scores and the most severe penalties.

As it becomes more widely recognized that one-size-fits-all content standards fit few or none, and that neither very general nor very specific content standards consistently work well, NCLB may ultimately force the conclusion that content standards, as currently conceived, are unworkable.[23]

Performance standards are also not working. High performance standards are producing unacceptable failure rates and litigation, while low performance standards have been shown to lower educational quality. For example, the low standards minimum competency testing of the 1970s has been roundly criticized for setbacks in critical thinking and for "dumbing-down" education generally. More recent experience of high standards has included massive failure rates and such absurdities as judging "not yet proficient" a valedictorian in a high-performing Michigan suburban high school, a National Merit Scholar accepted by MIT.[24]

As they struggle to cope with impossible strictures, some responsible educators move to protect their schools, their funding, their students, and their jobs, sometimes doing things for which they are called "cheaters."[25] The common (not universal[26]) experience is that the standards dream is resulting in unintended negative consequences: narrowed curriculum, teaching to the test, reification of test scores, deprofessionalization of educators, and intimidation and punishment of students, especially those who were not to be left behind.[27]

THE ASSESSMENT DREAM

From early beginnings in the nineteenth century, U.S. test developers have ardently believed that their large-scale tests could measure student achievement better than teachers could.[28] Identification of flaws in testing were ignored[29] or addressed with ever more technical explanations and procedural fixes that only psychometricians could hope to understand. What proportion of the public, including educators and educational policymakers, understands Kuder-Richardson formulae, standard errors of measurement, construct validity? Protected from public scrutiny by technical abstruseness, test developers have continued to base tests on outmoded social science theory—behaviorism—using test procedures that are little more than shell games and stipulating definitions that spin and twist meanings.[30] For example:

- Test *reliability* is highly touted by testing corporations for marketing and litigation purposes but, in fact, rarely calculated. Reliability procedures have been displaced by *internal consistency* procedures, with states, the courts, schools, parents, and the public none the wiser.[31]
- *Norm-referenced tests* (NRTs), the scores of which merely indicate distance from the average (norm), necessarily identify half of all test takers as below average. Recognized as destructive to student self-esteem and motivation, NRTs fail to indicate whether the students in a group might all be proficient, producing a high average and low scores for some proficient students, or might all be nonproficient, producing a low average and high scores for some nonproficient students. NRT scores have proved so open to manipulation that, fifteen years ago, every state was reporting scores above average, a mathematical impossibility.[32] Test makers responded with *criterion-referenced tests* (CRTs), not publicizing that CRTs were so saturated with NRT procedures as to be indistinguishable from them in practice.[33]
- Charged with *bias* against racial and ethnic minorities, English Language Learners, females, and the poor because of their low scores,[34] testers claim that differences in scores cannot be taken as empirical proof of unfairness but might be indicators of real group differences in achievement, ability, or aptitude. Faintly echoing eugenicists from a more blatantly racist era, they ignore the social, psychological, and economic consequences of low scores—denials of diplomas, denials of college admission, lowered aspirations, grade retention, and its well-researched trajectory toward dropping out. Such effects, they claim, are social, not technical, and therefore not relevant to measurement.[35]
- Scores from state tests designed to measure *individual student achievement* are routinely aggregated as indicators of district and *school quality*, purposes for which the tests are not designed or validated.[36] Testing corporations know that their tests are being put to inappropriate use by their state customers, in violation of the *Standards for Educational and Psychological Testing*, but they nevertheless continue to supply tests and related services for huge profits.

Implications

Despite the enormous divide between psychometrics and classroom assessment,[37] almost every educational measurement textbook claims that assessment improves learning. The reality often is that large-scale high-stakes assessment corrupts teaching and learning, resulting in narrowed curricula and teaching to the test,[38] "score pollution,"[39] teacher deprofessionalization,[40] student demoralization and stress,[41] and the loss of experienced teachers for the neediest students.[42]

The dream is that tests will provide better indicators of educational progress and achievement than teachers and schools do. They do not. Teachers' grades aggregated into GPAs predict college performance at least as well as college entrance exams.[43] The dream is that the tests are basically sound and that they are perfectible.[44] The nightmare is that they are not. Measurement error cannot be eliminated from a test, any test. The amount of error cannot even be known but only estimated. Surely, students should not be left behind or their teachers punished because of measurement errors.

THE ACCOUNTABILITY DREAM

The implicit theory of action is that test-driven accountability systems will, through score-based sanctions, improve student learning or raise test scores. The dreamers in state and federal government have failed to learn from actual experience or from research revealing that top-down reform can produce compliance without improving education.[45] They have failed to investigate whether their so-called incentives might actually function as insultingly obvious bribes and threats or whether they counterproductively produce competition and systemic game-playing. Standards for educational accountability systems have been developed, but accountability systems are not being held accountable.[46]

Implications

NCLB is a dangerous dream, especially for those children whom NCLB appears designed to help. In reality, teachers and children are being forced to bear increasingly high-stakes consequences triggered by scores laden with measurement error. AYP targets are especially unrealistic for chronically underresourced urban schools and the committed teachers who work with disadvantaged children.[47] Already, test-driven accountability is driving experienced teachers from low-scoring schools.[48]

There are better ways of ensuring accountability. Teachers practice better ways of understanding student achievement, more consistent with admonitions to use multiple methods of assessment than current state practices. Over a half-century, program evaluators have honed many better methods and approaches for determining educational quality.[49] Yet the pervasiveness of external test-driven educational accountability threatens the extinction of more promising and more effective strategies.[50]

Dreamy, high-sounding goals are not enough to maintain or improve educational quality. Perseverance toward even laudable goals becomes perseveration when mounting negative evidence is ignored. While universal education may be beneficial, universal education *standards* may not be. While compulsory education may be beneficial, compulsory *achievement targets* may not be. History, recent experience, and research offer critical cautions.

Naively, shortsightedly, quixotically, test-driven accountability continues and intensifies a century of testing's unintended negative consequences. The deepening Foucauldian nightmare[51] of centralized control driving teachers to become technicians,[52] of objectifying students as scores, and of education based on fear, surveillance, and punishment is avoidable. The United States may choose to rouse itself from its impossible modernist, scientistic dream, thereby avoiding a rude awakening to schools further segregated by income, to the abandonment of public education, and to huge numbers of students left behind educationally, economically, and societally.

Authentic Accountability: An Alternative to High-Stakes Testing

KEN JONES

Wouldn't it be a breath of fresh air if those who make the laws and policies about public schools showed a little understanding and common sense about what actually happens in schools and didn't just demand higher test scores? If they devised a system for holding schools accountable that acknowledged and addressed the daily challenges of teaching twenty-five or more children in one room, all of them different, all with interests, strengths, and weaknesses, all with real personalities, cultures, family backgrounds, hopes, and fears? If they honored the multiple purposes served by schooling in our democratic society?

As it is, educational policy is made by people who are remote from classroom realities and who seem to see public schools as problems to be fixed or abandoned rather than as democratic human enterprises needing to be supported. There is a notion abroad these days that we should treat schools like mini-corporations responsible simply for a bottom line of test scores. This kind of thinking is creating a depersonalized climate in our schools where children are often thought of in terms of their ability to test well rather than as the whole, complex people that they are or for the potential they have. To say that we want to hold schools accountable only for test scores is saying that nothing else matters—not what a school offers to students in terms of opportunities and challenges, not the quality of relationships that exists to sustain children and adults in the work that they do, not what capacities students demonstrate outside of the narrow curriculum that is tested, and not how responsive a school is to its parents and community. The existing school accountability system fits schools like a straitjacket. It ignores human nature and constricts the flow of ideas and innovation.

To be sure, school structures and cultures need to adapt to the changing needs of the modern world. The factory model that has existed for nearly a century is badly in need of transformation. So many of our students have been neglected and badly served that we must change the very nature of schooling. Indeed, this is a premise for much of the school reform that has been percolating in education for the past couple of decades. And yet these efforts have not made much difference in terms of transforming schools or improving the school experience for many disadvantaged students.

Are schools resistant to such change? Undoubtedly. Should schools be held accountable to change and improve so that they better serve the needs of all students and not just the privileged? Absolutely. Is the present accountability system designed to help schools make those changes for the better? Unfortunately, no.

What we can see more and more clearly is that state and federal policies have been terribly counterproductive. The use of high-stakes testing of students has been fraught with flawed assumptions, oversimplified understandings of school realities, undemocratic concentration of power, undermining of the teaching profession, and disastrous consequences for our most vulnerable students. Far from the noble ideal of leaving no child behind, current policies, if continued, are bound to increase existing inequities, trivialize schooling, and mislead the public about the quality and promise of public education.

What is needed is a better means for evaluating schools, an alternative to the present system of simply relying upon testing. A new model, based on a different set of assumptions and understandings about school realities and approaches to power, is required. It must be centered on the needs of learners and on the intentions of having high expectations for all.

PREMISES

Let's start with basic premises about the purposes and audiences of schools. For what, to whom, and by what means should schools be held accountable?

Schools should be held accountable for at least the following:

- *The physical and emotional well-being of students.* The caretaking aspect of school is essential to quality education. Parents expect that their children will be safe in schools and that adults in schools will tend to their affective as well as cognitive needs. In addition, we know that learning depends on a caring school climate that nurtures positive relationships.
- *Student learning.* Here we need to be sure that schools are attending both to student learning and to teacher learning. Student learning is complex and multi-

faceted. It includes not only disciplinary subject matter but also the thinking skills and dispositions needed in a modern democratic society. If we want to really understand what students know and can do, we must operate on the principle that one size will not fit all. Student learning should be measured in multiple dimensions using multiple means, including assessments developed and administered at local and classroom levels.

- *Teacher learning.* Having a knowledgeable and skilled teacher is the most significant factor in student learning and should be fostered in multiple ways, compatible with the principles of adult learning. Schools must be provided with sufficient time and funding to enable teachers to improve their own performance, according to professional teaching standards.
- *Equity and access.* Given the history of inequity with respect to minority and underserved student populations, schools must be accountable for placing a renewed and special focus on improving equity and access, and for providing fair opportunities for all to learn to high standards. Our press for excellence must include a press for fairness.
- *Improvement.* Schools should be expected to function as learning organizations, continuously engaged in self-assessment and adjustment with respect to meeting the needs of their students. The capacity to do so must be ensured and nurtured.

Schools should be held accountable to their primary clients: students, parents, and the local community. Current accountability systems make the state and federal governments the locus of power and decision making about school accountability. The primary clients should be empowered to make decisions about the ends of education, not just the means, provided there are checks to ensure equity and access and adherence to professional standards for teaching.

The means used to hold schools accountable should include multiple measures as well as customized measures. Measures of school accountability should be multiple and include qualitative as well as quantitative approaches, taking into account local contexts, responsiveness to student and community needs, and professional practices and standards. Because schools are complex and unique institutions that address multiple societal needs, there also need to be allowances for local measures, customized to meet local needs and concerns. A standardized approach toward school accountability cannot work in a nation as diverse as ours.

Given these premises, what is the proper role of the government in developing a school accountability system? It should create a system that focuses on:

- Improving student learning and school practices and ensuring equity and access, not on rewarding or punishing schools;
- Providing guidance and information for local decision making, not classifying schools as successes or failures;
- Reflecting a democratic approach, including a balance of responsibility and power among different levels of government.

A NEW MODEL FOR SCHOOL ACCOUNTABILITY

There is a framework for accountability currently employed in the business world called the Balanced Scorecard.[1] This framework describes a four-part measurement system designed to give a comprehensive view of the health of the organization. The premise is that both outcomes and operations must be measured in order to have a feedback system that serves to improve the organization, not just monitor it. It is in the spirit of the well-accepted business approach called total quality management, which holds that quality must be attended to all through the production process, not just at the end. Inputs matter as much as results. The four perspectives that form the framework for measurement in this system are (1) financial, (2) internal business, (3) customer, and (4) innovation and learning.

Applying this four-part approach to education, the following aspects of school performance can provide the components of a balanced school accountability model that attends to quality throughout the process of schooling, not just at the end: (1) student learning; (2) opportunity to learn; (3) responsiveness to students, parents, and community; and (4) organizational capacity for improvement. Each of these aspects must be attended to and fostered by an accountability system that has a sufficiently high resolution to take into account the full complexity and scope of modern-day schools.

Student Learning

Principles of high-quality assessment have been well articulated by various professional organizations.[2] They are not unknown, but they are ignored in the current high-stakes testing environment. A high-quality system (1) is primarily intended to improve student learning; (2) aligns with local curricula; (3) emphasizes applied learning and thinking skills, not just declarative knowledge and basic skills; (4) embodies the principle of multiple measures, including a variety of formats, such as writing, open-response questions, and performance-based tasks (not just multiple choice); and (5) is accessible by students with diverse learning styles, intelligence profiles, exceptionalities, and cultural backgrounds.

Assessment systems are based on learning theory. Currently, there is a misfit between what cognitive science and brain research have shown about human learning and how schools and educational bureaucracies continue to measure learning.[3] We now know that human intellectual abilities are malleable and that people learn through a social and cultural process of constructing knowledge and understandings in given contexts. And yet we continue to conduct schooling and assessment on the outdated paradigm that intelligence is fixed, that knowledge exists apart from culture and context, and that learning is best induced through the behaviorist model of stimulus-response.

In addition, assessment systems labor under the popular conception that they are a precise measurement system, similar to physical measurement systems in the hard sciences. Scientific measurement in the social and behavioral sciences cannot truly "objectify" learning and rate it hierarchically. Accurate decisions about the quality and depth of an individual's learning must be based on human judgment. While test scores and other assessment data are useful and necessary sources of information, a fair determination about a person's learning can only be made by other people, most preferably by those who best know the person in his or her own context. This is the concept in this country underlying the jury system; various forms of athletic evaluations, such as Olympic competitions, university tenure, and promotion; and other forms of performance evaluation. In schooling, test scores cannot stand on their own as the deciding factor of student success. Context must be taken into account. A reasonable process for determining the measure of student learning could involve local panels of teachers, parents, and community members who review data about student performance and make decisions about promotion, graduation, placement, and so on.

What is missing in most current accountability systems is not just a human adjudication system but also a local assessment component that addresses local curricula, contexts, and cultures. A large-scale external test developed by national testing corporations and administered by states is not sensitive enough to fully determine a student's achievement. District, school, and classroom assessments must also be developed as part of a comprehensive means of collecting data on student learning. The states of Maine and Nebraska are presently developing just such systems, with a great deal of effort being provided by local teachers and administrators.[4]

It is crucial to understand that locally developed assessments depend upon the knowledge and "assessment literacy" of teachers and that implementing such new measures for school accountability purposes will take new R&D investment.[5] Most teachers have not been adequately trained in assessment and need substantial and ongoing professional development training to develop valid and reliable tasks and effective classroom assessment repertoires. The value of such an investment is not only in the promise of improved classroom instruction and measurement. Research also shows that improved classroom assessment results in improved student achievement on external tests. In fact, there are indications that the difference gained in student achievement is greater from improved classroom-level assessment than it is from many other forms of instructional innovation.[6]

Lastly, legitimate and important efforts from state or federal governments to determine the effectiveness of the larger state school system can either support or undermine such local efforts. If state or federal agencies approach this need by way of requiring aggregated data from local to state levels, local decision making is necessarily weakened and an undue emphasis is placed on standardized methods. If, however, the state and federal agencies do not rely on aggregated results from local assessment systems to gauge the health of the larger system, much may be gained. In New Zealand, for example, a system of educational monitoring is in place that entails using matrix sampling techniques (much like the NAEP system in the United States) on tasks rather than testing every student on every topic. The New Zealand model includes not just written multiple-choice tests but also one-to-one videotaped interviews with students, team tasks, and independent tasks.[7] No high stakes are entailed for schools or students. The data is profiled and shared with schools for the purposes of monitoring statewide performance, providing teacher professional development, and developing model tasks for local assessments. Such a system supports rather than undermines local assessment efforts.

Opportunity to Learn

How can students be expected to meet high standards if they are not given a fair opportunity to learn? This is a yet unanswered question with respect to school accountability. Schools should be accountable to provide equitable opportunities for all students to learn, and we must develop ways to determine how well they do so.

At the heart of this matter is that the responsibility must be shared by the district and state. The inequitable funding of public schools, particularly the disparity between the schools of the haves and those of the have-nots, places the schools of disadvantaged students in unjust and often horrifying circumstances. Over the past decade, there have been lawsuits in various states attempting to redress this imbalance, which is largely a factor of dependence on property taxes for school funding. Yet not a great deal of progress has been made.

How should we define and operationalize the opportunity-to-learn construct? How will we measure it? How can an accountability system foster it?

At a minimum, one might expect that schools and school systems provide qualified teachers, adequate instructional materials, and sound facilities. This is the contention in a recent lawsuit, *Williams v. State of California*, in which the plaintiffs argue for an accountability system that is reciprocal, that includes accountability for the state system to provide adequate resources.[8]

But there is more to this issue than just funding. Oakes describes a framework that includes opportunity-to-learn indicators for access to knowledge, professional teaching conditions, and "press for achievement":

- *Access to knowledge*: teachers' qualifications and experience; instructional time; course offerings; class grouping practices; materials, laboratories, computers, and equipment; academic support programs; academic enrichment activities; parents' involvement in instruction at home or at school; opportunities for staff development; teachers' beliefs about the importance of challenging academic study for all students;

- *Professional teaching conditions:* teachers' salaries; pupil load/class size; teachers' time for professional nonteaching work; teachers' time for school-based goal setting, staff development, program planning, curriculum development, instructional improvement, collaborative research; teachers' involvement in decision making; teachers' certainty about their ability to influence and achieve school goals; teachers' autonomy/flexibility in implementing curriculum and instruction; administrative support for innovation; clerical support for teachers' noninstructional tasks;
- *Press for achievement:* focus on academics; graduation requirements; graduation rates; students' participation in challenging academic work; schoolwide recognition of academic accomplishments; teachers' expectations about student's ability to learn; uninterrupted time for class instruction; administrative advocacy and support for challenging curriculum and instruction; quantity and type of homework; the extent to which teaching and learning are central to teacher evaluation.[9]

Darling-Hammond stresses the "fair and humane treatment" of students in a set of standards for professional practice, including the following:

- Students should be treated with respect and dignity in an environment that stresses trust, fairness, and a climate of unanxious expectation;
- All students should be well known, as learners and as individuals, to those who have responsibility for their development. Teaching and learning should be personalized to the maximum extent feasible.[10]

As such standards for opportunity to learn are articulated, the accountability question arises as to how to monitor and report on them. Clearly, this cannot be done through the proxy of testing. What is needed is a means of observation in schools and classrooms in order to determine the degree of adherence to these standards. Two aspects of this must be considered: the quality of individual teachers and the quality of the school as a whole.

Teacher evaluation has received a great deal of criticism for being ineffective. The hit-and-run observations so often done by principals do little to determine whether teachers are meeting established professional teaching standards. Unions have been described as more interested in protecting their membership than ensuring high-quality teaching. A promising development that has potential for breaking through this impasse is the recent initiation of peer review processes by a number of teacher unions. Adam Urbanski, president of the Rochester Teachers Association and director of the Teacher Union Reform Network (TURN) has been a leader in advocating for and implementing such teacher evaluation processes. In a recent manuscript, he describes how the process should work:

There is a need for meaningful summative evaluations of teachers at key junctures: tenure and movement between career levels. There must also be useful formative evaluations in between. Evaluation methods should include the following:

- Some classroom observation by peers and supervisors structured by a narrative instrument (not checklist) based on professional standards such as those of the National Board for Professional Teaching Standards (NBPTS) and framed by the teacher's goals for the lesson/unit;
- Information from previous evaluations and feedback, such as structured references from colleagues and other supervisors;
- Portfolios that might include examples of teaching syllabi, assignments given, feedback given to students and samples of student work, feedback received from parents and students as well as colleagues, data on student progress, teaching exhibitions such as videotaped teaching samples, professional development initiatives taken, and structured self-evaluation.

A specially established committee of teachers and administrators should make all summative evaluation decisions about promotions or continued employment.[11]

In order to evaluate the performance of a school as a whole, a school review process will be necessary. Variations of inspectorates and school quality reviews have been developed in New York, Rhode Island, Maine, and other states, as well as in Britain, New Zealand, Australia, and other countries.[12] In order for such reviews to serve the purpose of school improvement, it is essential that observations and data collection be done in a "critical friend" manner through a combination of school self-assessment and collegial visitations. Findings from such a process should not be stated or used in a bureaucratic and judgmental way but, rather, should be given as descriptions to local councils charged with evaluating school accountability. As with all aspects of a learner-centered accountability system, the quality and effectiveness of a review system depends upon the time, resources, and institutional support given to it.

Responsiveness to Students, Parents, and Community

Current accountability systems take power and decision making away from the primary clients of the educational system and move them more and more toward state and federal agencies. As high-stakes testing dictates the curriculum, fewer choices are available to students. Parent or community concerns about what is happening in the classroom and to their children have become less important to schools than meeting state mandates.

Schools should be accountable for their responsiveness to students. A long-standing issue in education has been the lack of attention to student needs, whether that is individual learning styles, exceptionalities, group cultural norms and expectations, gender differences, or language barriers. It is well known that differentiation is needed in curriculum and instruction and that standardization creates inequities. In the world of special education, the individualized educational plan, which targets learning goals as well as means, is well accepted. In multicultural education literature and practice, the use of cultural context is deemed essential to engage students. Teacher standards, such as those articulated by the National Board for Professional Teaching Standards, highlight the need to respond to the needs of the specific students in a given teacher's classroom. Responsiveness to students means that curricula must be adapted, instructional time frames must be adjusted, student choices must be given. A prescribed curriculum for all, enforced by exit exams, gateway tests, and so-called grade-level expectations prevents this. What is needed is that each student is presented with important and challenging studies, not that one "best way" is set in place for all.[13] This is why local decision making about curriculum is critical.

One of the premises in the present definition of standards-based reform is that it is appropriate for states to set the learning goals and outcomes, monitor student achievement of these outcomes with a testing system, and then apply consequences based on the success or failure of students in this test. The understanding is that local districts and schools would be free to determine what curriculum to use in order to achieve these outcomes. Supposedly, schools and districts are given more freedom in this system than in an input-based control model that focuses on adequacy of materials, time-on-task, and other resource or methodology issues. In fact, as teachers well know, tests are based on content and assume a given curriculum. A high-stakes achievement test developed and administered at the state level must be based on a state curriculum framework that is very well specified, as a matter of validity. This inevitably preempts local curriculum choices.

Moreover, testing format and content often lead to a particular form of pedagogy. For example, a basic-skills multiple-choice test leads to more drill-and-practice in the classroom, whereas a more performance-oriented assessment that focuses on thinking skills leads to more writing and discussion. These effects are understood in the psychometric community and included within the parameters of consequential validity for a given test. It is unlikely that a low-level multiple-choice test or even a short-answer test is valid for the purpose of assessing learning standards that include the application of knowledge or complex thinking skills. Thus, a state test also strongly influences classroom pedagogy.

The concept that the present accountability system provides greater local flexibility and decision making about curriculum and pedagogy is an illusion.[14] Students do not see high-stakes testing as a means of improving their learning experience.[15] A learner-centered accountability system requires that decisions on curriculum and instruction be made locally.

Saying this, however, obliges us to acknowledge that one of the existing problems meant to be addressed by the present accountability system is the history of school unresponsiveness to students. The achievement gaps we are facing are painful evidence to many parents, community organizations, and educational policymakers that schools are not working well when left to make their own decisions about curriculum and instruction. If high-stakes tests don't improve this, what will work better?

We must look directly to parents and communities as the primary stake-holders for holding schools accountable. There are many examples of local community organizations, especially in urban areas, taking on the mantle of responsibility for insisting that schools are responsive to the needs of their children.

> Across the country, parents and community members in distressed, low-income neighborhoods are taking action to improve their local schools. They examine school performance data that show dismal student outcomes, and they raise demands to secure greater accountability as well as sufficient resources to en-sure that their schools can succeed. They get involved in school board elections, form coalitions, work with the media, and engage a broad spectrum of public actors to improve public education. All these efforts are making clear, strong impacts. They have won a new small-schools policy in Oakland, California; di-rected resources toward building new schools in the poorest, most underserved communities in Los Angeles; and brought new after-school programs to Wash-ington, D.C., schools. They have forced the removal of ineffective principals and superintendents in New York City and Mississippi, worked with teachers to improve student achievement in Chicago, and brought more rigorous math and reading programs to schools in Philadelphia.[16]

Using responsiveness to students, parents, and community as a form of accountability must go beyond PTA-like support efforts or many existing efforts to gain parent involvement, which are often focused on gaining par-ent support for existing school practices. It must also go beyond common efforts at gathering survey information about satisfaction. Real accountabil-ity to the primary clients for schools entails shifting power relationships.

Local school-based councils must be created that have real power to ef-fect school change. These councils would review accountability information from state and local assessments, as well as from school quality review pro-cesses, and make recommendations to school boards about school policies and priorities. They would hold school boards accountable for the develop-ment and implementation of school improvement plans. Questions about how to sustain such councils and ensure that they do not pursue narrow agendas must be determined. How councils are composed in urban settings will likely vary and be different from those in rural or suburban settings. Standards and acceptable variations for councils will be important topics for public discussion.

Schlechty describes a vision for such councils:

> Community leaders who are concerned about the futures of their communities and their schools should join together to create a non-profit corporation intended to support efforts of school leaders to focus on the future and to ensure that lasting values as well as immediate interests are included in the education decision-making process. It would also be the function of this group to establish a small sub-group of the community's most trusted leaders who would annually evaluate the performance of the school board as stewards of the common good and would make these evaluations known to the community. . .
>
> In a sense, the relationship between the school district and the monitoring function of the new corporation should be something akin to the relationship between the quality assurance division of a corporation and the operating units in the corporation. . . .
>
> When the data indicate that goals are not being met, the president of the corporation, working with the superintendent and the board of education, would seek to discover why this was the case, and would seek as well to create new approaches that might enhance the prospect of achieving the stated goals and the intended ends. It is not intended that the new corporation simply identify problems and weaknesses, it is intended that the leaders of this organization also participate in the creation of solutions and participate in creating support for solutions once they have been identified or created.[17]

Organizational Capacity

If schools are going to be held accountable to high levels of performance, the question arises: Do schools have the internal capacity to rise to those levels? To what degree are the resources of schools "organized into a collective enterprise, with shared commitment and collaboration among staff to achieve a clear purpose for student learning?"[18]

The issue of meaningful and ongoing teacher professional development is especially salient to whether schools are capable of enabling all students to meet higher standards of performance. While it is generally agreed that the quality of the teacher is at the heart of student learning, it is too often the case that time, resources, and high-quality professional development opportunities have been lacking. In many cases, teachers have been subjected to a training model that asks for faithful implementation of an innovation rather than an inquiry into how an innovation might be adapted to meet the needs of the specific context. More and more, teachers are asked to use allotted professional development time to do the work mandated by new accountability systems, rather than to develop their own professional knowledge and skills.

Little suggests that, in a climate of educational reform, the nature of teacher professional development must itself be reformed:

[T]he most promising forms of professional development engage teachers in the pursuit of genuine questions, problems and curiosities, over time, in ways that leave a mark on perspectives, policy, and practice. They communicate a view of teachers not only as classroom experts, but also as productive and responsible members of a broader professional community and as persons embarked on a career that may span 30 years or more.[19]

Little offers six principles for high-quality professional development:

1. It offers meaningful intellectual, social, and emotional engagement with ideas, with materials, and with colleagues, both in and out of teaching;
2. It takes explicit account of the contexts of teaching and the experience of teachers;
3. It offers support for informed dissent;
4. It places classroom practice in the larger contexts of school practice and the educational careers of students;
5. It prepares teachers (as well as students and their parents) to employ the techniques and perspectives of inquiry;
6. It is governed in a way that ensures bureaucratic restraint and a balance between the interests of individuals and the interests of institutions.

Schools must also attend to the issue of teacher empowerment. Teachers are increasingly controlled and disempowered in various ways. This leads to a decreasing sense of efficacy and professionalism and an increasing sense of job dissatisfaction and has become a factor in the drain from the profession behind the growing teaching shortage:

The teacher who has little control and power is the teacher who is less able to get things done and thus the teacher with less credibility. Students can more easily ignore such a teacher—indeed a lack of influence and credibility invites challenge. Principals can more easily neglect them. Peers may be more likely to shun them. In such cases teachers may feel that they have little choice but to turn to manipulative or authoritarian methods (that is, to adopt the "bureaucratic personality") to get the job done, which may simply exacerbate tensions with students and fellow staff. This, in turn, would likely lead such teachers to feel less commitment to their teaching job or to the teaching career.[20]

Hargreaves emphasizes that an important role for principals is to distribute leadership. Rather than take a heroic stance in leading schools into reform, it is important for principals to share power with teachers and others. This not only benefits teacher efficacy but works toward the institutionalization of change. It is a means of developing lasting organizational capacity.

To be an effective collective enterprise, a school must develop an internal accountability system. That is, it must take responsibility for developing goals and priorities based on the ongoing collection and analysis of data, monitor its performance, and report its findings and actions to its public. Many schools have not moved past the condition in which individual teacher responsibility rather than collective responsibility is the norm.[21] States and districts must cooperate with schools to nurture and insist upon the development of such collective internal norms.

THE NEW ROLE OF THE STATE

For this new model of school accountability to succeed, there must be a system whereby states and districts are jointly responsible with schools and communities for student learning. Reciprocal accountability is needed in which one level of the system is responsible to the others and all are responsible to the public.

The role of state and federal agencies, with respect to school accountability, is much in need of redefinition. Agencies at these levels should not be primarily in an enforcement role. Rather, their role should be to establish standards for local accountability systems, to provide resources and guidance, and to set in place processes for quality review of such systems. Certainly, there should be no high-stakes testing from the state and federal levels, no mandatory curricula, and no manipulation through funding. Where there are clear cases of faulty local accountability systems—a lack of appropriate local assessment systems; inadequate opportunities to learn; unresponsiveness to students, parents, and community; or lack of organizational capacity—supportive efforts should be implemented.

Are there any circumstances in which a state should intervene forcibly in a school or district? If an accountability system is to work toward school improvement for all schools, does it not need such "teeth"? This question must be addressed in a way that acknowledges the multilevel nature of this new school accountability model. One might envision at least three cases in which the state would take on a more assertive role: (1) to investigate claims or appeals from students, parents, or the local community that the local accountability system is not meeting the standards set for such systems; (2) to require local schools and districts to respond to findings in the data that show significant student learning deficiencies, inequity in the opportunities to learn for all students, or lack of responsiveness to students, parents, or communities; (3) to provide additional resources and guidance to improve the organizational capacity of the local school or district. Is it conceivable that a state might take over a local school or district in this model? Yes, but only after the most comprehensive evaluation of the local accountability system has shown that there is no alternative and then only on a temporary basis.

It is of great importance to the health of our public schools that we begin as soon as possible to define a new model for school accountability, one that is balanced and comprehensive. Schools can and should be held accountable to their primary clients for much more than test scores, in a way that supports improvement rather than punishes deficiencies. The current model of using high-stakes testing is a recipe for public school failure, putting our democratic nation at risk.

Evaluation of Schools and Education: Bad Practice, Limited Knowledge

Sandra Mathison and Marco A. Muñoz

SETTING: A conversation between an evaluation researcher and two school district evaluators about how evaluation in their school districts has been affected by the implementation of state mandated testing.[1]

INTERVIEWER: Well, I have been reading some literature on evaluation in school districts. There was a lot of research done in the 1980s, but there hasn't been much lately. I have been wondering if the increase in state-mandated testing has had any impact on what kinds of evaluation is done in school districts these days. You know, I asked a colleague of mine who is the director of evaluation in a large school district in the midwest about this, and she just smiled and said, "What evaluation?" This really piqued my interest. Like, for example, has there been a change in the kinds of evaluation problems you tackle?

EVALUATOR #1: We have become limited in what makes sense to evaluate. We have become almost 100 percent reliant on test scores as indicators of academic progress and achievement. The focus of most evaluations is: Does this program improve test scores?

EVALUATOR #2: Our state-testing program is helping us to move past anecdotal to factual information. We are becoming more precise and focused in our thinking and discussion. We are now able to say things like "according to the data generated on our children." I think the testing has helped us focus on what it is we should be asking, tracking, and evaluating.

INTERVIEWER: So, do the state tests play a role in framing evaluation questions?

EVALUATOR #1: Well, evaluation tends to be framed in terms of meeting standards in each subject area. Our evaluation questions are pretty much "Did the passing rates on the proficiency tests go up?" Most school district personnel are interested to know how a program and its specific components have helped "raise test scores," even though the *realistic* program goals were not to raise test scores.

EVALUATOR #2: There is a greater emphasis on the disaggregation of results by ethnicity, subsidized lunch status, length of time in district, first language other than English, and so on. More attention on school improvement, too, but there is still no consistent model for assessing how much and how well teachers are covering the targets of the state tests.

INTERVIEWER: And does this influence what kinds of data and data collection methods are used in the evaluation work you do?

EVALUATOR #1: It's the one-size-fits-all test use model. The variables selected tend to be quantitative in nature, data collection itself is highly electronic—all standardized test information, local assessment information, and grades are available electronically. The trade-off is that we do little qualitative data collection, as it is harder to link this type of information directly to standards.

EVALUATOR #2: Well, the one thing we now recognize is that data has to be collected more often. The state's program is yearly, and our thought is that data should be tracked each nine-week period. The state's testing program has raised our awareness of the advantages and limitations of criterion-referenced exams. We have grown in understanding large-scale assessments, and how they are created and scored. Likewise, the testing program has shown us that testing is not the only way to assess progress.

Also, the state testing program has encouraged us to start asking "why?" Why is one set of children doing better than another group? Why is one school out performing another? Why can Teacher A get a full year's growth from her children and Teacher B can't? The asking of why has led us to thinking about and using many variables to try to explain the variance in student scores. My thinking is that once we can control the variance, we can start making improvements. Variables aren't excuses any more. They are ways to get a better understanding of the phenomena around us.

INTERVIEWER: Has there been any impact on how evaluation information is disseminated or how evaluation findings are used?

EVALUATOR #1: Lip service is given to "using the results for improvement." Reports are geared to student performance on standards and meeting of district goals for improving the standards. An overall technical report is developed and summaries are used for public relations purposes. There is a tendency to explain away test results in terms of mobility or poverty of students. Also, the testing we do limits how likely we are to design studies that will pass peer review. We do some good work, but it might not be seen beyond the district because of limitations like no pre- and posttesting and no randomization.

There seems to be more passing around of paper and posting stuff on the Web but no real evidence of how much or how well managers or district decision makers are using results. I see a lessening of emphasis on areas that have indirect effects on improvement in the standards (for instance, behavior management training is less of a priority than training in writing and math strategies). I am all for holding people accountable, but I am troubled when someone wants to discipline a teacher for one year's data without looking into the qualitative reasons why that might have occurred. We seem to be designing "gotcha" accountability systems to try and trap staff (like having to log the number but not the type of writing assignments given in a month).

EVALUATOR #2: The testing mandates have made the reporting to the people uniform. We try to use test results as part of the picture but certainly not the entire picture. When I first started here, we did not want to report test scores to the school board, now we have to or they will see them in the newspaper. The district has to deal with data because their hand is forced by accountability mandates, by pressure from the media, by responding to issues of equality for minority students, and so on. And that is good. Reporting has caused those who would like to pretend that they don't need improvement to face the realities. This may be stressful, but it helps us to be better and more accountable. I find that many administrators and teachers find testing stressful because they now understand that "big brother" is watching what they are doing. I find this interesting because, in my experience, everyone has a "big brother" watching and holding people accountable. Why should education be any different? How did we let them go so long without having someone watching?

INTERVIEWER: It has really been interesting talking with both of you. It seems that state-mandated testing is a pretty significant factor in describing the practice of evaluation in school districts these days. What I find really interesting is how one of you sees these mandates as a constraint on evaluation practice, limiting the design of studies, data collection, ways of using the information. But the other sees these mandates as focusing the evaluation work, making it more precise and trustworthy and as a clear path to really improving the quality of schools.

Any last thoughts?

EVALUATOR #1: Not to make excuses, but many children in our schools face challenges unimaginable in suburban districts. But these issues are not taken into account in state "report cards." Teachers and principals feel they are being held accountable for factors they have no control over. Overall, I think the emphasis on improved school accountability is a good thing, but we need to be careful not to misuse the data or to completely forget about anything that is not directly written into a state standard.

EVALUATOR #2: Let me tell you a story. I worked with a committee of teachers on Title I evaluation to set target gains for Title I students. The teachers voted to set very low targets for Title I students so students would be more likely to reach them and the teachers would be less likely to be blamed. I find that education is too slow to respond when the evidence is present that someone just isn't the right person for the job. If an employee is not capable or doesn't have the desire to do the work, you let that employee go. In education, we seem to transfer people around first. This is unfortunate because children can't afford to wait until a bad teacher retires. It is my hope that testing will help us to move more swiftly and to make better decisions in this area.

STATE-MANDATED TESTING CONTRIBUTES TO BAD EVALUATION PRACTICE AND LIMITED KNOWLEDGE

The playlet illustrates that, like many stakeholders in education, school district evaluators have different perspectives on the value of the impact on state-mandated testing on their practice, that is, the ways in which students, programs, personnel, and schools are judged. What is common is an agreement that state curriculum standards and the student assessments associated with them have had a limiting and focusing effect on evaluation in schools.

There are a number of codes of professional conduct that apply to the work of evaluators in schools. There are *The Standards for Educational and Psychological Tests*,[2] *The Program Evaluation Standards*,[3] and the *Guiding Principles for Evaluators*.[4] Evaluators who work within or for schools are bound ethically, although not legally, by these various standards. Such, however, is not the case with educational policymakers and other parties interested in directing what occurs in the name of evaluating education, schools, school personnel, and children. Indeed, these professional standards are routinely violated by the rush to focus solely, or even primarily, on student standardized test scores as the evidence for making claims about the value of schooling.

Many high-stakes testing programs routinely lead to the violation of these professional norms in a number of ways. They

- invoke a fallible single standard and a single measure;
- are implemented and used to make high-stakes decisions before sufficient validation evidence is obtained and before defensible technical documentation is issued for public scrutiny;
- are employed without credible independent meta-evaluation;
- are flawed, both in technical adequacy and in accuracy of scoring and reporting;
- stimulate teachers and principals to manipulate test scoring and standards, change students' answers, send slow learners away on testing day, or otherwise invalidate test scores;
- assume that all children, including English language learners and special education students, learn in the same ways at the same rate and that they can all demonstrate their achievements on standardized tests;
- measure, for the most part, parental income and race, and therefore perpetuate racism, classism, and anti–working class sentiment.

The most serious problem with high-stakes testing is its insistence that education be evaluated in a narrow way. The practice of high-stakes testing in America is an effort to treat teaching and learning in a simple and fair manner but in a world where education is hugely complex with inequitable distribution of opportunity. Education requires decisions as to how children, teachers, and schools will be sustained, improved, and promoted, but high-stakes testing oversimplifies the decisions to be made. To follow the principle of "do no harm" requires evaluations of education and schools to examine consequences in real situations for all people affected. Current high-stakes testing policies and practices fail to provide the mechanisms of review, meta-evaluation, and validation demanded by the professional standards of evaluation.

As a consequence of the consistently bad evaluation practice and limited knowledge that standardized testing provides for judging the value of schools and the accomplishments of individuals, especially students, the American Evaluation Association has developed a set of expectations for what constitutes quality evaluation of schools, educational personnel, and students' achievement.[5] These are

- that both the wisdom and experience of professional teachers and fully validated standardized testing are important for sound educational decision making;

- that important evaluation decisions should be made on the basis of multiple criteria and multiple high-quality measures validated for specified uses;
- that test publishers involved in test development or implementation should be responsible for validation of representative high-stakes uses for which the tests are designed and that test publishers should publicly object and refuse future contracts with users when the publishers' tests are misused;
- that measurement specialists and advisors involved in high-stakes testing programs consider not only technical and theoretical but also consequential issues, such as the welfare of students, educators, schools, and society;
- that contractors for testing services, state or local, should demand appropriate validation studies and consistent high-quality services from test publishers and testing service providers;
- that educational policymakers and practitioners should use well-conceived systems of assessment and accountability that include multiple measures and continuously strive for better representations of what is taught and achieved;
- that state and local governance of education should draw on a wide range of perspectives as to what is best for students, schools, and society;
- that important decisions (for example, grade to grade promotion/retention, graduation, certification, classification, monetary rewards/sanctions) about students, teachers, and schools should not be made on the basis of any single test or test battery, no matter how many times it may be taken;
- that there is an urgent need to initiate and fund evaluations of high-stakes testing in all states and school systems where such policies have been enacted;
- that it is imperative that findings from these evaluations be provided to policymakers, parents, teachers, students, and the public about the consequences, positive and negative, of such policies;
- that evaluators of high-stakes testing, and programs in which high-stakes testing is prominent, should draw consistently on standards for utility, feasibility, accuracy, and propriety as found in the Joint Committee Standards for Program and Personnel Evaluation, AEA Guiding Principles, and Standards for Educational and Psychological Testing; and
- that government and educational institutions should avoid any legislative programs or mandates for high-stakes testing that violate professional testing and evaluation standards.

CONCLUSION

The assessment mechanisms associated with current school improvement efforts through standards-based educational reform have wide-reaching effects on all practices in schools. While it is most apparent how state-mandated assessments affect what happens in classrooms, there are areas of practice more hidden but equally affected. Such is the case with evaluation in schools. At its best, evaluation helps to examine what is good and bad about education in multifaceted and improvement-oriented ways through the involvement of a broad range of stakeholders. Evaluation, if done well, is democratizing. It requires that individuals and groups with a vested interest in that which is being evaluated engage in genuine deliberation about how to determine if the evaluand is good or bad, right or wrong. State mandated assessments have stripped the practice of evaluation of much of this potential for inclusiveness and improvement, and redirected resources to creating and maintaining student assessment systems including test administration, analysis, and reporting activities.

— II —

Perspectives on Standards
and Assessment

— 8 —

Teachers Working with Standards and State Testing

Sandra Mathison and Melissa Freeman

The current accountability strategies of school reform rely heavily on measuring outcomes, especially student achievement, and attaching consequences, either positive or negative, to various levels of performance. These accountability strategies affect everyone and every aspect of schools and schooling at local, regional, national, and international levels. This chapter examines the ways state curriculum standards and mandated student testing, the primary vehicle of accountability, affect teachers' work.

We have been doing research in elementary and middle schools and have spent a great deal of time in classrooms, talking with teachers and attending meetings with them.[1] What we find is a tension created by teachers' desire to be professionals, to act with integrity, and at the same time to give every child a chance to succeed. This tension seems illogical—surely, if a teacher is doing the best job she or he can, then every child will have a chance to succeed. What we find in these schools is that centralized curricular mandates and high-stakes tests force teachers to act in ways they do not think are professional.

Most teachers are not radicals. They do not seek complete autonomy and do not eschew the need for accountability (even bureaucratic accountability); they value direction and specificity, find some virtue in state-mandated tests, and are content within centralized systems that proscribe some aspects of their work. However, many teachers also perceive themselves as professionals with both the responsibility and capability of doing their jobs well and in the best interests of their students, and they find their professionalism assaulted by these school reform strategies.

Teachers may never have had much autonomy, and the professional status of teaching cannot be taken for granted. Teachers' work has historically received low pay, been perceived as relatively low status, and often operates within authoritarian and often petty school cultures. "Education has not suffered from any freedom granted teachers to run schools as they see fit; it has suffered from the suffocating atmosphere in which teachers have had to work."[2] Still, much educational research demonstrates the centrality of teachers in educational reform.

The current standards-based reform movement with its clear specification of content, pedagogy, and assessments adds to these demands, increases authoritarianism, and further erodes teachers' sense of professionalism. Researchers in Kentucky report that "the educators we spoke with resented the accountability measures as an insult to their professionalism."[3] Even though this is the case, teachers are not singular in their judgment of the value of these reforms. There are teachers who do not trust that other teachers can and will do their jobs. For those teachers, standards-based reforms and state-mandated testing are necessary to keep lazy, ill-prepared, or individualistic teachers on a common path with accountability.

TEACHERS' VIEWS ON CURRICULUM STANDARDS AND GUIDELINES

Many professional associations have adopted curriculum guidelines and standards. Organizations, such as the National Council of Teachers of Mathematics, National Council of Teachers of English, and the National Council for the Social Studies, have all created curricular guidelines to direct what should be taught and when in their respective subject matter. However, these guidelines have had a modest impact on what is taught in public schools because these organizations have no particular authority and limited persuasive power over state departments of education and local school districts. The imposition of state-developed curriculum frameworks or guidelines has, however, had a more significant impact on determining what teachers teach.

Although many state departments of education use strategies that allow for teacher participation in the creation of state curricular guidelines and standards, in general, most teachers feel distant from the process and the decisions.[4] In most states, a very small number of teachers, primarily from middle- and upper-middle-class communities, participate in the creation of state-content guidelines or standards. Indeed, school leaders and teachers in these communities know there is both prestige and advantage in being involved in this state-level activity. And these teachers are not selected to represent the diversity of communities served within the state—they are a sample of convenience. Therefore, teachers are required to adopt curricular standards

they have had little say in—within the current political climate, local preroga-
tives over curriculum have been all but eliminated. This may take very
dramatic forms, such as in California, where the use of whole-language approaches to teaching reading is forbidden and the emphasis is almost completely on phonics-based approaches. Usually, the redirection of what is
taught and how is more subtle.

There are two common responses to state curriculum guidelines, and often school districts adopt both. First, districts engage in a curricular alignment project—mapping what they have been teaching with what is proscribed
by the state. This is an especially common practice in districts with strong
leadership and in more middle- and upper-middle-class communities. Teachers, often through district or building curriculum committees, become involved in reviewing the curriculum, eliminating or adding topics, and
shuffling topics from one grade level to another. Teachers are drawn into
these activities, and their attention is focused on ensuring compliance with
the state expectations—they are not encouraged to engage in a critical review of the content standards.

In many cases, teachers become distracted from the big picture by focusing on a level of detail that probably doesn't contribute much to an overall
improvement of the quality of schooling. For example, we have seen teachers passionately discussing whether the solar system should be taught in third
or fourth grade, as suggested by the state standards. And the biggest concern, if it is moved to third grade, is that fourth- grade teachers will be denied
the opportunity to do the nifty, fun solar system fair they have traditionally
done with their students. Curriculum coordinators and school leaders direct
these curricular alignment activities to ensure that teachers' discussions stay
at this micro level, never venturing to suggest alternatives, adaptations, or
rejections of the state-prescribed sequencing of content.

Second, districts do textbook adoptions. Textbooks are presumed to be
a strong determiner of what is taught, and common adoptions are expected
to maximize the fit between the curriculum standards and what is taught.
They also ensure that teachers are covering the content that is proscribed
and on which students will be assessed. Textbooks are, therefore, also chosen to match the tests, not a difficult thing to do given that the textbook
and test publishers are often one and the same. These textbook adoptions
are often welcomed by teachers, especially in cases where there have been
few or woefully out of date textbooks. However, common textbook adoption also creates limits on what and how teachers teach—taking away at least
some of their professional autonomy to determine what is in the best interests of their students.

For example, in one urban school district, the adoption of basal readers
for elementary students supplanted the strategies teachers felt were most
appropriate for their students. The teachers recognize that the English Language Arts (ELA) test required more of their students than had been

expected in the past, so they used Title I money (federal educational funding targeted to schools with "disadvantaged" populations) to develop a curricular strategy. Teachers used trade children's literature magazines (*Ladybug* in third grade and *Spider* in fourth grade) as texts and developed multiple-choice and short-answer questions (like those on the ELA test) for each story. "We were making a huge effort to integrate. We were choosing materials and making selections do double duty with science or social studies, working around the themes so there was a whole integrated package." As the teachers were developing this trade magazine-based curriculum, the district curriculum committee adopted a basal reading series (Scott-Foresman's Reading series) that all teachers are required to use.

Teachers in this district think adoption of the basal readers is an insult and a distraction. Implicit in the textbook adoption (in both language arts and math) are messages from the district office that all teachers should be on the same page at the same time.

> A lot of teacher hours went into the curriculum that [the teachers] produced and then when we got our new reading series it was imposed on us. . . . [I]t is a mandate that you're on a certain page in a certain week across the district [and this] is unrealistic depending on the kids' abilities. So the teachers here just feel like all we're doing is frustrating our children. We are not teaching them the way that we as professionals should be allowed to help all of our children learn.

The teachers have more confidence in their own trade magazine-based curriculum to prepare their students.

While these new textbook adoptions may fill a void where there previously had been few resources, they can also create chaos and conflict. The teachers described in the previous paragraph find that districtwide textbook adoptions can create new problems or undermine teachers' previous work—in this case, with curriculum integration. As one teacher said: "As happy as I am to have a standardized curriculum across the district, this new reading program has no fourth-grade social studies content and no fourth-grade science content. None."

TEACHING IS CONSTRAINED BY STATE-MANDATED TESTING

There is ample research describing how state-mandated tests, particularly high-stakes tests, challenge and compromise the professionalism of teachers and change the "what" and "how" of teaching. Linda MacNeil's research in Texas illustrates a range of constraints on teachers' work, constraints that lead them to "exclude their richest knowledge from their lessons."[5] These constraints spring from the increased standardization and specification of important knowledge as that which is on the test. As a result, teachers adopt generic forms of content and presentation, develop a "test-based curriculum," separate content "for the test" and "real content," further fragment knowledge, and even give up on teaching altogether. In some cases, when a mandated test demands something that has not previously been a routine part of the curriculum, such as writing or problem solving, there is refocusing, although in ways driven pointedly by the test.

Teachers do not feel good about the constraints that testing places on their work. MacNeil describes teachers moving away from particularized child-centered teaching to teacher-centered generic teaching, because the latter reflects state-mandated curriculum and assessments. Dramatically, she concludes: "The reforms required that they choose between their personal survival in the system or their students' education."[6]

The teachers we have interviewed perceived their professionalism to be diminished. Perhaps one of the best ways to convey teachers' sentiments is to use their own words. The following poem was created from interviews with elementary teachers in New York State.

Most of our time in fourth grade is spent test-prepping
There is very little of the extra projects
The extra fun kinds of activities
That we used to be able to do
That goes by the wayside
Because we need to test prep

Being in fourth grade is almost an advantage
If I need materials I say
Oh it's test related
Then I can get them
If I have a child that I need to have looked at
Oh it's fourth grade

Seems to me there's more of an emphasis on something
Whether that's good or bad
I'm most uncomfortable with the effect
It's had at the mid-year
When it's time for us to decide
Is this child going to meet the criteria to move on to the next grade?

You take a child to a retention committee and say
This child might not necessarily be ready for the next grade
But professionally I know retention is not the answer
That is no longer weighted very heavily
When you as a professional say
I know the solution for this child is not retention
Especially on the third-grade level

What this test is testing is good
Kids should be able to read a passage
And respond to it in writing
That's basically what the test is asking kids to do
There's nothing wrong with that

What's wrong is the way the adults in the world
Take the scores and report them

It's a benchmark
If a child can't do it in fourth grade
And they can get it in fifth grade
Why should we penalize them?
The goal is to get them to be able to perform at this level
And if it takes them an extra year to master something
That's okay

We are not financial planners, where we are judged
In how many millions of dollars we brought in
We're not Wal-Mart
In how many sales we made
We are a service industry
So stop comparing success
With scores, growth, end products

What if you have a kid who got a two on the ELA
But was a knucklehead
An emotional disaster
Disruptive
But during the course of the year
In behavior
In courtesy and respect
Improved tremendously
Are you not a success then?
Did that kid not improve?

Are they measuring that?

Through outcomes-based bureaucratic accountability, teachers' work has come to be defined by the state-mandated tests, especially in English Language Arts, as well as by district directives geared to improve state test scores. But, for these teachers, it is not an either-or choice between personal survival and the students' education. These teachers confront the dilemma of being a good teacher, a professional, and helping kids to succeed, which is marked by performance on state tests. What we see repeatedly is that this dilemma is almost always resolved in favor of the students, that teachers sacrifice their professional integrity in order to help every child be as successful as she or he can be on the tests, even when they lack faith in the indicator. This resolution plays itself out in the classroom as well as around the administration and scoring of the state tests.

One thing teachers do is teach to the test. The many meanings of "teaching to the test" and the validity of the test itself conspire to create anxiety about the right thing to do. The basic tenet seems to be if a test measures what is important then teaching to the test is okay, but if the test is misdirected or poorly constructed or only a partial picture of what is important, then teaching to the test is not okay. The difficulty for teachers is that they often hold both views simultaneously. For example, if the test encourages teaching more writing or more problem solving than has been the case, teaching to the test (in the sense of taking curricular cues from the test content) is good. But the reading and writing on the test may be formulaic, focus on syntax, discourage creativity and exploration of language, and limit discussion—so teaching to the test is bad. Coupled with a context that often defines these tests as high-stakes tests, with serious consequences for schools (threats of state intervention), for teachers (shame and rewards), and students (possibilities of retention in grade, labeling), and teachers are left with little choice. The magnitude of the pressure is captured in the words of a Georgia assistant superintendent who said to a group of third-grade teachers, "You know this is your do or die year." So teachers teach to the test. Sometimes these are highly structured, orchestrated efforts, sometimes more haphazard, individualized responses.

And some teachers (and students and principals as well) cheat. While the degree of cheating is difficult to gauge, it is pervasive enough to make newspaper headlines with some regularity. The 2000 New York City cheating scandal has been widely covered in the media, but other high-profile, public cases of cheating have occurred in Texas, Kentucky, Connecticut, Illinois, and Rhode Island. Cheating can take many forms and without absolving teachers of wrongdoing, that they may find ways to "help" students, is in part a result of the stakes attached to the test performance. Is it cheating to erase stray marks that may misguide the scantron machine? Is it cheating to remind students to read the directions carefully? or have students do the test on scrap paper first so errors can be corrected as the answers are transferred to the test booklet or bubble sheet?

Teachers must watch their students take these tests and adhere to state department of education instructions about test administration. Sorting through how to administer the test, what questions the teacher can answer, and how the accommodations for special education students should be implemented is a dance the teachers do throughout the testing. And while teachers are mindful of following the rules, they interpret the directions differently. Some teachers are adamant about not answering any questions and watch in silence. Others encourage students to ask questions, hoping they will be ones teachers can answer: "Today when you are doing your questions, get your hand up and ask. Most of the time we could answer your question."

During the days of a test, teachers do quick checks on student scores, analyze the test questions, check up on students, talk with them about their perceptions, give them moral support, reprimands, and teach cram sessions based on the teacher's preview of the test. We observed a fourth-grade class, and after the first session of the math test, the teacher asks two boys, "How was it?" The students respond, "easy," "fun," "boring." And then two boys ask the teacher if $50 \times 50 = 250$. She has them figure it out and they find the answer is 2,500. She shows them another way to solve the equation. In another classroom just before the second day of the math test, the teacher is more focused. She hands out pencils that say "4th graders are #1" and tells them, "These are special pencils that only work on this portion of the test." But, before they begin the test, she gives the students a quick refresher on parallel lines, perpendicular lines, trapezoids, parallelograms, and hexagons. And she makes a last-minute plea that they remember what they have learned about probability and fractions.

In most states, there is a high level of security around the tests—they arrive at the school just in time for test administration, they are stored in locked vaults, and they are accounted for more carefully than most of the school's budget. Such precautions suggest the authorities expect cheating and violations of rules to occur. Recently, we were interviewed by a local upstate New York newspaper because teachers were suspected of having looked at the state test prior to its administration and therefore had had an opportunity to prepare the students for the specific test items. While we have no idea whether this is true or not, the suspicion speaks to a widespread anxiety about testing on the part of teachers, school administrators, and state officials.

Teachers find themselves focusing on some groups of kids more than others. In New York, children come to be known by the likely score they will receive on the state test—kids become solid 3s, 3s but potential 4s, 2s but potential 3s, and 1s and 2s. Teachers are pressured (by administrators and themselves) to focus on students most likely to improve their scores with specific and targeted instruction. Often the 1s and low 2s are left behind and the 4s don't get much attention either—students who are on the cusp of a score category become the focus of teachers' time and attention.

Moreover, they focus on subjects that are tested, those that "count." This means most instructional time is spent on language arts and mathematics, followed by science and social studies. Art, physical education, music, and drama are squeezed in if time and budgets permit—but often they do not. In a number of districts, recess, field trips, and other supposedly unnecessary aspects of education are eliminated or curtailed to decrease the time taken away from preparing students in tested content areas. While no teacher would diminish the importance of these subject areas, many bemoan the loss of opportunities for students to learn in less structured contexts, where students have more freedom of choice. The opportunities to explore personal interests and develop expertise through involvement in school drama productions, orchestra, or the school newspaper become diminished. Teachers sense a loss of the school's mission to educate the whole person.

The "one-size-fits-all" strategy that results from district textbook adoption, common curricula, and standardization weigh heavily on teachers, challenging the fundamental notions of individualized education and child-centered teaching. Teachers acknowledge they need to measure students' reading ability, mathematical knowledge and skill, and so on but feel they are caught on the horns of a dilemma of standardization and individualization. They are forced to ignore individual strengths and needs in an attempt to get all children ready to tackle the same test at the same time. "There are deep contradictions in the messages we are getting. Every kid is supposed to have—and, indeed, we are supposed to encourage them to build on their—individualized learning styles. The district actively supports individualized educational programs for children and then we are supposed to cram them through the test using the same approach for all children. Give me a break!" Teachers are more likely to subscribe to Susan Ohanian's view that "one size fits few"[7] when it comes to educational practices.

TEACHERS QUIT AND PUSH BACK, SOMETIMES

It is difficult to gauge the numbers, but more and more teachers talk of leaving the profession, of quitting the system that strips them of their professional rights and responsibilities and that requires them to work in ways they do not see as beneficial to students and to themselves. Teachers are fleeing grades in which high-stakes tests are administered and breathing easier when they are assigned an untested grade level.

Those teachers who stick it out sometimes engage in solitary and collective acts of resistance against the state mandates under which they toil.[8] Most of this resistance is to state-mandated tests because, in essence, those are the mandates that matter, much more so than state-adopted curriculum frameworks or guidelines. Teachers sometimes refuse to administer the tests, provide information to parents about state opt-out policies, publish the test items to expose their folly, write letters to the editor about the effects of state-mandated testing, and talk with legislators. But teachers resist at their own risk—at the risk of being sanctioned, reassigned to highly undesirable assignments, decertified, or fired. For these reasons, many teachers do not resist, even though they might want to do so.

Teachers are using their unions to take public stands through the adoption of resolutions about curriculum and assessment issues, and to pressure their state governments to opt out of the federal demands of No Child Left Behind (NCLB). For example, National Education Association (NEA) members in Alaska have recently sent a message to their state legislators and educational policymakers that the federal education dollars received through compliance with the testing (and other) requirements of NCLB are not worth the cost, financially and educationally.

CONCLUSION

Standards-based reform and high-stakes testing force many teachers into untenable situations fraught with dilemmas that are difficult to resolve and maintain teacher professionalism and help all children to succeed to the best of their ability. Repeatedly, in our research and that of others, we see teachers put in lose-lose situations. They act in ways that are inconsistent with what they believe to be best teaching practice in order to increase the likelihood that students will succeed as measured by the state tests, which, at least for many teachers, is a poor indicator of the achievement and success of children. Teachers must often do the wrong thing in order to do the right thing, sort of.

It is essentially a utilitarian ethic that underlies test-driven curricular reform, one based on means-ends arguments. The state departments of education, and indeed the federal government, adopt the view that the ends justify the means, and teachers too are drawn into this logic. The means are approaches to teaching and content that teachers might not choose—that do not represent good professional practice—and the state-desired ends (high test scores) are a poor but powerful proxy for the teachers' desired ends (the contextually appropriate success of every child).

We know that state-mandated curriculum and testing challenge teachers' professionalism, especially with regard to how they treat children. Of course, this is interesting only if these things matter. Teachers wonder if policymakers and politicians have any sense of children's individual differences and the centrality of that concept to teaching *and* learning. Current state standards-based reform and assessment policies and practices would suggest that policymakers and practitioners either have no sense of this or they don't care, or maybe they are trying to redefine these relationships. Through the currently proffered solutions to problems of education, policymakers/politicians/corporate CEOs eschew what teachers know about human learning and cognition, and much of what teachers know is helpful and harmful to children's achievement.

Are policymakers and politicians unaware that outcome-based bureaucratic accountability driven by state-mandated tests will reduce teacher professionalism and autonomy? That some research suggests lower performing schools will actually lose ground? and that these accountability strategies do relatively little to alter the fundamental injustices in schools and society, such as racism and classism? We don't know for sure, but we think probably not. There is a fundamental disagreement about what kind of work teachers and students should be doing in schools—work that requires real critical thinking that may contribute to the evolution of a just and equitable society *or* work that has the appearance of critical thinking and will contribute to oppression.

> By insisting that legitimate learning necessarily presents itself in and on the basis of test scores, such testing refuses to admit and accept differences (individual as well as cultural) in knowledge, values, experiences, learning styles, economic resources, and access to those dominant academic artifacts that ultimately con-

tribute to both the appearance of achievement and the status of cultural hege-mony upon which standards-based reforms depend. In effect, standardized test-ing encourages a singular and homogeneous public schooling—one antithetical to such contemporary ideals as diversity, multiculturalism, difference, and lib-eration—vis-à-vis an underlying and insidious mechanism or technology of oppression, one in which the interests of society's most powerful (the minor-ity) are privileged at the expense of those of the less powerful (the majority).[9]

The teachers we talk with are more angry or frustrated than better off as a result of state-mandated curriculum and testing, and there is little indica-tion that student achievement is advancing in genuine ways or that schools are being reformed.

— 9 —

"Parental Involvement": In Defense of What Kind of Vision for "Public" School?

MELISSA FREEMAN

INTRODUCTION

The belief that parental involvement is a key ingredient in student success has placed involvement, whether desired or not by parents, at the center of current standards-based educational reform. In turn, communities, or parents as a cohort of interested consumers of educational services, are often "cited" by state and federal officials as wanting higher standards and stronger accountability from public schools. But to what extent are parents really partners in the standards-based accountability movement? And when government officials speak of parents, what kind of parent are they talking about? This chapter focuses on the voices of two groups of parents in the current educational debate on accountability: one suburban (Orchard Hill)[1] and one urban (Park City). It is based on the idea that listening to parents talk about their experiences with testing can foster an understanding of how the culture of accountability affects different parents' understandings of their role as partners in their children's education and what those understandings reveal about their expectations of a public school system.

Current accountability strategies of school reform rely heavily on measuring student achievement on state standards through the use of state-mandated standardized tests and attaching consequences, either positive or negative, to various levels of performance. In New York State, these strategies include developing new learning standards in every subject area, publishing an annual report card on schools and districts, and mandating the use of statewide tests at the elementary and secondary levels. Fourth graders take an English language arts (ELA) exam, a math, and a science test. Fifth graders take a social studies test. Eighth-graders take all four of these subject tests plus an optional technology exam. And all students are required to take and pass five state-developed Regents exams to graduate from high school. Furthermore, different districts include their own standardized tests to measure math and English proficiency as well as a variety of other aptitude and achievement tests for placement purposes. So, while the discussions with parents upon which this chapter is based focus on the fourth-, fifth-, and eighth-grade state tests, the presence and impact of these other tests play an important role in understanding the context of their comments and concerns.

TWO DISTRICTS

The analysis in this chapter is based on interviews with parents in two school districts in upstate New York. In both districts, parents of elementary and middle school children were invited to participate in one-hour group discussions on the topic of state-standardized testing and were paid $25 for their participation. Four groups were conducted in Orchard Hill involving a total of thirteen parents, and six groups were conducted in Park City involving a total of thirty-seven parents. Table 9.1 and Table 9.2 provide an overview of district and participant demographics.

Parents in both districts believe that schools cannot successfully educate children without the support, involvement, and effort of parents. They agree that parental responsibilities include helping with homework, meeting with teachers, and advocating on behalf of their children when schools or teachers do not appear to be meeting their needs. Furthermore, they believe that parents who do not do these things are harming their children's chances at success. So the idea that I am putting forward, that parent involvement practices and expectations can actually harm a strong public school system, might seem questionable.

Involvement, like other social practices, is impacted by social status markers, such as class, as well as the social contexts within which it is practiced. And, like other practices, it can be harmful to the public if it conceals relations of power and oppression that play a role in creating and maintaining institutional structures that do not serve everyone equally. The parents' narratives reveal that parents in an urban, mostly working- and middle-class setting like Park City hold different conceptions of involvement and education than parents in a suburban, mostly middle- and upper-class setting like Orchard Hill. This suggests that the presence or absence of privilege may shape people's overall perceptions of themselves and others, as well as their beliefs about such things as standards, schooling, and accountability. Of significance here is whether the activities and beliefs of one group of people support and contribute to a system that is wrong for others.

Table 9.1
District Statistics from the Year 2000

	Park City	Orchard Hill
Population	62,288	17,765
Land area (sq. miles)	11.9	49.82
Per capita income	$29,458	$60,876
# Students	8,482	3,350
Student racial/ethnic origin		
Asian/American Indian	4.2%	0.8%
Black	30.1%	0.9%
Hispanic	9.3%	0.5%
White	56.4%	97.8%
Instructional expenditure/student	$11,031	$11,040
% Free lunches	48%	4%
% Passing 4th grade Math State Test	66%	93%
% Passing 4th grade ELA	50%	87%
% Passing 8th grade Math State Test	18%	69%
% Passing 8th grade ELA	27%	62%
Dropout rate	6.8%	1.6%

Table 9.2
Total Participant Demographics by District

	Park City (n = 37)	Orchard Hill (n = 13)
Ethnicity		
White	73.0%	100%
African-American	8.1%	
Asian	2.7%	
Hispanic	13.5%	
Native American	2.7%	
Gender		
Female	65%	69%
Male	35%	31%
Highest Education		
< Than High School	5.4%	0.0%
High School	16.2%	2.7%
Some College	40.5%	2.7%
College Degree	29.7%	86.4%
Graduate Degree	8.1%	8.1%

PARK CITY

The narrative accounts of parents in Park City center on relationships: their relationships with their children, their children's relationships with teachers, and the teachers' relationships with parents. Their primary concern is with the social and emotional well-being of their children as well as their general comfort level with schoolwork. A mother explains:

> I wouldn't want someone to say to me, "Well if your child doesn't pass [the tests] nothing's going to happen." I don't want to be an irresponsible parent, be like don't worry about it, because that's not how we're supposed to be. We want them to do their best and strive for their potential. But regarding the stress of the child who may not pass, I had a child that I know would do well on the test and then I also have a child that I know would not. And I felt just as much stress for my daughter who strives to do the best she can and was so worried about not being able to do the best and I had the same stress for my son who I know will not meet his potential.

Parents express being unsure of their or their children's capacity to succeed in a system that has intensified its educational requirements in ways that make it more difficult for children and families to keep up. Several parents share stories of children struggling to meet the state performance levels despite their efforts. Parents, such as this mother of twin fourth-graders, are frightened of what this will mean for their children's future:

> I'm lucky if I can get my sons to sit down after school and get their homework done. I'm lucky if I can get them to focus down enough to get their homework done. It's really hard because we do the reading thing. I read a page, one reads a page, the other reads a page. And it's like, "Ok mom, are we done now?" "No you guys got to do this." And then it's like screaming because they're screaming at me because they're bored; they don't want to do it. I just cannot get them to sit down 20 minutes. And it's like I can just imagine what's going to happen on the test because they're on medication and I don't feel that I should have to keep on increasing the medicine because they're not up to par or because they can't stay focused. That's not the answer either, to constantly medicate them. So what am I supposed to do? So this test really scares me because my children never failed a grade.

In response to these pressures, parents find themselves supporting their children while fearing the worst:

> I think that if the whole 4th grade is just focusing on the passing of the ELA, and in the end the child does not pass, it's going to be very devastating to somebody who is nine years old. And I try to reassure my child that a test cannot tell people what kind of a person you are. And I just express for her to do her best and we'll go from there.

Many parents in Park City feel that raising standards is enough change and pressure on their children and question the need for more tests. Some do so because they are skeptical that the tests offer any useful information about teachers, children, and schools, and see them as doing more harm than good. Others are amazed at the level of the work. A mother of a third grader comments:

> I think the hard part is because, have you looked at these books? When I came in for my parent-teacher conference, the teacher was like, "This is what the kids are supposed to be reading." And there are words in there that to me only an adult would use. So she's teaching them different shortcuts, which I think is great, but if there's that much pressure for them to learn this higher standard of curriculum, that's pressure alone. And then they have to prepare for these tests, too.

Others feel that if they are going to have tests, they appreciate the extra work the teachers are putting forth to prepare the children. A mother of an eighth grader states:

> On Saturday they gave an extra class for the test which was great. My daughter told me a few things that she learned. They gave some pointers on what to do during the test, which I think is helpful because if you're not prepared like that, you might not know how to do the format of the test. And you don't want to go in totally blank. So I think it's great that they prepare them.

And several parents, especially at the elementary level, are grateful for the extra attention teachers are paying to them. They report increased contact between school and home and increased information about what the curriculum looks like under the new standards. They convey a sense of empowerment as they share stories of learning new ways of assisting their children with homework:

> It's frustrating for parents when your child comes to you and they want you to help them with homework and you don't understand it yourself, which is how it was when my daughter was in third grade. I didn't understand the new math. I went to the teacher and I said, "Please show me, so I can help her." What they did last year and I believe they're having another one this year, they're having a math night for parents. And they gave us these books, and I use it this year to refer to, to help my son with his new math.

For the parents in Park City, current reform strategies have increased the pressure on children to perform and in doing so have added to the daily pressure on parents with little regard for the impact on the family. Several parents discuss this issue:

SAMANTHA: "They get so much homework."

JANICE: "But doesn't that make you frustrated? It does me because I'm thinking to myself, oh yes, I feel it is my job as a parent, but in a way I kind of don't because when I was in school my parents never had to sit down with me and say, 'Well this is what has to be done.' 'If you need help, ask your teacher,' that's the thing they used to tell me."

INTERVIEWER: "So why do you think you need to sit with your children now?"

JANICE: "Because it's harder for them."

SAMANTHA: "They make it, plus the teachers make it like they kind of make you do that. You're forced to do it."

JANICE: "I don't know if I want to say that though that you're forced to do it. I mean I want to help."

NORINA: "But the children do need the guidance and what the teachers give you is not, the children need a parental guidance to understand what it is that they need to do and then I find myself being short with my children, like I want to make dinner, I want to watch my movie, like I want to do my things and you know it's hard on the parents, too."

Of concern to parents in Park City is whether the heightened standards, testing, and pressure will serve the needs of the students and of the public. While some parents hope higher standards will mean their children will be better educated and therefore better prepared for college and employment, others fear that the impact of the system will be worse, not only for students who they fear will drop out and be left with nothing but also for the communities that will have to absorb those students. A father explains:

> When I went to high school there were three different options. Today the only thing that's out there is the standard thing: New York State Regents, that's it, you don't get no stinking diploma and any other diploma you get isn't worth it. And this is the same thing with these standardized tests. This is the only way you can be tested, the only thing that counts, and if you fall outside the norm, you're no good. And I think a lot of kids feel left by the wayside.

ORCHARD HILL

While parents in Park City express uncertainty about their ability to help their children succeed, Orchard Hill parents display confidence in their capacity to assist their children, even when their children may have more difficulties than others. A father of a son receiving special education services states:

> I don't see the standardized testing hurting anyone. My son in fifth grade is going to have a lot of challenges with the standardized testing. It is going to be a lot of work for my wife and me, probably, to help him along and help him to pass, and that's going to be a real challenge. But in the end, if we pull that off, in the end he will have learned more because of it.

Orchard Hill parents also care about their children, but their narratives are not focused so much on their children's emotional well-being as they are on the tasks their children have to accomplish. While parents in Park City ask their children to "do their best" as a way to provide them with emotional support, parents in Orchard Hill talk of pushing their children to strive for more than their best. A mother explains:

Well, sooner or later I hope that they'd be motivated to do it for themselves. Not just "I did my best." But when they're younger somebody has got to be watching and saying, "Well that's not good enough. I know you can do better."

Moreover, parents in Orchard Hill express few concerns that their children might fail and accept that if the system requires students to do something, they need to do it. School is "about jumping through the hoops," as one mother put it, so there is little point in resisting it.

My job is to reinforce whatever they learn in school. I mean there are things that go on that I disagree with but I don't share those with my kid, because this is where they have to be. This is their life and this is how it's gonna go.

This does not mean that they sit back and do nothing. While many of the parents in Park City express feeling uninformed about what is going on in their children's school and grateful for any guidance they receive from teachers, the parents in Orchard Hill talk about needing to be proactive, especially when it comes to getting their children into or out of particular classes or programs, as this mother did for her son:

My son, of course, he breaks the mold because he just marches to the beat of a different drummer. He will keep up with the science and the math, but writing is his thing. He loves it. He adores it. And last year we pulled him out of [an accelerated class] for other reasons and he was in a regular English class and it was tough for him. I mean we chose to do it and there were lessons that he learned about integrity and things like that that were valuable for him to learn. And this is the sort of thing when there's a big difference in motivation, instead of bringing the level up it's going to kind of drop.

Even when the results of their actions don't always match their goals, parents in Orchard Hill believe in a consumer-driven conception of involvement as opposed to the service-oriented conception shared by Park City parents. And so Orchard Hill parents are more likely to expect that when their children demonstrate excellence they should be rewarded accordingly and become frustrated when they need to fight for those rewards. A mother explains:

The middle school, they'll have an accelerated math class and there are 35 kids that actually qualify. They aren't going to take them all because they have one class. So they'll cut them. That's the problem I had. I had to lobby for my daughter to be in there even though all her scores were high.

Parents in Orchard Hill are also concerned about the impact of the tests and standards on the public school system. They understand that these might be difficult for certain people but feel that more harm than good would be done by eliminating them. A father explains:

We obviously are very, very fortunate here, you have a nice school, nice neighborhood, kids grow up in a dream-come-true type of area. And plenty of kids in the inner city don't have anything near to this. But the standardized tests, if they're not doing well then they need to fix the system. You don't want to try to make them feel better by giving them better grades or helping them out superficially. You've got to fix the problem. Not by lowering the test but by fixing the root cause of the problem.

PARENT INVOLVEMENT AS A CLASS-BASED DISCOURSE

The role parents play in their children's education is not innocent and can alter the practices and policies that are put into place for all children. For example, after middle school teachers in Orchard Hill switched to heterogeneous grouping for English, a group of vocal parents worked to overturn that decision by insisting that their gifted children had special needs. They organized and presented a plan to the board and succeeded in reestablishing a tracked system that included special classes for gifted and talented students.

Even individual activities, such as helping with homework, can play a role in creating and maintaining school structures that do not meet the needs of everyone equally. This occurs when those activities result in individual children receiving special privileges or protect a public education that does not serve the majority of the public. An example of this is the "expanded options for parents," one of the four principles upon which the No Child Left Behind (NCLB) Federal Education Act of 2001 is built. Many parents might think this will benefit public education since it seems to raise the capacity of parents to have more say in their children's education. However, what is touted as expanded options for parents primarily emphasizes parental choice to choose a better school over a failing one, not greater opportunities to work with educators to improve struggling schools or the choice to opt their children out of standardized testing.[2] Market-driven systems, such as currently designed standards-based educational reform systems, give the impression to parents that they have choices in how they wish to become involved in their children's education, but what they do is conceal the inequalities of resource and power that create differences in involvement, access, and parent and student opportunity in the first place.

Studies that have looked at the impact of class as a social discourse have found that social class influences the ways in which people relate to others and to institutions. For example, Benjamin DeMott[3] explains how the myth of equal opportunity and choice is so strong in American culture that it obscures how class-socialized behaviors contribute to acts of success or failure. He argues that the hidden social networks and the unequal distribution of resources, such as the knowledge that systems can be manipulated, are class related.

In a study that explored the ways in which parents made particular requests, Goldman and McDermott[4] point out that parents who make requests such as for particular teachers or placement in specific programs do so to guarantee that their child will get ahead in a competitive world. They conclude that what is gained is access to limited resources, which not only guarantee those resources for their own children but deny them for someone else's.

Similarly, Alfie Kohn[5] points out that the efforts of affluent parents to make sure their own children's needs are met actually works against any reform movement hoping to make sure all children's needs are met. What these studies suggest is that more attention needs to be paid to how class shapes our beliefs, actions, and interactions, as well as the way in which it alters our perceptions of ourselves and others.

It is important to note, however, that not all parents who attended the focus groups are poor in Park City and wealthy in Orchard Hill and that their narratives overlap in many ways. Moreover, most parents in both districts probably participate in ways that are neither overly demanding or manipulative, or abusive or neglectful. Despite this, the overall solutions and attitudes shared in each district display particular consistencies. I have already discussed the general influence of the local cultures of privilege and underprivilege. Add to this the impact of a system of accountability that supports and strengthens one of these orientations while weakening the other and the result is a structure that undermines a public school system that is intent on seeking real equality of opportunity for all.

IMPACT OF STATE-MANDATED TESTING

Parents in both districts agree that the state tests have impacted the way the curriculum is taught, and they agree that, for the most part, the impact on teaching has been a negative one. It has narrowed the experiences of children, increased the reliance of teachers on packets and formula teaching, and raised the pressure on children to conform in ways that do not work for many children. A mother in Park City comments:

> I teach preschool. Everyone learns differently. But there's a few of them who learn so drastically differently from the other children that the parents are concerned and want to put a kibosh on it. I'm really concerned that if you don't learn the way they want you to learn, you are advised to see a child psychologist. And it all starts as soon as you enter kindergarten. Why can't they learn differently? That's how they learn. They learn best differently. And because a lot of this testing has become so important it really singles them out.

This concern with individual learning styles is echoed in a different way by a group of parents in Orchard Hill:

GAIL: "I think the tests have a tremendous effect on what is taught in the classroom. The teachers have to teach to the tests and the kids practice the tests."

KATHLEEN: "And it might be things our kids already know and they're being taught it over and over."

MARION: "It's a waste of a year because they're not learning. They have no anxiety over taking the test."

KATHLEEN: "The other thing is that they seem to focus on a particular method which is geared toward this particular test and they teach no other method. And for my son, [this means] being forced to do a certain kind of math a certain kind of way rather than being able to take those intuitive leaps. I mean yes, he has to know how to do it that way, but it shouldn't be the only way that he's allowed to do it. You get no credit if you don't show your work in their style. No one can convince me there's a value added there."

Both groups agree that the tests are probably not a fair way to assess children and cite social class differences and differences in parent involvement as the primary reasons for why some kids will probably not do well on the tests. But their solutions for this issue are quite different and are based on very different conceptions of assessment as well as different expectations of education in general.

Park City parents advocate for the elimination of standardized state tests and view these as providing no new information to them about their children. They rely instead on personal and subjective forms of assessing their children's learning, as this mother relates:

> I think as a parent I know that my kids are learning whether they do good on that test or not. I can see just by the way they are coming home and the new things that they are learning every day. I see that. So that one test isn't going to change my mind that they're not learning.

Just as parental involvement for many Park City parents is about providing care and support to your child, learning occurs when you feel good about yourself and should be part of the daily experience. They worry that if school becomes too regulated and rigid, their children will not be motivated to or able to succeed. A mother explains:

> If there weren't any tests, I think my daughter could enjoy forth grade more. For Thanksgiving, the biggest thrill of the whole weekend was not having any homework to do. And I felt like dancing in the streets. I think if it wasn't so browbeaten into them, ELA, ELA, ELA, into them they would be getting a more rounded education this year. They would be able to focus on more than one thing. You learn through comfort. You learn when the pressure is off. It's a lot of pressure for somebody who's nine years old when their biggest thing should be, "Do you want to read *Berenstein Bears* tonight or *Little House on the Prairie*?" It's not that at all. Now it's "What is Laura Ingalls Wilder trying to say?"

Most parents in Orchard Hill, however, have little faith that a system without external, objective measurement would provide the information needed to assess the quality of their children's school experience. A father explains:

The state tests are a measurement tool. You need a measurement tool. It may not be the best one. I'm sure there are ways to improve it, but you know, good people have done the best they can to put together these state tests in general and you can't do without some method to measure performance. If you do that you run the risk of teachers going off on their own little tangents teaching and you have no way to realize what's going on until the kid is into the next year and he hasn't learned what he needed to learn. So you need to have a measurement tool.

These parents hold different expectations for school. Rather than view school as primarily a social experience where people develop and grow, school is a stepping-stone to life in a market-driven world and should reflect the competitiveness of that world. Another father explains:

You know, in general life really isn't fair. I just can't get upset about demographics. You know every kid, no matter where they come from, every kid is going to have to go out into the real world eventually. And you can't be tailoring everything to every kid.

On the other hand, parents in Park City are becoming less and less convinced that the state testing system is meant to inform school reform efforts, as they see increased evidence that the emphasis on testing and test scores is diverting people's attention away from important issues like equality of resources. A father explains:

The purpose of setting a benchmark for a test is not to provide resources to those who failed to reach it, but to somehow, either through embarrassment or pressure, get them to do something else to reach it without any additional resources. And therefore it is very easy for a spokesman to say, "All this school really needed to do is buckle down and work harder." And while that may be functionally true, it doesn't address the situation where there are serious gaps between resources and the number of people who haven't reached basic reading skills.

However, parents in wealthy districts such as Orchard Hill generally support the idea put forth by politicians that more resources is not the answer for failing schools. In their view, success in a competitive world is more of an attitude than an ability and point to the need for each district to come up with its own solution. A father explains:

When you think about it, high-income neighborhoods, the schools generally look better and there's more money, just because there are more local taxes these schools are better off. On one end it's not fair to say, okay, you have these high-income areas, let's take more tax money from them and give it to the low-income areas. I don't think it adds more to their resources, it's just that it's the attitude; there's a predetermined perception of what their lives are going to be like, and what they seek. So their perceived self-concept [of] themselves [is] lower in low-income areas than in affluent areas. So the only way to bridge that gap, to change that, is not so much the school, I don't think they can do that. They haven't been able to do that, and I don't think you can ask them to do it; you need to change the parent."

While attitudes and self-concepts may be important factors in determining children's success in school, images of success ride on other such images, and these have to be maintained at a certain cost. Privilege, for example, "dream-come-true" communities and schools that reflect consumer and market-driven values, not only enable success and achievement, they are seen as rewards for success and achievement. And so parents in Orchard Hill are protective of what they have. Their primary worry is not that standards and testing might hurt nearby communities but that too much publicity of their own community success, which they believe is accurately depicted by the test scores, might cause it harm by drawing people to the district who may not share its values and would compete for its resources.

Parents in Park City do not share this concern. They don't believe that the test scores provide an accurate statement about what their schools have to offer and feel the state's accountability system is harming their community by perpetuating false images of failure. They relate being pleased with their school district and appreciate, for example, its multicultural nature and the way the district values technology and the arts. Their primary concern is not whether people come or go but that a system that places emphasis on competition and test results undermines their own values of achievement, including the importance of respect and tolerance for others.

A standards-based accountability system that is based on a conception of achievement that is aligned with the views of people who do whatever it takes to outperform the rest cannot successfully provide a quality education for all children. In fact, it does the opposite by discouraging a public response that embraces the challenge of a quality public education as everyone's challenge and everyone's concern. It does this by supporting and maintaining unequal and segregated educational experiences and practices that reward privileged schools and districts for maintaining their advantage and punish underprivileged schools and districts when their students are unable to make up their disadvantage and meet the standards set forth by the state tests.[6]

IN DEFENSE OF WHAT KIND OF VISION FOR PUBLIC SCHOOL?

A view of education for all that rides on students passing high-stakes tests is a view that continues to favor the privileged over the underprivileged and is not a view that seeks a strong education system for all. The viewpoints shared here should not be taken to mean that parents in Orchard Hill never care about others, while parents in Park City never seek advantage for their own children. What seems clear, however, is that the belief in personal effort and merit obscures the deep-seated advantage of privilege. By externalizing the success and failure of schools and districts into comparable points on a scale, the state's accountability system succeeds in displacing the conversation away from issues of resource and access and placing them squarely where they least belong: on the individual school, the individual teacher, and the individual parent.

Parents become the repositories for the failure and success of schools, and they also become allies to the state's accountability system. Many parents in higher-income areas such as Orchard Hill create alliances between themselves and their schools. They participate in the school's agenda by making sure their children do well on the state tests even if these are not considered "ideal" learning experiences, in exchange for getting what they want for their children such as smaller class sizes and above-average educational resources and opportunities. What these parents seek is a way to maintain advantage for themselves and their children and keep choices and options open. Based on consumerism, the idea is to keep available the right ingredients to use for every situation that arises. They do this by working with the system, maintaining strong networks, and competing for the best products. In other words, they are quite comfortable in a market-driven society.

Standards-based reform initiatives not only function in a similar way, they also encourage activities that reinforce merit- and competitive-based structures. The embracing of market conditions for public schooling has resulted in having more resources offered to areas that need it least while depriving other areas of much needed resources. This occurs when good teachers flee struggling neighborhoods because the pressure is too high; when monetary rewards are provided to schools that reach a particular performance level; and when children who fail the tests are deprived of participating in other essential experiences like enrichment classes and field trips. In this kind of system, the more you have to begin with, the more you get in the end. The rhetoric of "standards for all" hides the oppression that is occurring in its name.

All people struggle for a place in the materialistic world of social practices, a piece of the American pie, so to speak, so the struggle to succeed and define oneself within social spaces is relational and is impacted by the power relations and oppressive practices of the larger society. People are at a disadvantage when their cultural values and social expectations conflict with the values of the institution within which they are trying to find footing. Parents who are content when their children are happy in school, do the work expected, and get along with their peers find their values and goals bypassed by a system where success is defined by a point of reference that means little to them.

Furthermore, it is important to realize how an image of involvement that is based on choice and competition, on this "go, go, go" mentality, as one Park City mother put it, contributes to silencing the voices of parents who are involved in other ways. A parent in Park City shares her values:

> I go periodically to the PTO meetings with other PTO presidents and the Superintendent, and we get into these conversations. We just feel that the important thing is to teach a child in the classroom what we were taught; respect and understanding, sharing, all those things that were emphasized when we were growing up are no longer there because they have to meet this curriculum. And

the kids aren't learning some of the basic rules of life that we were taught. I mean, how important is the ELA going to be when they're 30 years old and working?

Improving schools for all requires that people look beyond advocating for their own child or school, and advocate instead for a system that seeks real equity of opportunity for all. It means rejecting market conditions for our public schools, conditions that place both parents and children on unequal ground before they have even begun to compete. And it means rejecting standards of assessment that not only delocalize public input but also isolate successful and failing schools and districts from each other. It is far more difficult to establish a democratic, inclusive, and open social relationship between the public and its schools in a climate of competition and blame than it is in a climate of cooperation and trust. Understanding how the practices of the powerful can work against a strong public school is crucial for developing and sustaining relationships between parents and schools that have as a goal to protect and work toward a public educational system that improves schooling for everyone, not just a privileged few.

Leaving No Child Left Behind: Accountability Reform and Students with Disabilities

Margaret J. McLaughlin
and Katherine M. Nagle

INTRODUCTION

Appreciating the issues surrounding students with disabilities within a standards-driven system requires an understanding of the ambiguities between the concept of individual rights as it has evolved during the latter part of the twentieth century in the United States and an educational system that promotes a normative view of equity. Essentially, both concepts emerged from an interpretation of the constitutional guarantee to the right to life, liberty, and the pursuit of happiness. The concept of individual rights assumed that "all" individuals would equally enter into and profit from societal organizations. This early interpretation of individual rights in the United States argued against government's regulation of economic or social structures, including schools, and education was constitutionally deferred to the individual states.

A fundamental shift in this construct of individual rights began when reformers began to view government's neutrality or abstention from interference with the individual as harmful to many. People of color, the poor, and the disabled were not protected under the earlier concepts of individual rights and, in fact, were denied access to the same rights that others had.[1]

This shift in interpretation had a powerful impact on public education. The 1954 *Brown v. Board of Education* decision established that the right to education was an individual property protected under the U.S. Constitution. The Brown decision established that black children not only had a right to education but also that they had a right to the same education received by white children, citing that "separate but equal" schools were inherently unequal due to stigma and deprivation of interaction with children from other backgrounds.[2] The federal courts not only intervened to establish an individual right to an education but also began to define a uniform and egalitarian form of education.

This premise of equity is an important theme in current federal and state standards-driven educational policies, such as Title I of the No Child Left Behind Act (NCLB), the 2001 reauthorization of the Elementary and Secondary Education Act. The current reform framework includes the creation of *common* standards, challenging assessments, and enhanced accountability for student performance.[3] Central to these reforms is the notion that *each* student is entitled to instruction that is grounded in a common set of challenging content standards and that schools and individual students must be held accountable for achieving equally high levels of performance on these standards.

The Brown decision also provided the precedent for the federal special education legislation that entitles each eligible child with a disability to a "free and appropriate public education" in the "least restrictive environment." The 1975 legislation, The Education of All Handicapped Children Act (PL 94-142), guaranteed that all children with disabilities must be given an education; it must be provided in the least restrictive setting; education must be individualized and appropriate; it is to be provided free; and procedural protections are required. Subsequent reauthorizations of the act have extended the protections and added provisions (including changing the name of the act to the Individuals with Disabilities Education Act [IDEA]) but the central guarantees remain unchanged. To provide a context for considering how the concept of individualized education can be juxtaposed with standards-based education, we must consider who receives special education and the meaning of the entitlement to an "appropriate" education.

Who Receives Special Education?

The IDEA and accompanying regulations prescribe a number of procedures for determining the extent and nature of the special education provided to individual students as well as set criteria for determining what constitutes a disability under the law. Federal law requires that individual states develop regulation and procedure for how the state will operationalize the disability categories. The resulting federal and state definitions and the procedures for determining disability vary from state to state and sometimes even across districts within a state.

Federal and state statutes and rules use classification as a means for controlling the allocation of resources and for assuring that the legal protections and entitlements are targeted at the members of a protected class. Yet the classification of students as disabled and eligible to receive special education and related services has generated much controversy and debate over the years.[4] Among these are the long-standing issue of disproportionate representation of certain racial and ethnic populations and males in special education and the burgeoning number of students classified as "Specific Learning Disabled." For example, during the past decade, the number of children classified as having specific learning disabilities has increased by almost 38 percent.[5]

Presently, students with disabilities ages six through seventeen account for 11.5 percent of the estimated total student enrollment for grades pre-K through grade twelve.[6] Of the thirteen disability categories covered under IDEA, four categories account for 87.7 percent of students with disabilities ages six through twenty-one. The specific learning disabilities category accounted for half of the students served, speech or language impairments for 18.9 percent and mental retardation and emotional disturbance accounted for 10.6 percent and 8.2 percent, respectively. The one characteristic shared by these students is academic underachievement in one or more areas.

For more than 50 percent of the school-age students currently being served in special education, referrals from classroom teachers, or parents are the primary mechanism for triggering eligibility. Professional judgment or family advocacy becomes critical in determining access to special education. Research has confirmed extreme variability across states in both classification rates and factors that contribute to classification, such as definitions of disabilities, assessment procedures, and administrative decision making.[7]

The Entitlement to an "Appropriate" Education

The cornerstone of federal special education law is the individual student's entitlement to a "free appropriate public education" (FAPE) (20 U.S.C., 1401[8]). As defined through regulation, FAPE means special education and related services that are provided at public expense, under public supervision, and are provided according to an individualized education program (IEP). By law, each child's IEP must include a written statement of a child's present level of performance; a statement of annual goals and short-term objectives and benchmarks; a statement of all special education and related services that will be provided and the extent to which the child will participate in general education; and schedules for annual review. At the time of passage of PL 94-142, Congress clearly indicated that the requirement for individualized programs was essential to achieving the ambitious goals of the legislation.[8]

State and federal courts have played a significant role in defining what constitutes an appropriate education. The Supreme Court's decision in *Board of Education of Hendrick Hudson Central School District v. Rowley* (458 US 176, 1982) held that in order to be appropriate, the special education and related services provided to a child with a disability must be designed in conformity with the procedures and timelines and must be reasonably calculated to confer educational benefit.[9]

Analyses of applications of the Rowley standard disagree as to the consistency of interpretations. However, most would agree that a child's education is deemed appropriate if he or she is making progress based on some judgment of his or her capabilities and that there is no requirement to maximize potential or move toward any performance standard.[10] The idea of "benefit" is very ambiguous and can result in disputes over the appropriateness of any child's IEP.

Recent broad changes in federal and state special education policies attempt to align special education with the broader educational system. Current special education reform ideology is less concerned with bureaucratic conventions and adherence to rigid rules and procedures and is more focused on achieving specific levels of student performance. Public educational policy is shifting from concerns solely about equal access to education to ensuring equal access to an adequate education, defined in terms of educational attainments or outcomes. For students with disabilities, the expectation is that they will access the standards, participate in assessments, and be included in educational accountability systems the same as their nondisabled peers. The intent of all of this legislation is to ensure that no group of students receives differential treatment within the schools, under the assumption that individual students should have equal opportunity to achieve the same outcomes.

CURRENT POLICY REQUIREMENTS

Current policy requirements for standards-based reform relating to students with disabilities are found in two federal laws: IDEA 97 and the NCLB. Both pieces of legislation contain provisions requiring the participation of students with disabilities in state assessments and disaggregated public reporting of those students' performances.

Standards-Based Reform and IDEA

The 1997 reauthorization of IDEA contained a number of new provisions designed to align special education accountability more closely with reform efforts already taking place in regular education. These provisions mark a departure from the traditional rights-based model of special education accountability systems, which focused on compliance with specific procedures and timelines.[11] Policymakers, concerned with the low expectations and poor postschool outcomes for students with disabilities placed a strong emphasis in IDEA '97 on linking the educational program of children with disabilities to the general curriculum by adding components to individual education programs (IEPs). Although the term *general education curriculum* is not defined in the law, the regulations define it as the same curriculum as for nondisabled children [34 C.F.R. § 300.347(a)(1)(i)].

Consistent with the requirements for greater access and progress in the general education curriculum, IDEA '97 presumes children with disabilities will be included in state and district assessments. Specifically, states and districts are required to include students with disabilities in local and statewide assessments with accommodations where appropriate [§612(a)(17)(B)(I)] and to document this on individual student IEPs. If a student with a disability will not participate in the state assessment, the IEP must include a statement of why that assessment is not appropriate for the child and how the child will be assessed [§614(d)(1)(A)(v)]. For those students with disabilities who are not able to participate in state assessments even with accommodations, states were required to develop an alternate means of assessment no later than July 1, 2000.

States and districts are required to report the performance of students with disabilities on state and district assessments with the same frequency and in the same detail that they use to report the performance of nondisabled students [§612(a)(17)(B)(iii)]. In addition, states must report the performance of students with disabilities on any alternate assessment. Other accountability provisions new to special education include the requirement that states establish performance goals and indicators for students with disabilities and report progress toward these goals to the U.S. Secretary of Education and the public every two years.

These IDEA provisions indicate that state and local assessments are regarded as educational benefits that contribute to a student's opportunity to learn. Moreover, the intent of these provisions is to ensure that schools are accountable for the achievement of students in special education as well as those in regular education.

Students with Disabilities and NCLB

The shift toward more focused, standards-based accountability in special education, evident in IDEA, received additional impetus with the new Title I requirements of NCLB. Lawmakers recognized that defining success based on average student progress masked achievement gaps between student groups and enabled schools and districts to appear successful even though groups of their students were struggling.[12] Under NCLB, states must assess at least 95 percent of all students and students in each of five target groups, including students with disabilities. In addition, states must publicly report disaggregated subgroup performance as long as student confidentiality is maintained. However, schools are only accountable for groups that are large enough to allow statistically valid and reliable conclusions to be made regarding their performance on state assessments.. This minimum number for subgroup accountability is determined by each state.

States must set separate annual yearly progress (AYP) targets in mathematics and reading/language arts ensuring that all groups of students remain on a trajectory toward proficiency by 2013–2014. These targets increase overtime and must be the same for all schools serving the same grades and for all groups of students within schools. NCLB includes a "safe harbor" clause that can be applied to any subgroup or subgroups of students that fail to meet the statewide goal. In this situation, the school can still make AYP if the percentage of students below proficient falls by 10 percent, and the subgroup or subgroups in question meet the 95 percent participation requirement and makes progress on the other required additional indicator.

One aspect of NCLB that has proved problematic for students with disabilities is the requirement that state assessments measure grade-appropriate performance in reading/language arts and mathematics. Recognizing that grade-level assessments would not be appropriate for some students with disabilities, especially those with severe impairments, the NCLB regulations give states and school districts the flexibility to measure the achievement of students with the most significant cognitive disabilities against alternate achievement standards and to count the "proficient" scores of these students as proficient in the calculation of AYP [200.13(c)(1)(i)]. However, to ensure that alternate achievement standards are not used as a loophole to evade accountability for large numbers of students with disabilities, the number of proficient scores on alternate achievement standards at the LEA and state levels must not exceed 1 percent of all students in reading/language arts and in mathematics (Federal Register, Vol. 68, No 236, Tuesday, December 9, 2003, Rules and Regulations, pg. 68703).

An alternate achievement standard is an expectation of performance that differs in complexity from a grade-level achievement standard. The final regulations make clear that alternate achievement standards are appropriate for only a small percentage of students with disabilities. Under NCLB, individual states are allowed to define alternate achievement standards as long as they are aligned with the state's academic content standards, promote access to the general curriculum, and reflect professional judgment of the highest achievement standards possible [34 C.F.R. § 200.1(d)].

Issues Related to Students with Disabilities in Standards-Based Reform

Several issues challenge the full participation of students with disabilities in current reforms. The issues can be broadly categorized as (1) conceptual and (2) technical. Among the conceptual issues is the tension between the concept of an "individualized" education as determined by the IEP team and the notion of common content standards and performance expectations. A related issue is how to ensure that students with disabilities have authentic opportunities to achieve the common standards. Technical issues primarily center on assessments and include the effects of assessment accommodations and the nature of the inferences drawn from the performance data of students with disabilities.

Standards and IEPs. Historically, students with disabilities were largely segregated from the mainstream of education or their educational services were driven by the IEP and, at best, only loosely coupled to the general curriculum or classroom instruction. Clearly, the more time a student with a disability spends in the regular classroom the greater the likelihood that he or she will be exposed to and have the opportunity to progress in the general education curriculum.

Currently, over 95 percent of students with disabilities are served in regular school buildings, while 4 percent, or over 230,000 students with disabilities, are in separate schools or settings. The percentage of students with disabilities educated within the regular classroom at least 80 percent of the school day increased to 47.3 percent in 1999–2000. However, over 20 percent of all students with disabilities are educated in special classes within the regular school buildings, and an additional 28 percent receive special education outside the regular classroom between 21 percent and 60 percent of the school day (U.S. Department of Education, 2002). These data provide some indication of the challenges associated with ensuring that students with disabilities receive an opportunity to access the standards-based instruction. These opportunities are "controlled" by the IEP.

As noted earlier, the IEP defines what is "appropriate" for a student with a disability, including the specific goals and areas of special education as well as the setting in which that education is to be delivered. The IEP team decides how a student participates in general education instruction and assessments, including what accommodations the student will require. The IEP remains the primary mechanism for the delivery of a free and appropriate education to students with disabilities. However, the IEP team is no longer the sole determinant of a student's educational experiences, as the teams now operate in an environment in which the state's academic content standards, achievement standards, and assessments must be addressed.

If students with disabilities are to reap the benefits of standards-based reform, they must have access to the general education curriculum over the long term. Data from the annual reports to Congress discussed earlier have important implications for the participation of students with disabilities in standards-based reform and performance-based accountability mechanisms. Although the vast majority of students with disabilities are being educated in regular school buildings, there is a paucity of information relating to curriculum and assessment of students with disabilities in separate settings.

As an example, a recent study of accountability policies and practices in private and public day treatment and residential schools for students with emotional disturbance revealed a number of problems. These included lack of knowledge of state standards and assessments and policies regarding the participation of students with disabilities and low assessment participation rates.[13]

Placement in a regular school is no guarantee of access to the general curriculum. Over 20 percent of students with disabilities served in regular school buildings may have little or no access to the general education curriculum as taught by general education teachers because they are educated outside the regular classroom for almost the entire school day. In addition, over a quarter more of all these students spend one-fifth to two-thirds of their time outside the regular classroom. This means that opportunity to access standards is highly dependent on the general education curricular knowledge of the special education teacher. Even those students with disabilities who are educated in general education classrooms may be only physically present. Unless instruction is appropriately differentiated, needed supports are in place, and teachers possess the necessary knowledge and skills to work with diverse learners, this one factor alone is insufficient to provide meaningful access to curriculum and to higher levels of achievement.[14]

In order for students with disabilities to reap the rewards of participating in the school reforms to which all students are entitled, schools must provide these students with content-based instruction that is designed carefully to meet their individual learning requirements. Effective instruction for individuals with disabilities has been shown to incorporate three critical features: individually referenced decision making, intensity, and explicit instruction. Individually referenced decision making is perhaps the signature feature of effective practice for individuals with high-incidence disabilities. Individual decision making fosters high expectations for learning; requires teachers to reserve judgment about the efficacy of an instructional method for a student until the method proves effective for that individual; and necessitates a form of teacher planning that incorporates ongoing adjustments in response to the individual student's learning. Disturbingly, however, research suggests that, although successful interventions designed to provide access to the general curriculum exist, the extent to which these practices are used is largely unknown.[15]

Assessments and Students with Disabilities

A cornerstone of current standards-based reform is the increased accountability for student performance. Accountability systems that have evolved over the past decade are based on the critical assumption that student performance can be accurately and authentically measured.[16] The primary tool used to implement the accountability is a state assessment. Students with disabilities participate in assessments in the following ways: (1) assessments are taken in the same way as with other students, (2) assessments are taken with accommodations, and (3) students take an alternate assessment.[17]

Assessment accommodations. Students with disabilities have a legal entitlement to assessment accommodations under three federal laws, the IDEA, Sec. 504, and the Americans with Disabilities Act. An assessment accommodation represents a change in testing materials or procedures that are designed to offset the impact of a student's disability and allow him or her to participate in an assessment. An accommodation should not alter the content or the achievement standard.

There is no set of universally approved assessment accommodations, and state policies on accommodations vary tremendously.[18] Some accommodations are believed to change what is being tested, yielding scores that are considered invalid. These kinds of accommodations may be referred to as "nonstandard" or "invalid." It is not uncommon to find an accommodation that is permitted in one state but considered invalid in another. Such variations in state accommodation policies reflect a lack of agreement in the field regarding which accommodations pose a genuine threat to validity.[19]

Because a nonstandard accommodation may affect scores, states may remove these scores from summary reports, flag them, or report them as "basic" or zero scores.[20] This leads to a situation in which a student with disabilities takes a test but "participates" in name only because his or her score is removed from any aggregate performance report.[21] Research on the impact of accommodations on score validity indicates that an accommodation uniquely interacts with an individual student's disability and support needs, such that it is impossible to generalize about the effects on validity.[22] In addition, accommodations are often "bundled" such that an individual student rarely receives one accommodation but rather a set.[23] For example, a student who receives extended time may automatically be assessed in a separate setting within a small group and perhaps have instructions read aloud.

Decisions about accommodations rest with the IEP team and are, by definition, individualized and idiosyncratic. An IEP team can also specify an accommodation that has not been approved. Currently, within Maryland, reading aloud in the third- and fourth-grade reading assessment invalidates a student's assessment score, and the student is placed at the basic level of proficiency. During the 2002–2003 school year, in one large suburban district, 89 percent of the third-grade students with disabilities received accommodations that invalidated the results of the reading assessment, placing them at the basic level of performance and providing no meaningful measure of their reading or accountability data for their instructional program.

Until recently, performance of students with disabilities was not reported separately, and it was very difficult to determine how many were participating in state assessments. For example, in 1997, only around 50 percent of states could report how many or what percentage of students with disabilities participated in their state's assessments.[24] Today, participation is increasing, but we still face issues related to understanding the performance of students with disabilities. According to *Education Week*'s survey, thirteen of the thirty-seven states that provided participation rates for students with disabilities tested 95 percent or more of their special education students in reading and math in grades four, eight, and ten.[25] Overall, participation rates for students with disabilities ranged from 40 percent to 100 percent.

Inferences from performance trends. One of the cornerstones of NCLB is that all students and student subgroups must be proficient on state assessments in reading/language arts and mathematics by 2014 as measured by performance on yearly state assessments and the state's additional academic indicator. If a school does not make annual yearly progress for two consecutive years, the decision is made to label it as a school in need of improvement and thus subject to interventions and sanctions. Based on the absence of an increase in the percentage of students scoring proficient from year to year, the conclusion is reached that the school is ineffective. However, even when assessments are well designed and properly administered, school test results are inexact and changeable.

Fluctuations in test results at the building level often occur from year to year for reasons that have very little to do with the quality of instruction and effectiveness of the school.[26] One of the greatest sources of unreliability in test results is student variability across grades, that is, grade three students in year one can be very different from grade three students the following year.[27] For example, changes in the population of students being tested because of student mobility or an influx of immigrants or refugees can produce significant year-to-year variations in average test scores. Other possible factors contributing to the volatility of test scores are changes in teaching staff or inclement weather on testing day.[28] Kane and Staiger estimate that variations in student population and other external factors not related to student learning are responsible for more than 70 percent of the year-to-year fluctuations in average test scores for a given school.[29]

Figlio argued that schools that make large test-score gains one year are likely to do worse the following year and vice versa. Schools with a "poor draw" one year tended to bounce back in the next; conversely, schools with an unusually high achieving group in the testing grade tended to revert to more average performance the next.[30] The crucial fact to remember is that test scores need to be thought of as estimates rather than precise measurements. A rise or fall in average test scores in one year does not necessarily mean that a school is less or more effective that year. Thus, any decision as to the effectiveness of a school should be based on how well it educates different groups of students over the years. This allows schools that fail to meet AYP due to essentially random events to be differentiated from those that demonstrate consistent patterns of failure for all students or target populations over several years.

This inherent volatility in year-by-year test results is especially pronounced for small groups; indeed, measurement experts have expressed concerns about calculations of trends for small populations of students, such as students with disabilities.[31] There is legitimate apprehension about the likelihood that test scores from small groups will exacerbate sampling variation, leading to imprecision in assessment results. NCLB takes this into account by allowing school systems to exclude from AYP calculations those subgroups in which the number of test takers is too small to yield statistically reliable information.

Kane and Staiger point out that although reliability is greater when sample sizes increase, there is no magical sample size above which subgroup results are statistically reliable.[32] Indeed, the interpretation of the minimum threshold differs from state to state based in theory on the technical qualities of the assessment. However, although increasing the minimum subgroup size could help school systems reach more defensible conclusions about school quality, it can also mean that many schools will not be held accountable at all for some students or that they may be held accountable one year but not the next because certain subgroups become "invisible."

An additional matter in understanding performance of students with disabilities in the aggregate is the year-to-year changes in the cohort. To evaluate whether students with disabilities are benefiting from standards-based reform, clear and consistent comparison groups are necessary.[33] For students with disabilities, the assumption of consistent groups is likely to be violated due to movement of students in and out of special education. The composition of this group can change dramatically across grade levels and from year to year, which directly impacts academic achievement.

Researchers have calculated the annual turnover rate in special education to be between 25 and 30 percent. While mobility occurs with all populations, the mobility in and out of special education is related directly to academic achievement. Ysseldyke and Bielinski found that the achievement scores of those students exiting special education were roughly 0.5 standard deviations higher than those remaining.[34] Furthermore, students entering special education averaged as much as 0.75 standard deviations below those exiting special education

SUMMARY AND CONCLUSIONS

The dominant vision of standards-based reform policies rests heavily on high expectations for all students and universal access to common and challenging standards-based curricula. These policies shift the goal of equity from one of equal physical access to the same educational setting to ensuring equal access to the same educational attainments or outcomes. This concept of equity requires that students with disabilities meet the same standards, participate in the same assessments, and be included in educational accountability systems just as their nondisabled peers. This vision and attempts to realize it are redefining the meaning of special education and the core legal entitlements. Still, many fear that this vision will bring serious unintended consequences. For example, recent research in four states and eight school districts suggests that many educators subscribe to the belief that it is unfair to expect students with disabilities to participate in state assessments and perform at the same level as their peers without disabilities.[35] Similar findings were reported from a national survey of 800 special and regular educators carried out by *Education Week*:

> While a vast majority of teachers believe their special education students make "significant academic progress over the course of the school year," most question whether such youngsters should have to meet the same academic standards and testing requirements as others their age. . . . More than eight in 10 teachers believe that most special education students should be expected to meet a separate set of academic standards, rather than the same standards as others their age.[36]

Also, many parents and advocates fear that, as substantial numbers of schools and school districts fail to meet the new accountability targets under NCLB because of the performance of students with disabilities, these students will become the scapegoats for the system. Indeed, the previously noted *Education Week* survey indicates that thirty of the thirty-nine states with complete assessment data had achievement gaps of thirty percentage points or more between special and general education students on their statewide reading assessments. In some states, this gap reached fifty percentage points.

The extent to which students with disabilities truly have an equal opportunity to participate in standards-based reform is dependent on a number of factors. First, states must continue to move toward developing state accountability systems that are meaningful and valid for students with a range of abilities. Such systems should include assessments that are aligned with state content standards and appropriately document the performance of all students and provide a reliable systemwide measure of whether—and what—all students are learning.

Too often in the past, students with disabilities were excluded from accountability systems, the consequence of which was that they did not have an equal opportunity to be challenged and learn the same important content. Regardless of where students with disabilities receive instruction, they must have access to a challenging standards-based general education curriculum.

Much of the responsibility for realizing the vision of standards-based education rests with individual principals and teachers. Both general and special education teachers will need to increase their capacity to provide equal access to content standards to all students. This will require increasing both their content area knowledge and instructional expertise.

Finally, perhaps the greatest barrier to the full participation of students with disabilities in standards-based reform lies in successfully challenging existing beliefs about the abilities and potential of this group of students. Given the high-stakes nature of current standards-based educational reform, how students with disabilities will be accommodated and how they will fare will likely continue to be controversial for some time. However, in all deliberations, care must be taken to keep the promise of meaningful and equitable educational opportunity.

The Accumulation of Disadvantage: The Consequences of Testing for Poor and Minority Children[1]

Sandra Mathison

This chapter discusses the ways standardized testing puts children of color and children living in poverty at a disadvantage. This disadvantage begins early in the school career of a child and repeats itself again and again. Education, when driven by standardized testing, is not the great equalizer it is so often portrayed to be in the mythical world where merit counts most.

TESTING IN K–12

Testing starts early and it occurs often in the life of an average student, even more often if a student is at either end of the achievement spectrum, that is, gifted or with learning disabilities. In a recent analysis of the U.S. Department of Education's Early Childhood Longitudinal Study, Kindergarten Cohort (ECLS-K), Lee and Burkam conclude: "There are substantial differences by race and ethnicity in children's test scores as they begin kindergarten. Before even entering kindergarten, the average cognitive scores of children in the highest SES group are 60% above the scores of the lowest SES group. Moreover, average math achievement is 21% lower for blacks than for whites, and 19% lower for Hispanics."[2] Setting aside the unjustified confidence in the meaningfulness of standardized test scores for young children, this report illustrates just the beginning of a lifetime of characterizations and decisions that will be made and, indeed, institutionalized for children of color and those living in poverty.

Beginning in kindergarten, test results are used to sort, track, and monitor the abilities, achievements, and potentials of students. Assessments, based in part on standardized test results, are essential for monitoring the progress of children, for making instructional and curricular decisions, and for evaluating programs and policies. The danger is that standardized test results will be weighed more heavily than they ought to be, that decisions once made cannot or will not be reversed, and that other compelling information may be ignored.

The uses of standardized testing are more far ranging than most people realize. While there is considerable variation from one district to the next, children will be administered at least one but typically many more standardized tests within a single year. The following table (Table 11.1) illustrates the testing experience of a child from kindergarten through high school in an upstate New York school district.

The Case of High-Stakes Tests

What are high-stakes tests? They are tests that have serious consequences attached to the results—these consequences may be for students, teachers, principals, schools, and even states. For students, these consequences include whether they will graduate from high school, whether they will be promoted to the next grade or retained, whether they will spend their summer in school, or whether they will be required to participate in tutoring that extends their time in school substantially. Although high-stakes tests can confer rewards as well as sanctions, and indeed a number of states provide financial rewards for high or improved test scores, more often there are punishments. These punishments can be direct (such as taking over or closing schools, replacing administrators or teachers, or withdrawing accreditation) or indirect (such as publishing test scores in the local newspaper, shaming, or job reassignment).

Although high-stakes testing has become a national phenomenon, there are some clear patterns illustrating who is most likely to be subjected to these tests. High-stakes testing is disproportionately found in states with higher percentages of people of color and living in poverty. A recent analysis of the National Educational Longitudinal Survey (NELS) shows that 35 percent of African-American and 27 percent of Hispanic eighth-graders will take a high-stakes test, compared with 16 percent of whites.[3] Looked at along class lines, 25 percent of low SES eighth graders will take a high-stakes test compared with 14 percent of high SES eighth graders.

The Quality Counts report[4] indicates that of the eighteen states that require passing a standardized test to graduate, eleven are in the south, that is, states with substantial minority populations. As more states adopt high school graduation tests, this relationship will weaken some—twenty-six states in all will have such a test—fourteen of those are in the south or southwest

Table 11.1
An Illustration of Testing in the Life of a Student

Grade	Test
Kindergarten	Boehm Test of Basic Concepts
1st	Gates-MacGinitie Reading Test*
2nd	Gates-MacGinitie Reading Test*
	Stanford Diagnostic Math Test*
	Terra Nova (reading & math)
3rd	Gates-MacGinitie Reading Testing
	*Stanford Diagnostic Math Test
	*Terra Nova (reading & math)
	School & College Ability Test (SCAT)**
	Cognitive Abilities Test (CogAT)
4th	Gates-MacGinitie Reading Test*
	Stanford Diagnostic Math Test*
	School & College Ability Test (SCAT)**
	NYS English Language Arts Test
	NYS Math TestNYS Science Test
5th	Gates-MacGinitie Reading Test*
	Stanford Diagnostic Math Test*
	Terra Nova (reading & math)
	School & College Ability Test (SCAT)**
	NYS Social Studies Test
6th	Terra Nova (reading & math)
	School & College Ability Test (SCAT)**
7th	Terra Nova (reading & math)
	Cognitive Abilities Test (CogAT)
8th	NYS English Language Arts Test
	NYS Math Test
	NYS Science Test
	NYS Social Studies Test
	NYS Foreign Language Test
	NYS Technology Test
9th	Regents Exams:
10th	English Language Arts
11th	Mathematics
12th	Global History & Geography
	U.S. History & Government
	Science, Language other than English
	PSAT
	SAT

*For remedial students only.
**Johns Hopkins Talent Search test for gifted program.

regions of the country. States that currently use high school graduation exams to grant or withhold diplomas are Alabama, Florida, Georgia, Indiana, Louisiana, Maryland, Minnesota, Mississippi, Nevada, New Jersey, New Mexico, New York, North Carolina, Ohio, South Carolina, Tennessee, Texas, and Virginia. States that are developing high school exit exams are Alaska, Arizona, California, Delaware, Hawaii, Massachusetts, Utah, Washington, and Wisconsin.

Not only are students of color more likely to take high-stakes tests, they also score lower than white students. From the websites of a sample of any state departments of education (for illustrative purposes Massachusetts, New York, and Kentucky are described here), one can demonstrate this conclusion. Last year in Boston, 43 percent of white students failed the tenth-grade math test; 85 percent of Hispanic students failed. In Schenectady New York, 62 percent of children of color failed the fourth-grade ELA; 41 percent of white students failed. In neighboring Albany school district, 68 percent of children of color failed this test, compared with 33 percent of whites. In Kentucky's Jefferson County public schools, scores on reading tests demonstrate the same relationship: 63 percent of white fourth graders were proficient, compared with 34 percent of African-American children; 54 percent of white seventh-grade students were proficient, compared with 27 percent of African-Americans; and in eleventh grade, 37 percent of whites were proficient, compared with 13 percent of African-American students.

The remainder of this discussion will focus on three outcomes of high-stakes testing and the ways in which minority children are particularly disadvantaged:

- the disproportionate impact of state testing on dropout rates for minorities;
- the bizarre effect of monetary rewards for students; and
- the diminishment in the quality of education as a consequence of testing for all, but especially for minority students, when differential performance on tests is translated into the "achievement gap."

The Impact of Testing on Dropout Rates for Minorities

Both graduation tests and tests given earlier in a student's career are having substantial impact on the numbers of students who are dropping out of school. The increased dropout rates are based on two factors, the graduation tests themselves and the impact of increased rates of retention in a grade, especially in eighth and ninth grades.

Graduation Tests. The numbers of states requiring graduation tests is on the rise, and by 2008, more than half of the states plan to have such a test in place. (See Figure 11.1.) This represents a dramatic increase in a less than thirty-year period. In 1983, when *A Nation at Risk*, the flash point for the standards-based and test-driven educational reform movement, was pub-

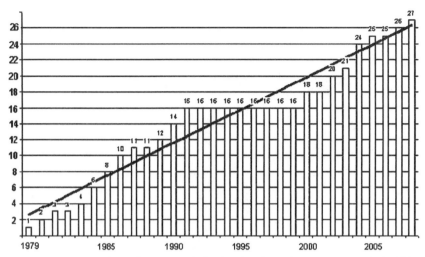

Figure 11.1 Number of states with high school graduation tests, 1979–2008. *Source*: Amrein & Berliner (2002).

lished, three states had minimum competency testing in place (Florida, North Carolina, and Nevada) that amounted to a graduation or exit test. *A Nation at Risk* called for rigorous tests to assess exiting high school students. The concerns about a decrease in high school graduation rates is particularly pointed given that most teenagers graduate.[5] The proportion of all students who obtain a high school diploma has steadily increased in the last fifty years, with more dramatic increases for minorities. It is this context that suggests backsliding in national educational aspirations with the advent of high-stakes graduation tests.

Arizona researchers Audrey Amrein and David Berliner report actual or estimated percentages of students who take and fail high school graduation tests in eighteen high- stakes testing states.[6] They find a considerable variability across states: a low of 0.5 percent in Virginia, where the basic skills graduation test is administered in sixth grade, to a high of 10 percent in New York and 12 percent in Georgia. In addition to students who take the test and fail to graduate, considerable numbers of students either drop out or take the GED. An examination of data from the National Center for Education Statistics illustrates that, nationwide since 1985, there has been a more than 20 percent increase in the number of GED test takers, mostly for people nineteen years of age or younger. So, while failing the graduation tests may keep a substantial number of students from receiving a high school diploma, these tests reverberate down in schools and influence decisions made by schools about students and decisions made by students about schooling.

Retention in Grade. There are two grade levels at which retention is most common: first grade, when underage boys are retained to permit them time to "mature," and again in eighth and ninth grade, when students are on the cusp of entering high school. Students of color are retained at high rates and there is an unhealthy interaction between grade retention and the presence of high-stakes testing. Analyses of the NELS data indicate the mere presence of a high-stakes test is a strong predictor of higher dropout rates.[7]

Walt Haney found that "Only 50% of minority students in Texas have been progressing from grade 9 to high school graduation since the initiation of the TAAS testing program. Since about 1982, the rates at which Black and Hispanic students are required to repeat grade 9 have climbed steadily, such that by the late 1990s, nearly 30% of Black and Hispanic students were 'failing' grade 9. Cumulative rates of grade retention in Texas are almost twice as high for Black and Hispanic students as for White students."[8] One conclusion from this study is that retaining students in ninth grade boosts the tenth-grade TAAS scores (because the potential low scorers are excluded) *and in effect* keeps many of these students from ever taking the test, as the likelihood they will drop out of school increases dramatically.

In Massachusetts, with the implementation of a tenth-grade high-stakes test, the overall retention rates for ninth graders jumped from 6.3 percent in 1995 to 8.4 percent in 2001. In 2001, twelve districts held back 20 percent of ninth graders. The districts with the highest ninth-grade retention rates, between 27 and 38 percent, enroll a majority of nonwhite students.

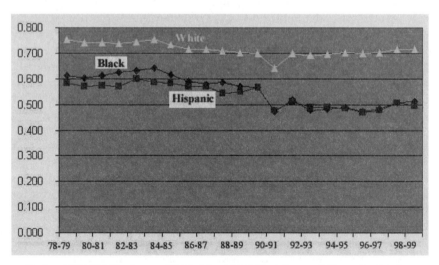

Ratio of TX HS Graduates Divided by GD 9 Enrollment 3 Years Earlier for Whites and Nonwhites (Black and Hispanic), 1978–1999

Figure 11.2   Illustration Differential School Graduation. *Source*: Haney (2000).

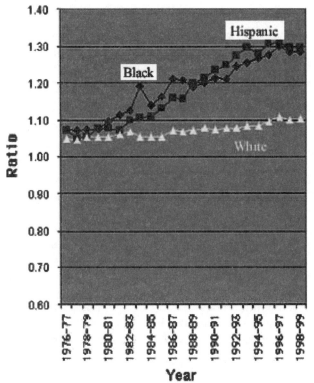

TX Grade 8 to 9 Progression Ratios by Ethnic Group
1977–1999

Figure 11.3 Illustration of Differential Retention in
Grade Effects. *Source*: Haney (2000).

Parallel to these changes in retention rates are increases in the number of
students dropping out of school. Being retained in a grade, especially in
middle and high school, at least triples a student's likelihood of dropping
out of school.

If students persist and take a high school graduation test, those who do
poorly on the test are more likely to drop out of school, *and* this poor test
performance disproportionately affects students with high grades. In other
words, students who have by other indicators done reasonably well in school
are disproportionately influenced by poor test scores to drop out of school.
It appears that high-stakes testing contributes substantially to grade retention in middle and high school and to the failure of students to graduate
from high school.

The Bizarre Effect of Monetary Rewards for Students

Six states give scholarships to students for high performance on state-mandated tests—California, Delaware, Michigan, Missouri, Nevada, and Ohio. These scholarships provide neither incentives nor opportunities for minority students to go to college, in spite of the rhetoric to that effect. Scholarship money goes to students who would have attended college anyway—they maintain the status quo with regard to access to a college education.

Michigan's Merit Scholarship Program is a good example of this scenario. It is worth noting that the Treasury Department administers the testing program in Michigan. Using money from a settlement with cigarette companies, Michigan awards scholarships based on performance on the Michigan Education Accountability Program, or MEAP. In Michigan, one in three white, one in five Native American, one in five Hispanic, and one in fourteen African-American test takers receive scholarships. In the Detroit area, 80 percent of students in affluent suburban districts, which are white, compared with 6 percent of students in the Detroit city schools, received scholarships. Not only does the Michigan scholarship program reward those already college bound, it does so by diverting money that should have gone to Michigan's poor and indigent who are suffering from tobacco-related diseases. The ACLU, MALDEF, and the NAACP are currently suing Michigan state for these and other corrupting effects of high-stakes testing in that state.

The Diminishing Quality of Education for All Children and Especially for Minority Students as Manifest in the "Achievement Gap" Rhetoric

There is a great deal of research to be done to fully understand the impact of high-stakes testing on the quality of education and schooling, but the short-term conclusion researchers are drawing is that high-stakes testing not only does not improve education but, indeed, diminishes its quality. A local newspaper carried a critique of state testing from a middle school student:

> The statewide test bombards the schools with pressure. . . . In the second week of school we get things from the teacher like, "This was on the test last year so listen up". . . . The pressure restricts teachers from doing their job. . . . They can't help struggling students fully understand the material because when the student starts to finally kind of get it, it's time to move on so they can get the entire curriculum taught. . . . The test pressure just about kills some kids. I have never heard a student say, "All this pressure from the test gets me fired up!" More often, I see kids cracking. They start freaking out . . . the test is taking

away the real meaning of school. Instead of learning new things and getting tools for life, the mission of the schools is becoming to do well on the test.

This seventh grader's words capture much of what researchers are finding out about the impact of high-stakes testing, or what is more generally called outcome-based bureaucratic accountability. As reflected in this student's comments, high-stakes testing is contributing to the

- deprofessionalization of teachers;
- narrowing of the curriculum;
- adoption of curriculum driven by tests that underrepresent the purposes of schooling;
- of teaching only what is tested;
- elimination of project-based student work, field trips, recess;
- creation of unproductive stress.

High-stakes testing has these negative effects on many children, but it is especially so for children of color, because they are disproportionately exposed to and punished by the effects of high-stakes tests. In addition, because the use and impact of tests is ubiquitous, we are diverted from thinking about causes; from thinking about the basic technical shortcomings of the tests, as well as the scoring, standard setting, and interpretation; and from the interests served by these test-based accountability schemes. An obvious manifestation of this diversion is the rhetoric of the "achievement gap."

Is there really an achievement gap? The rhetoric of the achievement gap adopts a deficit model of those scoring lower on tests, often seeking explanations based on differences in natural abilities, a harkening back to the early eugenics of standardized testing, or at least to the identification of cultural deficiencies among those doing less well on the tests. This rhetoric leads to a search for solutions in those deficient children and families, solutions that, by and large, advocate doing more of the same that apparently isn't working now, for example, tutoring, grade retention, extended school days/years, and the adoption of pedagogies that de-skill both teachers and students by, for example, the adoption of direct instruction techniques and phonics-only curriculum. These strategies might lead to short-term gains in test scores but do not result in meaningful learning.

The rhetoric of the achievement gap looks for solutions that alter children and families of color and those living in poverty but not for solutions that alter teacher competencies, curriculum, pedagogy, school organization, or school finance. Alternatives to the search for how to remedy poor and minority children and families might be:

- fundamental restructuring of schools (e.g., alternatives to authoritarian and top-down management of schools);

- improvement of school climate (e.g., enough paper, books kids can take home and even keep, toilet paper in the bathrooms, air conditioning, adequate space, classrooms instead of trailers, quiet places for one-on-one interactions with students, "Books, supplies, and lower class size!");
- curricular alternatives (e.g., afro-centric or latino-centric curriculum);
- decreased class size or small schools;
- reform of school financing (e.g., elimination of local property taxation as a major component of school financing);
- attention to the racial profiling inherent in school discipline policies and practices;
- the courts' role in resegregating schools, creating what the Harvard Civil Rights Project calls apartheid schools;
- much greater caution about using hastily developed, unvalidated tests that are used by policymakers in ways that violate professional standards and are frequently inaccurately scored.

The "achievement gap" is more accurately a *test score gap*. It's also an *opportunity gap*. A visit to an affluent white suburban school and one to an urban primarily minority school will illustrate that there is a *resources gap*, and that same visit will also reveal an *income gap*. Focusing on the test score gap without attention to these other gaps will do little to alleviate the inherent racism in educational opportunity and achievement.

COLLEGE ENTRANCE TESTS

In the face of great odds, children of color and living in poverty do complete high school and aspire to attend postsecondary education, where they encounter another potential setback in the form of college entrance tests. Based on a lack of validity and the differential performance of minority and poor children, there has been increasing criticism and rejection of both SAT and ACT scores for college admissions.[9] Still, many colleges expect students to take these admissions tests, and Tables 11.2 and 11.3 illustrate the disadvantage for minority students and the impact of income on test scores. With regard to the impact of family income on test scores, middle-class children are less likely to gain advantage than are poor or very wealthy children. Sacks concludes, "There is little doubt that the prevailing paradigm about merit has consistently reproduced social and economic advantages for the 'dukes of the system,' the relatively few who conform to widely held views of merit."[10]

College admissions scores are used for more than admissions, however. Scholarship awards are also based on SAT or ACT scores. In a letter to Florida's Governor Jeb Bush, FairTest, MALDEF, and others outline the problems:

Table 11.2
2002 College Bound Seniors SAT Scores

Ethnic Group	Verbal	Math	Total	
African-American or Black	430	427	857	
Mexican or Mexican-American	446	457	903	
Puerto Rican	455	451	906	
Other Hispanic or Latino	458	464	922	
American Indian or Alaskan Native	479	483	962	
White	527	533	1060	
Asian, Asian-Amererican, Pacific Islander	501	569	1070	
Other	502	514	1016	
Family Income				
Less than $10,000/year	417	442	859	
$10,000–$20,000/year	435	453	888	+29
$20,000–$30,000/year	461	470	931	+43
$30,000–$40,000/year	480	485	965	+34
$40,000–$50,000/year	496	501	997	+32
$50,000–$60,000/year	505	509	1014	+17
$60,000–$70,000/year	511	516	1027	+13
$70,000–$80,000/year	517	524	1041	+14
$80,000–$100,000/year	530	538	1068	+27
More than $100,000/year	555	568	1123	+55
ALL TEST-TAKERS (Approximately 1.3 million)	504	516	1020	

Source: College Board, *College-Board Seniors National Report*, 2002.

While African-Americans comp[o]sed 14.4% of all SAT and ACT takers, they received only 3% of all Academic Scholars Awards (100% funding) and only 8.3% of Merit Scholarship Awards (75% funding). Latinos, who made up 13.7% of all test takers, earned only 8.7% of the Academic Scholars Awards and 12.3% of Merit Scholarships. White students, by contrast, comp[o]sed 53.4% of test takers, yet received 76.3% of the Academic Scholars Awards and 71.5% of Merit Scholarships.

The use of SAT and ACT score cut-offs to determine eligibility is a major reason why proportionately few African-American and Latino students received these lucrative scholarships. Students must score 1270 or higher on the SAT, or 28 or higher on the ACT, in order to qualify for Academic Scholars; the Merit Scholarship Award eligibility is set at a SAT of 920 or an ACT of 20. Yet in Florida the average SAT score was 857 for African-Americans and 952 for Latinos, both of which are more than 300 points below the cut-off for the Academic Scholars Award. For Whites in Florida, the average score was 1044. Other measures of academic preparation, such as grades, do not demonstrate

Table 11.3
2002 College Bound Seniors ACT Scores

Ethnicity		
African-American/Black	16.8	
American Indian/Alaskan Native	18.6	
Mexican-American/Chicano	18.2	
Puerto Rican/Hispanic	18.8	
Other	19.2	
Multiracial	20.9	
Asian-American/Pacific Islander	21.6	
Caucasian-American/White	21.7	
Household Income		
Less than $18,000/year	17.8	
$18,000–$24,000/year	18.6	+0.8
$24,000–$30,000/year	19.4	+0.8
$30,000–36,000/year	19.9	+0.5
$36,000–$42,000/year	20.4	+0.5
$42,000–$50,000/year	20.8	+0.4
$50,000–$60,000/year	21.3	+0.5
$60,000–$80,000/year	21.8	+0.5
$80,000–$100,000/year	22.4	+0.6
More than $100,000/year	23.3	+0.9
ALL TEST-TAKERS (1.1 million test-takers)	20.8	

Source: ACT High School Profile Report: H.S. Graduating Class of 2002 National Report.

such a great racial disparity. It is the high test score minimums, particularly for the Academic Scholars program, that put receipt of these awards far out of the reach of many students of color.[11]

The move away from needs-based and toward merit-based scholarships, such as in the Florida example, is happening in all parts of the country with similar results. In the Introduction to their edited collection, Heller and Marin parody the deleterious effects of such scholarships:

Imagine someone reacting to higher education's current situation by saying that what we needed were large new programs to subsidize white and middle- to upper-income students to attend college, and that it was not necessary to raise need-based aid even enough to cover new tuition increases. We would give some minority students entering awards because of their relatively high grade point averages from inferior segregated schools. However, we will take their aid away when they cannot get a "B" average in a vastly more competitive college setting and blame them for not being up to the task. A huge amount of money would go into this new program, far more than was spent for the need-based scholarships in some states. We would get the money from an extremely regressive tax—a state lottery that drew money disproportionately from poor and minority players. In other words, poor blacks and Latinos would end up paying a substantial part of the cost of educating more affluent white students, who would have gone to college even if they had not had the additional financial incentive. And to add insult to injury, colleges would cut their own financial aid funds, or shift these resources to give more money to high scoring students. In cases where the financial aid made more students eager to go to a particular institution in the state, rather than an out-of-state school where they would have to pay tuition, the in-state institution could raise its selectivity ratings by excluding students with lower scores, students who would usually be minority and from less affluent families.[12]

PROFESSIONAL LICENSURE TESTS

For minority and poor students who pursue professional degrees, graduating from high school, getting into college, and being able to afford it may mean being faced with yet more standardized tests to obtain a license to practice their chosen profession. For example, if a person aspires to be an accountant or a doctor, lawyer, teacher, social worker, or police officer, she or he must pass a standardized test required either by a professional association or a state regulatory agency.

In 1994, the *Journal of the American Medical Association* reported that women and minorities were more likely to fail Part I of the National Board of Medical Examiners test.[13] In 1996, the Louisiana State Police Commission agreed to discontinue a written entrance exam for police cadets and to develop a new test that does not discriminate against African-Americans in a settlement with the U.S. Department of Justice. After repeated tries, 97 percent of whites and 78 percent of African-Americans passed the bar exam as reported in a study by the Law School Admission Council in 1998. In the late 1980s, it was clear the most commonly used teacher test, the National Teachers Examination, barred disproportionate numbers of minority teacher candidates from teaching. This trend continues as forty-two states now require a teacher licensure test. In 1999, PRAXIS passing rates nationwide for white candidates were 82 percent and 46 percent for African-Americans. A National Research Council report on teacher testing finds the tests lacking in validity, job-relatedness, and likely to compound the desire to attract more minorities to the teaching profession.[14] And so the story goes for other employment-related tests for dockworkers, insurance agents, plumbers, pharmacists, and so on.

BUILDING A K–16 RESPONSE TO THE DISADVANTAGE
CREATED BY STANDARDIZED TESTING

There is every reason to believe that access and quality of schooling is differentiated in this country and that differentiation is along race and class lines. Standardized testing plays a substantial role in maintaining this differentiation beginning in kindergarten on through school and into access to professions and jobs. This is a K–16 issue, not one isolated in either public schools or higher education.

A number of professional organizations that represent K–12 educators and professors have developed policy statements reflecting caution and concern about the impact of standardized testing, although these statements focus on testing in K–12. For example, the American Educational Research Association (AERA), American Psychological Association (APA), American Evaluation Association (AEA), International Reading Association (IRA), National Council for Teachers of English (NCTE), National Council for Teachers of Mathematics (NCTM), and College and University Faculty Assembly of the National Council for the Social Studies (CUFA/NCSS) have issued statements that caution against the use of singular measures for important educational decision making, that outline the detrimental effects of tests on teaching and learning, and that point out the inherent racism and classism of standardized tests.[15] These statements, as well as the complementary research agendas and political action campaigns, represent one step in building solidarity among practitioners (K–12 teachers and administrators) and researchers to defend public schools.

This K–16 alliance also includes parents, and the rise of grassroots organizations that combine the knowledge and resources of educators, researchers, and parents are on the rise.[16] Some grassroots organizing and resistance to standardized testing has been facilitated by FairTest, a not-for-profit advocacy organization devoted for many years to "ending the abuses, misuses and flaws of standardized testing and to ensur[ing] that evaluation of students and workers is fair, open, and educationally sound. [FairTest] places special emphasis on eliminating the racial, class, gender, and cultural barriers to equal opportunity posed by standardized tests, and preventing their damage to the quality of education." FairTest sponsors the Assessment Reform Network (ARN), "a national project created to support parents, teachers, students and others who are working to end the overuse and misuse of standardized testing in public education and to promote authentic forms of assessment." The goal of the ARN "is to open the doors to disadvantaged children by removing barriers to achievement, while improving the quality of education for everyone," through facilitating an exchange of ideas, resources, and strategies among a wide audience.

Researchers are now beginning to see the common threads that can support examination and critique of testing as it employed across the K–16 educational spectrum. There is little reason to believe that current test-based reforms in precollegiate, collegiate, and professional education will redress the inequities between white and minority students and between those living in poverty and those not. Indeed, this testing has the potential to further deepen and divide Americans along race and class lines.

— 12 —

Educational Leaders and Assessment-Based Reform[1]

WILLIAM A. FIRESTONE

The recent passage of the federal No Child Left Behind legislation is only the most recent chapter in a history of increasing emphasis on educational standards. An important part of that history has been the use of tests to both measure and to enforce the implementation of those standards. Advocates argue that assessments appropriately focus policy on educational outcomes and can become useful spurs to raising educational achievement and increasing educational equity. Opponents argue that testing—especially when linked to high stakes—narrows the curriculum, increases stress in the lives of both teachers and students, pushes some students out of school, and shifts attention from learning to raising test scores as an end in itself.

Partisans on both sides tend to ignore the substantial variation in response to state tests. This variation comes from a number of sources, including the design of the state tests, the stakes linked to those tests, students' age, their family background, and the leadership for responding to state assessment policy. This chapter focuses on the latter factor. I argue that while educational leaders could help ensure that schools adjust to state tests in more constructive ways, they have difficulty in doing so. I first look at the testing problem from the leader's perspective. The challenge for leaders is not that they are overwhelmed by testing but that testing is just one of many problems they face; an appropriate balance must be achieved. Next, I consider how leadership is configured in schools and districts. Here the problem is that leadership is fragmented, coming from different offices at the district level as well as from building principals. The cacophony of leadership can add to the challenge of generating a constructive response to testing. Finally, I argue that reformed educational practice comes not from responding to the external pressure of educational tests but from a shared, internalized sense of accountability for students' achievement and well-being.

COMPETING PRESSURES

Standards and assessments provide weak guidance for local practice because they must compete with so many other issues. Both empirical and conceptual analyses point to the weak position of tests as guides to practice. We recently surveyed elementary principals in New Jersey about the fourth-grade test in that state. The survey began with a pair of open-ended questions asking principals to list the big issues they faced in their schools and the issues that that their districts faced. The school-level issues that principals mentioned most often were—from most to least frequently cited—enrollment changes, aligning the curriculum with the state standards and tests, facilities, pressure to improve test scores, funding, and staffing. Only two of these (aligning the curriculum with the standards and pressure to raise test scores) are related to the state testing program. Principals believed that the same six issues were important to district leaders, except that the top three district issues were enrollment shifts, funding, and facilities, none of which related to testing. From the principal's view at least, districts could deal with testing and curriculum only when the larger financial and demographic issues had been addressed.[2]

Analysis of the meaning of accountability also points to the weak guidance offered by testing. To many observers, accountability and testing are interchangeable; testing is, after all, the way accountability is enforced. Yet, this is a narrow definition of accountability. A broader view based in policy analysis suggests that accountability is present any time one person must render an account to another, especially where the latter has some authority or control over the former. School administrators face a wide variety of accountability pressures, including bureaucratic, political, professional, and market accountabilities, although, in specific instances, the lines between specific kinds of accountabilities can be blurred.[3] Bureaucratic accountability occurs when people in a role are held accountable for meeting specific rules and regulations. Testing programs represent a new kind of bureaucratic accountability. In the older form, schools and districts were held accountable for providing certain inputs, such as safe buildings or certified teachers. Testing policies hold schools accountable for outcomes, such as having a certain percent of students scoring at a proficient level on an assessment. In fact, the publication of test scores is the rendering of a highly abstract form of account.

Probably the oldest form of accountability is political accountability. This is most obvious in the account school leaders must provide to an elected school board. Historically, schools have been accountable to their local communities. The formalization of that accountability in school boards was codified some time ago. Yet the political process creates pressures for things that are quite different from high test scores. In fact, where accountability to the community is higher than accountability through test scores, district administrators may be distracted from instructional issues by a variety of turf issues and local sensitivities. In rural areas, schools are often valued as a source of community cohesion and, in both rural and urban areas, they are an important source of jobs. Sometimes parents view safety and moral education as more important that the cognitive achievements measured by test scores and valued by professionals. Finally, a major concern for the public is the cost of education. Raising test scores is not popular when it becomes too expensive.[4]

Professional accountability may also conflict with the accountability embedded in tests. Occupations are said to be professionalized when they combine a body of specialized knowledge with commitment to certain moral standards. Professional accountability may be especially important when the knowledge in question makes it difficult for the layperson to monitor and assess the work of the professional. It includes entrance requirements to the field and various forms of peer oversight.

Neither teaching nor school leadership are fully professionalized, but great strides have been made in the last two decades to develop standards of professional practice. One of the most important developments was led by the National Council of Teachers of Mathematics, whose *Curriculum and Evaluation Standards for School Mathematics* provided a model for other disciplinary groups to follow.[5] The Interstate School Leaders' Licensure Consortium Standards for School Leaders have received less attention. However, they attempt to clarify the meaning of professional educational leadership and are being institutionalized in systems for accrediting schools of education.[6]

Professional standards—especially with regard to content—may not align well with state tests for two reasons. First, the vision of deep knowledge of a subject area is difficult to operationalize through state tests. Consider the difficulty of developing reliable, cheap-to-score items that measure the vision of "mathematical power" or the "ability to explore, conjecture, and reason logically, as well as the ability to use a variety of mathematical methods effectively to solve nonroutine standards."[7] This vision contributed to considerable experimentation with the use of portfolios and performance assessments for state assessments. However, the use of such alternative assessments, while instructionally quite useful, proved too unreliable for high-stakes testing and too expensive for the amount of testing now required since the introduction of No Child Left Behind.

The second problem is political. Challenging standards are not well understood by the public, so they are vulnerable. At one point, California used a testing system that was highly influenced by the national mathematics standards, but after a major political backlash, led by university mathematicians and conservative elements, that state intentionally moved away from those standards.[8] The Texas state tests that were President George W. Bush's model for the No Child Left Behind legislation were poorly aligned with the mathematics standards.

What are we to make of this picture of testing, as one pressure among many that local educational leaders and teachers must respond to? How does it square with the picture of overwhelming pressure coming from high-stakes tests that has been portrayed by other researchers?[9] I suggest that the problem with past research is that it has followed one source of accountability—state testing—into the school without considering other accountabilities. This has, in fact, been the major problem with most research on any kind of educational accountability: It only looks at one source at a time.

In fact, educators interpret state policies in light of other accountabilities they face and their beliefs about effective educational practices, among other things. As an example of the complexity of this process, one superintendent in a state with a high-stakes testing system doubted that his district would be sanctioned by his state for low test scores. He worried, though, that low scores would undermine public confidence and impede budget passage. His understanding of the state standards and professional definitions of effective teaching in some areas was rather limited. To the extent that he understood state standards, he did not support them. Thus, he communicated to his staff the political importance of raising test scores without support for some of the practice innovations that standards advocates wanted to accompany the state's assessments. The central office staff communicated that interpretation to others throughout the district.[10] This example illustrates how the interpretation of several, sometimes competing, accountability demands, when filtered through personal beliefs, can lead to interpretations that the designers of accountability systems may not support.

FRACTURED LEADERSHIP

Leaders might cope with competing accountability pressures if they spoke with one mind. In fact, leadership in school districts is fragmented. This is not the distributed leadership that has become such a buzzword, a way for teachers and leaders to share the challenge of change.[11] Rather, it is the situation when schools and districts are staffed with a number of leaders, attending to different external constituencies and with overlapping yet different internal responsibilities. The result is a great deal of leadership with the potential to pull in different directions.

One part of this problem is the division of labor between school and district leadership. This became apparent in our study of teacher responses to state testing in New Jersey.[12] This study asked what factors encouraged teachers to spend more time on test preparation and two kinds of instruction: (1) didactic teaching that featured memorization and practice but that did not necessarily allow for student exploration of ideas; and (2) inquiry-oriented instruction that promoted such exploration and understanding of the concepts studied more than practice. Test preparation had two dimensions that reflected the two different approaches to instruction. Didactic instruction was associated with short-term test preparation—that is, cramming in the month before the test was given. Inquiry-oriented instruction was associated with what we called "embedded" test preparation, or test preparation that was integrated into regular instruction and spread throughout the year.

Districts provided the major structuring for curriculum and instruction. Their contribution was to lead the development of district curricula and to plan professional development. Both of these activities affected teaching. Where the district used professional development time to help teachers learn how to prepare for the state test, not surprisingly, the amount of teaching devoted to test preparation increased. Because New Jersey's state test included a mix of performance-oriented items that had some room for students to explain and justify their work, and multiple-choice items that emphasized recall, test-focused professional development included a mix of more drill-oriented and more exploratory instructional activities. Not surprisingly, teachers who reported a lot of professional development focusing on the test also said they did more of both didactic, drill-oriented instruction and inquiry-oriented teaching. Where the district emphasized professional development focusing on subject matter, teachers reported engaging in more inquiry-oriented instruction and less didactic instruction. Curricular investments also influenced teaching. Easy access to textbooks encouraged didactic instruction, while access to calculators and science kits was associated with inquiry-oriented instruction.

Principals did not provide the same strong guiding hand with regard to curriculum or professional development, although they might "work in collaboration with the district." The principal's instructional involvement was more informal. For instance, principals generally avoided using formal authority, such as the right to supervise or to influence teaching. They were more likely to make suggestions to help teachers improve their practice. These might include advising a teacher on how to handle a classroom disturbance or discussing other issues relating to classroom management.

Some principals were more supportive than others, but that support was general and diffuse. It included providing funding to get discretionary materials and time for professional development. It also included arranging for teachers to get additional training, but principals rarely provided such training themselves. They were supporters, encouragers, and facilitators, but not instructional experts. As one teacher explained,

> Our principal is very helpful. He's allowed us to go to some workshops and he's given us the freedom to choose some effective professional development opportunities, and he's really been supportive of that in terms of time.

Strangely, principal support was associated with teachers spending more time on both short- and long-term test preparation and inquiry-oriented but not didactic instruction.

In sum, both principal and central office leadership influenced teaching, but different mechanisms were used to provide leadership, and the two were not always aligned. A major problem for district leaders is to decide how much influence to decentralize to the school building. Because even relatively weak interventions by the principal can noticeably influence teachers, there is an argument for granting considerable local autonomy. However, if principals' interpretations of state tests and how to raise scores are at odds with those of the district's—which is quite likely especially where principals are generalists and district leadership comes in substantial measure from content specialists—the resulting contradictory signals may confuse teachers and undermine any effort to move in any direction.[13]

Moreover, especially as they become larger, district offices may offer fragmented guidance to teachers. Spillane describes how even where district offices have one unit responsible for curriculum and instruction, it may be divided into offices for curriculum, assessment, professional development, and assorted subject areas.[14] Moreover, guidance coming from the curriculum and instructional unit may differ from that coming from offices for Title I, children with disabilities, and English language learners. Curriculum guides may predate state tests, and locally selected standardized tests may not be well aligned with the state tests. The array of professional development opportunities offered during the course of the year may align with state tests to differing extents, and—as these examples indicate—individual units within the central office may differ in their understanding of and support for state tests. Under these circumstances, teachers may receive extremely confusing guidance on how and whether to respond to state tests.

Confounding the fragmentation among different offices is the difficulty of controlling or even orchestrating the factors that influence teaching and learning. A recent review lists over twenty different "pathways" through which teaching and learning might be influenced. These are categorized into four broad areas: supervising and training teachers, curriculum and assessment, organizing the system, and supporting students.[15] Some pathways, such as providing breakfast for students, affect teaching indirectly. With others, district influence is at best shared. Testing is actually an excellent example of that. While school and district leaders have little influence over state-mandated tests, these leaders may require additional tests beyond those administered by the state. Moreover, teachers make their own decision about in-class assessments at the end of units and at other times. School and district leaders usually influence teachers' assessment primarily through the professional development they offer. Similarly, teacher hiring practices are influenced by state licensing requirements, and professional development may be partially regulated by the state as well as negotiated with the teachers' union. These examples suggest that even if leaders were of one mind, they would have to share influence over some of the most powerful means for influencing teaching and learning.

In sum, leadership fragmentation is the norm in American school districts. Within the same district, leaders pay attention to different sources of accountability, rate their importance differently, and come up with different coping strategies. Moreover, control over critical pathways for influencing teaching is shared and contested. A coherent approach to multiple sources of accountability—including state tests—that is shared by most school and district leaders and is implemented in a consistent way to give teachers common guidance appears to be the exception to the rule. Yet it does happen. A few recent case studies suggest that school and district leaders can develop a common vision of the meaning of state tests and how to respond to them that integrates those tests with the other responsibilities those leaders have.[16] To learn more about the conditions under which this congruence of leadership happens, I turn to the next section.

INTERNAL ACCOUNTABILITY

The rise of testing is part of a larger worldview that doubts that American schools are performing well or have either the tools or motivation to do better. In this view, schools need external motivation to improve, and that motivation should come through accountability policies, including—but not limited to—testing. Moreover, in this view accountability is equated with responsibility to some external authority or source of pressure. Paradoxically, schools that respond most effectively to the pressure coming from state testing regimes may do so because of a strongly developed sense of *internal* accountability.

In the prevailing view, internal accountability is an oxymoron. There cannot be accountability without external oversight or pressure in some form. Yet a few researchers have identified schools with high levels of internal accountability, that is

> where essential components of accountability [a]re generated largely within a school staff. Staff identify clear standards for student performance, collect . . . information to inform themselves about their levels of success, and exert . . . strong peer pressure within the faculty to meet the goals.[17]

Internal accountability requires a shared culture with strong professional norms governing expectations for students. It also suggests a well-developed capacity for teachers to collaborate around shared values. Thus, this concept supports research linking strong school professional communities with improved student performance.[18] It also fits with the research on transformational leadership, which suggests that leaders can promote this sense of internal accountability.

At this point, evidence from a few studies suggests that schools that have strongly developed internal accountability respond to external accountability demands in ways that promote student learning, as measured by tests.[19] However, the research also raises a number of questions and suggests a variety of pitfalls. Internal accountability is not a magic bullet. While some schools develop internal accountability to a set of norms holding that all children can achieve high standards, in other schools the established norms are that many children cannot succeed. In these schools, low expectations abound, and internal accountability may impede reform and improved teaching. Thus, not only is internal accountability important, but it is also important to have accountability for the right internal standards.

There are a whole set of questions about the factors that contribute to internal accountability for high expectations. For instance, strong building leadership seems to be necessary to help develop internal accountability that copes constructively with state accountability systems. However, it is not so clear whether leadership from the principal is sufficient. In some cases, "distributed leadership" that brings teachers into the equation in a more active way is also necessary. How feasible is such distributed leadership when local norms promote low expectations for many students?[20]

There are also questions about the interaction of external and internal accountability systems. Strong external accountability systems clearly get schools to focus on state testing regimes. However, it is not clear whether strong external accountability promotes internal accountability that is aligned with the external accountability. In some cases, it seems to. However, schools that have special missions, like magnet schools or special-purpose high schools, may be torn between well-defined historical internal accountability for goals at odds with state tests and the tests themselves.

It also appears that schools have to have the capacity to respond to new external challenges before they will take responsibility for those goals. That is, if teachers do not have the knowledge or capacity to work together to develop new instructional approaches, they may not develop internal accountability aligned with external expectations. Moreover, the need to respond rapidly to external accountability demands may actually undermine efforts to develop the capacity that would allow internal accountability to develop. Teachers become so busy making short-term accommodations in curriculum or scheduling, required by people who think they know how to address external mandates, that they never develop the fundamental knowledge (about both content and how to teach it) in tested subjects that would allow them to help their students succeed. Without that knowledge, they are unlikely to respond effectively. All these problems may be most extreme in schools with large concentrations of low-income students, limited funding, and the greatest difficulty in hiring expert teachers.

These findings suggest that claims that testing and other forms of external accountability will benefit poor and minority students are overstated. The situations where state testing will promote a strong sense of internal accountability are very special. They require a preexisting capacity to make changes suggested by the state tests, the absence of commitments at odds with those tests, and leadership that finds a way to redefine tests as indicators of forms of student learning that teachers find important.[21]

High schools also create special problems. Their departmental structure works against developing norms that are shared schoolwide. Each department develops its own identity around its own subject area. Moreover, without careful leadership, the burden of responding to state tests will fall on the departments that teach those subjects, and other departments will atrophy.[22]

The evidence for the potential of internal accountability at the school level is stronger than that for district internal accountability. Even though district leaders have greater access to the factors that influence teaching—curriculum, materials, and professional development—the influence that such access brings is limited by both the distance between district leaders and teachers and the fragmentation of offices so common in larger districts. Nevertheless, a few recent qualitative studies of districts unusually successful in raising student achievement point to a greater potential for district instructional leadership than pessimists had thought. In these studies, districts have influenced teaching through a combination of shared norms as well as the orchestration of such policy pathways as textbooks, curriculum guides, and professional development. Normative influences include the creation of a district-level professional community with a strong culture emphasizing the primacy of student instruction for all units, including the financial office. While the details of this normative message vary and the ways it is generated differs, it is present in many accounts. Also unclear is the role of personal influence. It seems unlikely that strong district internal accountability can be achieved without a superintendent who is strongly and visibility committed to promoting student achievement. It seems equally improbable that such accountability will survive without a team of leaders at the top of the organization that share this fundamental commitment and provide an understanding of how to achieve it.[23]

The exploration of district internal accountability is so limited that the contribution of state testing to its development has not been explored. We can speculate that the publication of state test scores is likely to make student achievement more relevant to the highest levels of district leadership (and school board governance), where the focus is usually more on questions of resources and politics than teaching and learning. However, as at the school level, it seems likely that linking high stakes to tests will encourage the use of short-term expedient measures to raise scores. The deeper changes in school culture and capacity that have greater potential to link increased test scores to increased student learning would seem to require more time and freedom for local consideration than high-stakes venues permit.[24]

CONCLUSION

Testing is just one of many problems that school leaders face. They must constantly cope with changes in funding, enrollments, the varying ideas of good practice coming from professional reformers, and the preferences of voters. They face bureaucratic accountability—including that coming from testing regimes but also the regulations stemming from state and federal government—political accountability (to voters and parents), market accountability, and professional accountability. These accountability pressures push leaders in quite different directions.

Moreover, leadership itself is fragmented. It comes from superintendents, a variety of district offices, principals, and teachers. All these leaders identify different problems and propose different solutions. It is no wonder that teachers often close the door and try to teach as they see fit. But doing so is becoming increasingly difficult, as the content taught, the materials used, and even the pacing through the content are increasingly specified from some central source.

The reform problem for educational leaders is not so much how to cope with testing as how to ensure that all children receive a high-quality education. From that perspective, testing is a mixed blessing. While it gets student achievement on the agenda, the way it defines achievement matters. The tests that promote more challenging conceptions of achievement are rarely used by states for accountability purposes, and recent changes in federal policy work against such tests. The stakes associated with tests need to be appropriately calibrated. If they are too high, educators will resort to short-term test preparation. If they are too low, the test may be ignored.

For high and equal achievement to be achieved, leaders must focus on student outcomes more or less regardless of the testing regime in question and in spite of a variety of other accountability pressures that they face. This means constructing a definition of the outside environment where improving student achievement is possible and desirable, creating consensus on that definition first among appropriate leaders and then among others, and finally creating the material conditions—well-educated teachers, appropriate materials, curriculum, and instructional practices—to ensure that learning occurs.

The Mismeasure and Abuse of Our Children: Why School Officials Must Resist State and National Standardized Testing Reforms

William C. Cala

They hesitate and they regret, and sometimes they petition; but they do nothing in earnest and with effect. They will wait, well disposed, for others to remedy the evil that they may no longer have to regret. At most, they give only a cheap vote, and a feeble countenance and god-speed, to the right as it goes by them. There are nine hundred and ninety-nine patrons of virtue to one virtuous person.

—Henry David Thoreau

THE RATIONALE TO RESIST

Each time I interview prospective candidates for administrative positions, I ask several questions that give me a fairly good snapshot of the person sitting before me. It is critical that the person hired relates well to students, parents, peers, teachers, and the community. By the end of the interview, I generally have a sense of the candidate's position on standardized testing and its relationship to children and learning. In those few cases where the candidate has been politic and evasive, I bluntly posit the questions on high-stakes testing (HST) directly. In the summer of 2003, such an encounter brought me to a new level of frustration. Regardless of the manner in which I queried a prospective assistant principal, she deftly dodged a direct answer better than most politicians on cable talk shows. Specifically, I was attempting to determine how much pain and suffering she believed a child should endure before an educator raises a voice of protest. In other words, "How much damage to children will you permit before your conscience engages your mind and voice to speak out and object to the abuse that our children are experiencing?" To my dismay, this candidate would follow the direction of the government on this issue until no child remained standing.

Unfortunately, this type of behavior by current and prospective leaders is more the norm than the exception. Over the years, I have tried and supported multiple strategies to stop the abusive practices of using HST as gatekeepers to the futures of our children—a push for a national diploma; countless legislative bills; resolutions in local, state, and national organizations; and the dissemination of the data detailing the specific damage to children since the onset of HST as a national direction. Perhaps the lack of knowledge of the harm being done to children deters school leaders from leading. Under this assumption, I have focused the efforts of my research and action on (1) collecting, with precision, the negative consequences of the testing reform for our children, (2) disseminating this information widely and often, and (3) taking tangible, concrete actions in opposition to HST.

DAMAGE TO STUDENTS

The damage to students nationwide has been prolific. Research by Angela Valenzuela, Linda O'Neil, Walter Haney, and others has highlighted the burgeoning dropouts, retentions, and push-outs across the country (particularly in Texas, the mother ship of all HST reform). My primary focus has been on the frightening effects of testing in New York State since it began HST reform in 1995. New York State's own Regents Report Card shows the following.[1]

- Since 1995, the rate of students leaving high school for GED programs increased by 30 percent;
- From 1998 to 2000, the number of students dropping out increased by 17 percent;
- Since 1995, 1,440,000 students repeated ninth grade;
- English Language Learner dropouts have become the minority group with the highest dropout rate. Prior to 1996, they were the highest diploma-earning minority.

In a well-publicized study[2] by Advocates for Children that appeared in *The New York Times* and *New York Post*, it was uncovered that 160,000 students in New York City alone were pushed out of high schools to hide the dropout rate between 1998 and 2001. Approximately 100,000 additional push-outs have occurred since 2001. A recent Manhattan Institute study[3] paints the following bleak picture for New York State:

- Only 46 percent of African-Americans graduate from New York State high schools, placing New York twenty-seventh out of the thirty-one states with statistics;
- Only 40 percent of Hispanics graduate from New York State schools, placing New York second to last in the country;
- The graduation rate for whites in New York is 78 percent, or fourteenth out of thirty-seven states;
- New York State's total graduation rate of all races is 64 percent, or thirty-ninth out of fifty states.

Negative statistics have increased dramatically as well for Students with Disabilities (SWD) in the state of New York.

- From 1998 to 2001, SWD dropouts increased from 7,600 to 9,600 (26.3 percent increase). Nationally, the dropout rate decreased by 5.6 percent[4];
- New York's SWD classification rate is 14.8 percent[5];
- IEP diplomas increased by 22 percent.[6] (These certificates of completion of the Individualized Education Plan are not high school diplomas.)

These numbers clearly demonstrate significant problems that have arisen as a result of the HST reform, but other indicators are more difficult to collect and calibrate. For example, data relating to mental health issues are very difficult to assemble and less likely to be part of a mandated data collection scheme. However, if one peruses medical journals or recently published books on mental health, a disturbing trend is unearthed. Dr. Marilyn Benoit, president of the American Academy of Child and Adolescent Psychiatry, stated, "I am seeing more families where school work that is developmentally inappropriate for the cognitive levels of children is causing emotional havoc at home, and the pressure on teachers to teach to tests and outperform their colleagues is translating into stressful evenings for parents and children."[7] In *The Depressed Child—A Parent's Guide for Rescuing Kids*, by Dr. Douglas A. Riley, the realities of the negative effects of HST are made very vivid. One chapter is titled "External Stress and Death Thoughts: The SOLs" The SOLs are the state of Virginia's mandated standardized tests (Standards Of Learning). The following is a chilling passage from his book:

> When I was a child, the term "SOL" referred to a phrase that cannot be mentioned here. Suffice it to say that if you were SOL you were seriously out of luck, so to speak. In Virginia, the SOLs have left many children feeling SOL, to the extent that this spring when the tests were administered across several grade levels, we had a flood of parents of worried, stressed-out children calling my office for appointments. Among them was one preadolescent boy who had told his mother that if he did not pass his SOLs he intended to kill himself.[8]

Riley believes that the area of illness due to the testing craze is the tip of the iceberg. He relates the story of his local ambulance corps where suicide attempts and overdoses coincide with the delivery of report cards. Perhaps I would question the plausibility of this statement if I had not heard the very same information from the director of our local ambulance corps in Perinton, New York.

DAMAGE TO TEACHERS AND SCHOOL LEADERS

The ill effects on teachers and administrators are equally disturbing. In New York, fourth and eighth grades are the critical testing years. It is noteworthy that teachers of these grades are fleeing the profession[9] or requesting grade-level changes. One of the most disturbing concerns is the cheating done by teachers across the country—cheating out of desperation to satisfy the bureaucrats who are force-feeding this reform; cheating to raise test scores to keep jobs; cheating to prevent children from being labeled as failures. Associated Press writer Michael Gormley reported that there were "21 cases of proven cheating by teachers from Buffalo to Long Island" in New York state from 1999 through the spring of 2002.[10] The proven cases represent only a small sampling of the total picture. Gormley suggests that cheating is not reported due to the consequences for those reporting cheating by peers and administrators.[11]

When faced with the capricious moniker of *failure* due to HST, a school principal is often put in an impossible situation. In many city and rural schools mired in inextricable poverty and social morass, principals will never compare favorably with their wealthy suburban counterparts. There are no city or rural miracles, although the nation was sold the "Texas Miracle" by Rod Paige, former Houston Independent School District superintendent and current Secretary of Education in the George W. Bush administration. We have subsequently learned that the *miracle* was nothing more than a *mirage*. More aptly stated, it was a fraud.[12]

As a group, teachers and administrators care deeply for the children in their charge. Some educators care so much that they become obsessed and, far too often, depressed over the challenge and demands of HST. This became all too real on April 11, 2002, at Simington Elementary School in Gwinett County, Georgia. The body of Principal Betty Robinson was found next to a .38 caliber revolver. Ms. Robinson was described as a great leader, admired for taking care of her faculty and caring very much about her school and the success of her students.[13] Just prior to her suicide, Simonton Elementary had been named one of four Gwinett schools receiving federal Title I funds for low-income students that had not improved its test scores enough. It was reported that the day before she took her life, Ms.

Robinson had been in a meeting in which her school's poor performance was discussed.

WHY EDUCATORS DO NOT FIGHT

Knowing the ill effects of HST, the question we have to ask is why educators do not fight back. Part of the answer may lie in the work done by social psychologist Stanley Milgram in the 1970s. His book *Obedience to Authority* resonates today. Social psychologist Thomas Blass describes Milgram's work about how far people would go in following the orders of a person in authority.[14]

> The subjects believed they were part of an experiment supposedly dealing with the relationship between punishment and learning. An experimenter—who used no coercive powers beyond a stern aura of mechanical and vacant-eyed efficiency—instructed participants to shock a learner by pressing a lever on a machine each time the learner made a mistake on a word-matching task. Each subsequent error led to an increase in the intensity of the shock in 15-volt increments, from 15 to 450 volts. At some point in the study, the learner began to complain of heart problems and to demand that the shocks stop. Each time the teacher tried to stop, the experimenter (the authority figure) would insist that the experiment go on. To everyone's surprise, over 60% of all subjects followed the experimenter's commands to go on, even after the learner ceased responding entirely.
>
> In actuality, the shock box was a well-crafted prop and the learner an actor who did not actually get shocked.

Why do so many educators (administrators, teachers, etc.) who clearly understand and are able to articulate the damage of New York's current reform, when told to administer and follow the orders of State authority, follow like sheep being led to the slaughter? When I spoke with a superintendent from Nassau County, Long Island, he said, "Bill, they've [superintendents] all given up down here; they're now just trying to raise test scores."

When reading poll results that support these HST reforms, I cannot help but think of Milgram's *Theory of Obedience* and why we are in the mess that we find ourselves. People who are doing a job as instructed by an administrative figure are following the instructions, not their own moral code. The feelings of duty and one's own value system are clearly separated, and the sense of responsibility shifts in the mind of the subordinate from himself or herself to the authority figure. Milgram noted this in his work in 1965, and this may account for the failure of administrators and teachers to resist the testing tyranny.

With numbing regularity good people were seen to knuckle under the demands of authority and perform actions that were callous and severe. Men who are in everyday life responsible and decent were seduced by the trappings of authority, by the control of their perceptions, and by the uncritical acceptance of the experimenter's definition of the situation, into performing harsh acts. . . . A substantial proportion of people do what they are told to do, irrespective of the content of the act and without limitations of conscience, so long as they perceive that the command comes from a legitimate authority.[15]

A further rationale for the failure to resist the testing tyranny can be seen in "An Allegory of Educational Testing in New York State." It is an essay I wrote that appeared in the March 2003 edition of the *Phi Delta Kappan.* I parallel Dava Sobel's book *Longitude: The True Story of a Lone Genius Who Solved the Greatest Scientific Problem of His Time* to the present-day situation in New York, where educational leaders stubbornly resist thoughtful alternatives to the "scientifically based" high-stakes testing model.

Sobel's account was of John Harrison, who discovered how to determine longitude at sea but whose discovery was repeatedly rejected by the leaders of the time in Great Britain. Harrison's discovery was unacceptable simply because he was just a country carpenter and not a real scientist. Great Britain was losing sailors by the hundreds each year due to the inability to determine longitude at sea, so the discovery of longitude was crucial to the future of the country. The British Parliament even passed the Longitude Act, offering a king's ransom to the person who made such a discovery. Unfortunately, the Board of Longitude (BOL), which was responsible for determining a winner, was composed of scientists, who looked upon anyone out of the mainstream of science with disdain. Harrison was clearly out of the mainstream.

For forty years, Harrison's attempts to be heard and awarded the prize were denied by the BOL, even though his test runs proved to be incredibly successful. Each time he presented proof of success, the BOL added more requirements, new resolutions, new regulations, allowing time for the "real" scientists of the day to solve the problem.

The "real" scientists never did discover a solution. In spite of Harrison's successes, the BOL remained unmoved. Finally, at the age of eighty, Harrison was granted the prize money by Parliament, not by the BOL.

State education commissioners and state boards of education have exquisitely mirrored the blindness and arrogance of the Board of Longitude. Educational plans that have been proved to work with the cities' poor and disenfranchised have been scuttled in favor of unproven testing regimens. For example, in New York, there are twenty-eight Consortium schools that have been outperforming their inner-city counterparts for thirty years; yet, the State Board of Regents is putting them out of business by prohibiting the very effective practice of performance assessment in lieu of HST. As another example, states and the federal government continue to define their own scientific research in the area of reading. Phonics appears to be the only method that will win the prize of public money, in spite of the successes of blended reading approaches. Irrespective of learning, only higher test scores will yield the Title I prize money. In light of this bureaucratic bullheadedness, is it any wonder that teachers, administrators, and parents remain silent?

The cynic in me adds one more rationale as to why leaders do not object, protest, and resist reforms that are palpably hurting countless children. It lies in this quotation from Upton Sinclair: "It is virtually impossible for a man to understand what he is paid not to understand."

STRATEGIES OF RESISTANCE

> The ultimate measure of a man is not where he stands in moments of comfort and convenience, but where he stands at times of challenge and controversy.
> —Martin Luther King, Jr.

Earlier, I noted some very compelling reasons why educators must resist the ubiquitous HST reform that has plagued our children, teachers, and communities. No matter what the reasons are for teachers and administrators to opt into a conspiratorial silence and no matter how understanding we may be of the comfort and absence of conflict that the failure to act brings us, we can never permit this reticence to trump the needs of those disenfranchised by this abusive testing regimen. Over the past decade, a small group of colleagues[16] and I have used a number of strategies that, in isolation, will *not* make a difference, but when utilized in concert *can* and *do* move mountains. I have identified seven strategies that are essential to any effort to change bureaucratic mandates.

1. Getting the Facts
2. Speaking Out Often
3. Writing
4. Targeting the Power Brokers
5. Building a Better Mousetrap
6. Using the New Three "Rs"
7. Believing in the Power of One

All these strategies are "at risk" behaviors! If you are a parent, you are at risk of being criticized by school personnel, politicians, or neighbors as a whining liberal. If you are a teacher, you will be accused of being lazy and not wanting to be held accountable. If you are an administrator, you will be painted with the "dumbing-down" brush and accused of being an apologist for the status quo. (Fortunately, I work in a high-performing school district and avoid that particular attack; however, I would not have been able to take HST resistance as far as I have if I were from a high-need, low-performing school.) Any strategy that jeopardizes the power of one's position will have consequences for those attempting to make the change. Some strategies have more substantial consequences than others, but *all* consequences must be endured if we expect to stop the mismeasure and abuse of our children.

Getting the Facts

What I find most disconcerting is the lack of basic understanding educators have about the assessment process. In short, most educators (teachers and administrators) are incapable of carrying on a conversation about the mechanics of standards-based assessments. This is not a knock on our profession but rather a comment on the convoluted nature of the standards-based testing system. Item Response Theory (IRT), for example, is a standards-based tool used to weigh the difficulty of test questions. Plugging IRT into the Google search engine yields an overwhelming 578,000 hits! Imagine a teacher faced with reading an article on IRT with the following titled subtext: "A Hyperbolic Cosine Latent Trait Model for Unfolding Polytomous Responses."[17]

A typical tactic of the "standardistos" (author Susan Ohanian's moniker for high-stakes test panderers) is to use the language of the psychometricians or to employ psychometricians themselves to defend their tactics. The strategy has worked well by shutting up commonsense opposition. So how do we become educated and how do we compete in the debate? Getting the necessary knowledge does not require a degree in statistics and measurement. It does require, however, a knowledge of the purpose of the particular tools used by the testmakers. In looking at the issue of IRT, we need not know about "polytomous responses." It is helpful to know, however, that IRT is a process whereby the difficulty of each question on a test is rated on a scale (1 through 4, with 1 being easy). If we look at a real test situation, we can see how common sense, combined with a general knowledge of the nomenclature of testing, provides us with the knowledge to fight and defend, using the strategies of resistance.

In 2002, when the New York State Regents physics test was given to high school students, the result was that three times as many students failed as in previous years. Common sense immediately sends a signal that something is wrong. Armed with the definition of IRT and a strong need to know, several educators requested details of the process under the Freedom of Information Act and uncovered the problem. Simply stated, one person in the state, the chief psychometrician, threw out the work of a large group of teachers who performed the IRT process and changed the passing score to a much higher number. One need not be a Ph.D. in measurement to realize that something untoward had happened. It is noteworthy, however, that possessing the rudiments of terminology along with a passion to uncover the truth can lead to a wealth of incredible information to fight HST.[18]

While understanding that knowledge of the testing process is important, I believe "Getting the Facts" relative to the damage to students and public education that has occurred since the beginning of the HST reform is more critical. Getting the "real" numbers is not that difficult, but it does take drive and perseverance. For example, in the spring of 2003, the New York State Education Department put out a press release stating that students with disabilities (SWD) were now earning more diplomas than in the past and that the HST movement was responsible for this wonderful accomplishment. If you have been in or near the vicinity of a school over the past several years, it is clear to any observer that students with disabilities are not benefiting as a result of HST; in fact, there are numerous class action lawsuits across the country attempting to restore the rights of SWD lost under No Child Left Behind's HST program. Again, common sense tells us that there is more to this picture. My first step was to get the facts. I searched New York's State Education Department website to find the full annual report on SWD. Next, I went to a second source, the state's annual Report Card, which lists all data inclusive of SWD information. Then, I went to the federal Office of Special Education Programs's website to look at New York data that are required to be submitted to the federal government by the states. Within a short period, I was able to compare three sources reporting the same information. What I found were large discrepancies in the classification rate of students with disabilities and a wealth of information that the state intentionally ignored in its glowing press release of April 28, 2003. I discovered that the number of students getting diplomas had increased slightly over a one-year period, but the long-term statistics on diplomas were flat. The real disasters were buried. In fact, from 1998 to 2001, SWDs who dropped out of school increased from 7,600 to 9,600 (26.3 percent increase), while nationally, the dropout rate among SWDs *decreased* by 5.6 percent. Furthermore, IEP diplomas (certificates of completion that are not high school diplomas) increased by nearly 22 percent.

Over the years, I have discovered that reports of successes relating to HST are nearly always suspect. The medical profession uses the term "Index of Suspicion" when diagnosing medical problems. HST progress reports by state departments of education are high on my "Index of Suspicion" relative to the disease of dishonesty. There are two important points to remember in the quest to get the facts: (1) always maintain your Index of Suspicion when examining data relative to HST, and (2) assume that any report claiming victory that emanates from departments of education and defy your sense of logic is either false or selective cherry picking of the facts.

Finally, endless information is available on the Internet. It is possible to obtain nearly all of the source information you need at your desktop. Search engines such as Google are invaluable as you search for and get the facts.

Speaking Out

Speaking out can take many forms. Silence has but one. In my circle of colleagues (superintendents), the depth of understanding of the issues surrounding the care and instruction of children is so obvious in one-on-one conversations. In previous years, such conversations led me to believe that a unified statement about HST, endorsed by superintendents, would not only be viable but also essential to the education of the general public and desired by superintendents. I was only partially correct. Certainly, a unified statement of fact supporting the American Educational Research Association's position on HST, for example, would go a long way in informing the public of the ethics of assessment. This information is vital to the public and its ability to make judgments about each state's own testing program. I miscued thinking that a group of caring, compassionate, educated individuals would take their ethics public. It has become very clear, in my experiences, that superintendents, in general, have such tenuous jobs and that security trumps will, courage, and the ability to do the right thing. Building-level administrators and teachers are equally reluctant to speak out, as they are regularly pressured by their superiors to produce higher test scores. Unfortunately, test scores have become the sole measurement of a good school. Yet the need to speak out has become all the more critical and essential.

Considering the reluctance of educators to speak out, the role of parents becomes ever so important. Parents need to express their concerns at PTA meetings, to boards of education, to their children's teachers, and to their building-level administrators. Getting involved on listservs is a powerful way for parents and educators to speak out across the country. The resources available via the pooling of minds through this venue are enormous. For example, FairTest hosts the most potent listserv in the country with its Assessment Reform Network (ARN) at http://www.fairtest.org. Setting up a listserv on your own is easy and free. In the Rochester, New York, area we have set up a listserv on testing through Yahoo for the Coalition for Common Sense in Education. Area parents and educators converse daily and share speaking-out strategies and other tenets of resistance.

The remaining resistance strategies naturally flow as the necessary implements for speaking out. The important principle to remember is that silence solves nothing and will infinitely exacerbate the problem.

Write, Write, Write

The pen is mightier than the sword. It is an old axiom that is more relevant today than ever before. Personal conversations are valuable; however, practically speaking, the written statement is the most functional way of conveying well-formed and reasoned position statements. It serves little purpose to gather the facts and not disseminate the fruits of your labor. Information needs to be shared with

- Newspapers;
- State Education Department officials;
- Governing boards of state education departments;
- Local and state legislators;
- Education committee chairs of state legislatures;
- Radio;
- Television.

Most newspapers provide two avenues for readers to get their views in print—letters to the editor and the guest essay. You need not be an expert in the field to have your work published; however, carefully reasoned and adequately researched articles stand a better chance of being printed. The general rule of print media is no more than one article in a thirty-day period. Do not be afraid to submit articles on a regular basis. Having different people from your group write on an alternating basis is very effective as well. Education and government officials get a lot of mail. If you want your views to be read, it is imperative that the document you send is in a very readable format.

- Make your communication short. Do not run on page after page when you can say what you need to say in a few words;
- Use bullets to highlight your facts. Keeping the facts separated this way enables the reader to get the facts easily;
- Source your information whenever possible. Without providing documentation that validates your position, your work will be viewed as rhetoric or simple opinion.

Target the Power Brokers

When speaking out and writing to effect a change, it is important that the message reaches those who have the power to make a difference. Who makes educational policy and law at the state level? Who has influence with whom? How are state governing boards assembled? Are they elected or are they appointed? Who appoints them? Is the state education superintendent/commissioner elected or appointed? Who appoints him or her?

Answering these questions is an important part of getting the most mileage out of one's efforts. For years, many of us in New York have attempted to be heard by the commissioner of education. As our requests went unanswered, we moved our efforts to the people who appoint the commissioner, the Board of Regents. Recently, when these efforts proved to be futile, we moved our effort to the state legislature, which appoints members to the Board of Regents. In New York, the majority party in both houses has the responsibility to appoint members to the Board of Regents, so we knew where to focus our efforts. Subsequently, our efforts have now focused on the legislature.

One particular strategy that we have employed with some success was calling for public hearings on the effects of HST in New York. Many of us fought long and hard for these hearings to become a reality. As a result of our perseverance and persistence, five hearings were held in Rochester, Albany, and New York City in September and October 2003. The legislature has in turn placed significant pressure on the Board of Regents to reexamine the entire concept of multiple assessments versus the high-stakes testing model now in place. The Board of Regents delayed implementation of the total HST plan in New York as a result and is carrying on discussions that, prior to the hearings, would have been unthinkable. The Board of Regents is now examining alternatives to exit exams—an unthinkable notion before the hearings.

Additionally, the scrutiny of individuals making arbitrary and capricious assessment decisions in the state department of education by legislators and the Board of Regents has begun in earnest. Recently, the top two assessment officials in the state have been either forced to retire or move out of public sector education. This movement did not take place through silence but through the efforts of those speaking out loudly and often. Had there not been bold and outspoken efforts by a few activists from Rochester and New York City there would have been no progress. Knowing the power brokers and getting the message to them is absolutely essential if we expect to move decision-making bodies.

Building a Better Mousetrap

What is your plan to measure student performance by objective measures? This is the most common response to those who voice opposition to high-stakes testing, and it is a fair question. In fact, criticism without a viable option resonates as hollow rhetoric. Being aware of sensible, successful, and proven alternatives is part of getting the facts, and essential if we expect to initiate a change in the testing-to-learn model. While HST proponents refuse to recognize them, there are many models of success throughout the country. As I mentioned earlier, the Consortium schools in New York are a splendid example of schools that produce high output in areas of abject poverty. Most of these twenty-eight schools serve poor neighborhoods, students with English as their second language, and an overwhelming percentage of students of color. Schools such as Urban Academy of Manhattan, Fannie Lou Hamer of the Bronx, and School Without Walls in Rochester serve poor inner-city populations with demographics among the worst in their respective school systems; yet they overwhelmingly outperform their counterparts.[19] These schools have never used standardized tests to achieve high graduation rates, college acceptance, and extremely high attendance.

Another highly successful model, and one I have written about in various publications, is the model proposed by Ron Wolk. The Wolk model maintains the use of standardized tests but puts them in proper perspective. His system consists of a 135-point grading system, with 40 points allotted to standardized tests. The remainder of the points is assigned to teacher evaluations, community service, extracurricular activities, attendance, and performance by exhibition.

Providing a commonsense alternative to HST is the only answer to eliminating it. A "better mousetrap" already exists; one need not reinvent it.

When All Else Fails: The New Three "Rs"—
Resist, Refuse, Revolt

Earlier in the chapter, I related the interview question I posed to an assistant principal candidate—How much damage to children will you permit before your conscience engages your mind and voice to speak out and object to the abuse that our kids are experiencing? To take this question one step further, we must ask how much damage to children will we permit after trying every means of resistance available to us within the parameters of the system. When we have spoken out incessantly, have written hundreds of letters, have targeted the power brokers to no avail, is it time to give up? Do we accept as fact that the abuse of our children is a part of the fabric of our democracy? It is at this point that commitment to principle is categorically defined.

How committed are we to a principled stand? Are we able to resist by refusing to perform duties that will lead to children being left behind and thrown away? Are we willing to put our jobs in jeopardy?

There are two poignant examples of courage, where individuals refused to follow the arbitrary mandates of silence in their districts and, subsequently, put their jobs on the line for the benefit of kids. These two courageous men are George Schmidt of Chicago and James Hope of Gwinett County, Georgia. George Schmidt published questions from standardized tests that had been administered to students in the Chicago public schools. He published these questions in the newspaper *Substance* to point out their poor quality, lack of value, and the damage that they would do to the children in the Chicago schools. As a result of his actions, he was fired. The case continues to wind its way through the courts to this day. Hope also provided to the media some educationally unsound questions from the Gateway test that was mandated in Gwinett County. His story is equally unpleasant. The district did everything in its power to fire him and went so far as to have him put under police surveillance. The district's efforts to fire him were overturned by the courts; however, the district continues to apply pressure on Hope to this day.

Both men fought within the system until it became clear that no means other than the use of the new three "Rs" could be effective to protect their children. Their actions caused incredible personal and familial pain. The financial burden of legal defense has been overwhelming. Was it worth the pain and suffering? Has their anguish helped others? These are difficult questions to answer, but there is no doubt that their courage is making a difference in their own states and nationally as the incredible weaknesses of the testing reform of the No Child Left Behind Act is exposed. The courage of the Schmidts and the Hopes of the world give the rest of us the courage and the avenues to speak out and lobby the power brokers for the changes necessary to provide a learning environment free from abuse. There comes a time when refusing to follow regulations that result in damage to children becomes a necessity. Both these men reached that point. However, the question remains about whether others possess the courage required of the new three "Rs".[20]

The Power of One

There is no doubt that in uniting our minds, spirits, and muscle, we can change the world. All too often, though, we find ourselves protecting our security and not willing to take the risks necessary to bring about change. Earlier I stated that resisting and speaking out almost always carry inherent risks. In many cases, the greater the risk, the more likely we are to bring about a desired change. What does one do when, universally, there is support for a position but no commitment to any action other than perfunctory lip service? Do you stand alone? For how long? What are the potential consequences? The best explanation of the "Power of One" can be seen in a real drama that I lived in the spring of 2003.

For nineteen consecutive years, the New York State legislature failed to pass its budget by the mandated April 1 deadline. The late passage of the state budget negatively impacts public schools as they send their budgets to the public for a local vote in May. Within the state budget package is the requisite state aid to schools necessary to determine the local tax burden. In years past, this budget delay presented various difficulties, but these difficulties were adequately managed by local school districts, as schools were able to predict with reasonable accuracy the state aid they would receive. As a result of the fiscal crisis in our state since September 11, 2001, predicting no longer worked. In fact, in 2001–2002, there was a net loss in aid to schools, and Governor George Pataki refused to approve a budget. Schools did their normal projecting, which was a compromise between the governor's and the legislature's budgets. For the first time, these predictions did not work. The money never came. Large city schools were decimated. The Rochester City Schools received $25 million less than they had predicted. As a result, across the state, scores of teachers and programs were eliminated. Eventually, some of the lost money was returned to schools during the school year. This did not help very much, as the damage had been done—the programs and people were eliminated. It became very clear that an on-time budget was imperative and that past practices would no longer work.

After nineteen years of late state budgets and the disaster caused by the 2001 late budget, the Fairport, New York, Board of Education passed a resolution stating that it would not hold its local budget vote until the state had passed its own budget. The board wrote to all 700 New York School Boards and superintendents asking for support by joining this resistance. In spite of the enormous public support for the Fairport position (editorials across the state and country praised this bold move), not one board joined the Fairport movement. Not one! We received countless letters and phone calls from schools offering private support, but not one was willing to take the risk involved in the Fairport resolution. Yet the Fairport board stood its ground. This solo stance was reported in *The New York Times*. On April 13, 2003, the front page of the "New York Region" bore Jane Gross's bold story, "A Small School District Rises Up against Albany." This was the turning point of the battle. The story sent chills through the legislature and the governor's office. As Fairport maintained its position, Commissioner of Education Richard Mills threatened to remove the superintendent and the Fairport board if the school board did not hold its vote at the preordained time. It soon became evident that the legislature did not want the "blood" of Fairport on its doorstep. The movement from April 13 forward defied history and conventional state politics. When the legislature (both the Republican Senate and the Democratic Assembly) realized through the *New York Times* story that a delayed budget would mean the acceptance of the governor's budget (a budget that would destroy nearly every gain of the past decade) and that Fairport would hold firm in its position, they did something no one would have imagined. Immediately, both houses began talking of passing a law that would permit local schools to vote two weeks later. This would give the legislature time to pass an aid package that schools would be able to incorporate into their own spending packages and would provide local taxpayers with intelligent information on local taxation. No one believed that this law would be passed. It did pass, and overwhelmingly in both houses. Popular opinion, however, led people to believe that delaying the school votes was a far cry from a state budget agreement with the governor's signature. All had to be accomplished within a few days, and everyone knows that the state government just can't move that quickly. This time it did move quickly. To nearly everyone's surprise, a budget that both parties agreed upon was adopted. However, the biggest hurdle lay ahead. The governor labeled the budget as irresponsible and promised to veto it, and he did. Could the legislature override the governor's veto? Impossible! A veto override had not occurred in the state for over twenty years. The governor went on a television campaign to convince voters that the legislature should not override the veto. He made personal appearances to business alliances to garner support, but community sentiment was not with the governor. The people of New York wanted an on-time budget and a budget that did not gut schools and social services. The legislature read the communities well, indeed. In a historic vote, the governor's veto was overridden. In fact, the Republican Senate unanimously voted to override the veto of its own Republican governor.

There is no doubt that Fairport resolution was an impetus for this historic action, and, privately, many legislators admitted that without Fairport's stand, nothing, *nothing*, would have changed. The Power of One is enormous—one school board, in one town, moving the entire state. Imagine what we can do if we were to join hands in resisting HST!

Again I must stress that silence is not an option. Our children are being abused and discarded in ever-increasing numbers due to an unfeeling, thoughtless, high-stakes testing reform. When we look at the damage inflicted on our children, it should be clear that we can no longer passively accept the blind authority brought to light by Stanley Milgram's experiments. We cannot accept the baseless standards mission heralded by state and federal governments. We must fight this tyranny with our voices, our minds, and our will, using every strategy available to us. We must resist even if it means refusal. When I am speaking to a group of parents, educators, or community members or when I am giving testimony to legislators or governing educational boards relative to the ills of high-stakes tests or when I am marching in protest to the actions of bureaucrats who have promoted this abusive reform, I can hear the words of Frederick Douglass repeating themselves over and over in a continuous loop—"If there is no struggle, there is no progress. Those who profess to favor freedom, and yet deprecate agitation, are men who want crops without plowing the ground. They want rain without thunder and lightning. They want the ocean without the awful roar of its waters."

Our failure to speak out and resist makes us unwitting coconspirators in a plan to destroy our children and the prized institution we know as public education. We must not remain silent.

Notes

GENERAL EDITOR'S INTRODUCTION

1. Portions of this section draw upon E. Wayne Ross, "Remaking the Social Studies Curriculum," in *The Social Studies Curriculum: Purposes, Problems, and Possibilities*, rev. ed., ed. E. Wayne Ross (Albany: State University of New York Press, 2001).

2. John Dewey, *Democracy and Education* (New York: Free Press, 1966), p. 87.

3. Robert W. McChesney, Introduction to *Profits over People: Neoliberalism and Global Order*, by Noam Chomsky (New York: Seven Stories Press, 1988).

4. Madison quoted in Chomsky, *Profits over People*, p. 47.

5. For an explication of these issues see Edward S. Herman and Noam Chomsky, *Manufacturing Consent: The Political Economy of the Mass Media* (New York: Pantheon, 1988).

6. Noam Chomsky, *Media Control: The Spectacular Achievements of Propaganda* (New York: Seven Stories Press, 1997).

7. A. A. Lispcom and A. Ellery, eds., *The Writings of Thomas Jefferson*, vol. 16 (Washington, DC: The Thomas Jefferson Memorial Association, 1903), p. 96.

8. Dewey quoted in Noam Chomsky, *Class Warfare* (Vancouver: New Star Books, 1997).

INTRODUCTION

1. Dwight D. Eisenhower (text of an address delivered from the Oval Office on "Science in National Security," November 7, 1957), http://www.eisenhower.archives.gov/dl/Sputnik/Sputnikdocuments.html.

2. The projects included, for example, Biological Sciences Curriculum Study, Physical Sciences Study Committee, and projects known collectively as the "new math" and "new social studies."

3. William H. Schubert, "Historical Perspectives on Centralizing the Curriculum," in *The Politics of Curriculum Decision-Making*, ed. M. Frances Klein (Albany: State University of New York Press, 1991), pp. 98–119.

4. David C. Berliner and Bruce J. Biddle, *The Manufactured Crisis: Myths, Fraud and the Attack on America's Schools* (New York: Perseus, 1995).

5. Larry Cuban, "Reforming, Again, Again and Again," *Educational Researcher* 19 (January/February 1990), pp. 3–13.

6. This list is largely based on analysis by Elliot W. Eisner, "Educational Reform and the Ecology of Schooling," *Teachers College Record* 93 (Summer 1992), pp. 610–27.

CHAPTER 1

1. There are a number of sources that provide a history of mental measurement and the role of testing in schools. See Stephen Jay Gould, *The Mismeasure of Man* (New York: W. W. Norton Books, 1981) and David A. Goslin, *The Search for Ability: Standardized Testing in Social Perspective* (Russell Sage Foundation, 1966).

2. Goslin, p. 63.

3. There are a number of resources that chronicle the development of NAEP. See, for example, http://www.nagb.org/pubs/95222.pdf.

4. Goddard's case example for his theories was the Kallikak family. This pseudononymous and poor family, whose ancestry he traced to an upstanding man and a tavern wench, was from New Jersey. From this union grew the "good" and "bad" lines that fortified his heritability of intelligence arguments. The photographs Goddard used to demonstrate the moronic lineage of the Kallikak family would later be revealed to have been altered, with dark lines about the eyes and mouth to give an appearance of evil or stupidity. See Gould for a more complete discussion of this event.

5. For a history of the "Lippmann-Terman debate," see N. J. Block and G. Dworkin, eds., *The IQ Controversy* (New York: Pantheon Books, 1976).

6. Richard J. Herrnstein and Charles Murray, *The Bell Curve: Intelligence and Class Structure in America* (New York: Free Press, 1994).

7. Hernsteinn and Murray, p. 96.

8. See, for example, Randy Hoover's extensive analysis of student test data in Ohio, *Forces and Factors Affecting Ohio Proficiency Test Performance: A Study of 593 Ohio School Districts*, http://cc.ysu.edu/~rlhoover/OPT/index.html, as well as Peter Sacks's critique of the SAT, *Standardized Minds: The High Price of America's Testing Culture and What We Can Do to Change It* (Boudler, CO: Perseus Publishing, 2000). See also Mathison's chapter in this volume, "The Accumulation of Disadvantage."

9. George F. Madaus, "A National Testing System: Manna from Above," *Educational Assessment* 1, no. 1 (1993), pp. 9–26.

10. Robert Linn, "Assessments and Accountability," *Educational Researcher* 29, no. 2 (2000), pp. 4–16.

11. See Popham's chapter in this volume on this conceptual confusion.

12. National Commission on Excellence in Education, *A Nation at Risk* (1983).

13. Ibid., p. 5.

14. The goals and their rationale are published under the title *The National Education Goals Report: Building a Nation of Learners* (Washington, D.C.: National Education Goals Panel [NEGP], 1991).

15. McREL, *Content Knowledge,* 3rd ed.: *A compilation of content standards for K–12 curriculum in both searchable and browsable formats,* http://www.mcrel.org/standards-benchmarks/.

16. Ibid. See section on Purpose.

17. See especially Popham and Mathison and Freeman, in this volume.

18. See Mabry in this volume for a more complete discussion of the dilemmas and impossible dreams entailed in NCLB.

19. See, for example, the sophisticated database created by Achieve, Inc., that permits the identification and comparison of curriculum standards and assessments across the entire nation, heralded with the motto of "aligning standards for student achievement," http://www.aligntoachieve.org/.

20. Chad W. Buckendahl, Barbara S. Plake, James C. Impara, and Patrick M. Irwin, "Alignment of Standardized Achievement Tests to State Content Standards: A Comparison of Publishers' and Teachers' Perspectives." Paper presented at AERA, New Orleans, 2000.

21. The Education Commission of the States has supported the exploration of alternative models of accountability (see http://www.ecs.org/ecsmain.asp?page=/html/IssuesK12.asp) and in the edited volume *Redesigning Accountability Systems for Education,* (New York, Teachers College Press, 2004), Susan Fuhrman and Richard Elmore explore the nature and limits of current outcomes-based accountability. See also the Annenberg Institute for School Reform's "accountability toolbox" at www.annenberginstitute.org/accountability/toolbox/. See also, Robert E. Stake, *Standards-Based and Responsive Evaluation* (Thousand Oaks: Sage, 2004).

22. Kenneth Sirotnik, "Promoting Responsible Accountability in Schools and Education," *Phi Delta Kappan* (2002), http://www.pdkintl.org/kappan/k0205sir.htm.

CHAPTER 2

1. Commission on Instructionally Supportive Assessment, *Building Tests That Support Instruction and Accountability: A Guide for Policymakers,* (Washington, DC: Author, 2001), http://www.aasa.org; http://www.naesp.org; http://www.principals.org; http://www.nea.org, and http://www.nmsa.org.; *Illustrative Language for an RFP to Build Tests That Support Instruction and Accountability,* (Washington, DC: Author, 2001), http://www.aasa.org; http://www.naesp.org; http://www.principals.org; http://www.nea.org; and http://www.nmsa.org.

CHAPTER 3

1. Copyright 1999 by Alfie Kohn. This chapter was originally published in *School Administrator*, November 1999, and is reprinted with permission.

CHAPTER 4

1. Some of the early recommendations were to develop a more comprehensive system of preschool education and to eliminate early tracking of students. Germany is the only developed nation that still tracks children early on into different instructional programs, beginning at age ten.

2. The original TIMSS took place in 1995 in grades four, eight, and twelve. In 1999, to get an idea of how much the fourth graders had gained, some countries participated in testing only eighth graders, who would have been in the fourth grade at the time of the original study. In this country, the two studies are usually referred to as "TIMSS" and TIMSS-R" (for "repeat"). In other nations, they usually carry the designation TIMSS-95 and TIMSS-99.

3. Otto Von Bismarck said that there are two things you shouldn't watch being made, sausage and legislation. If one reads Harriet Tyson-Bernstein's *America's Textbook Fiasco: A Conspiracy of Good Intentions,* one might be tempted to make textbook construction a third item in Bismarck's list.

4 Gerald W. Bracey, "The TIMSS 'Final Year' Study and Report: A Critique," *Educational Researcher* (May 2000), pp. 4–10.

5. The TIMSS Reports may be obtained from The TIMSS International Study Center at Boston College or on the Internet at http://www.csteep.bc.edu/timss. The five major reports are *Mathematics Achievement in the Primary School Years, Science Achievement in the Primary School Years, Mathematics Achievement in the Middle School Years, Science Achievement in the Middle School Years,* and *Mathematics and Science Achievement in the Final Year of Secondary School.*

PISA data can be found at the U.S. Department of Education website, http://www.nces.ed.gov/surveys/pisa or at the website of the Organization for Economic Cooperation and Development, http://www.pisa.oecd.org.

PIRLS data can be found at the U.S. Department of Education website, http://www.nces.ed.gov/surveys/pirls or at timss.bc.edu/pirls2001.html.

CHAPTER 5

1. No Child Left Behind Act of 2001, Public Law No. 107–10 (2001).

2. National Research Council, *Scientific Research in Education* (Washington, DC: National Academy Press, 2002).

3. GOALS 2000: Educate America Act, Public Law No. 103–227 (1994).

4. "1994 ESEA: The State of State Compliance," *Education Week,* April 17, 2002, p. 29.

5. David C. Berliner and Bruce J. Biddle, *The Manufactured Crisis: Myths, Fraud, and the Attack on America's Public Schools* (Reading, MA: Addison-Wesley, 1995); Susan H. Fuhrman and R. F. Elmore, "Understanding Local Control in the Wake of State Education Reform," *Educational Evaluation and Policy Analysis* 12, no. 1 (1990), pp. 82–96.

6. In Iowa, the only state that has not adopted standards-based testing, nearly all districts administer the norm-referenced Iowa Test of Basic Skills (ITBS); see Linda L. Mabry, with K. Daytner, and J. Aldarondo, *Local Administration of State-Mandated Performance Assessments, Research Report to the Proffitt Foundation* (Bloomington, IN: Indiana University, 1999).

7. Michele Bachmann, "Legislation to Opt-out of 'No Child Left Behind' Makes First Deadline," *News from Senator Michele Bachmann* (April 9, 2004), http://www.senate.leg.state.mn.us/caucus/rep/membernews/2003/dist52/20030409_NCLB_Deadline.htm.

8. Los Angeles Independent Media Center, "National 'Opt Out' Day Focuses Attention on No Child Left Behind Act" (September 28, 2003), http://la.indymedia.org/news/2003/09/85462.php (accessed January 27, 2004); D. Taylor, "No Child Left Behind?" *Utah Independent Media Center* (October 4, 2002), http://www.utah.indymedia.org/news/2002/10/2966.php.

9. D. A. DeSchryver, "NCLB and NEA: United at Last," *The Doyle Report* 4, no. 4 (January 26, 2004), http://www.thedoylereport.com/spotlight/feature#4010.

10. Jean Piaget, *The Language and Thought of the Child* (New York: World, 1955); Michael Glassman, "Dewey and Vygotsky: Society, Experience, and Inquiry in Educational Practice," *Educational Researcher* 30, no. 4 (2001), pp. 3–14; D. C. Phillips, "The Good, the Bad, and the Ugly: The Many Faces of Constructivism," *Educational Researcher* 24, no. 7 (1995), pp. 5–12.

11. Howard Gardner, *Frames of Mind: The Theory of Multiple Intelligences* (New York: Basic Books, 1983).

12. Grant Wiggins, "A True Test: Toward More Authentic and Equitable Assessment." *Phi Delta Kappan* 70, no. 9 (1989), 703–13; Grant Wiggins, "Standards, Not Standardization: Evoking Quality Student Work," *Educational Leadership* 48, no. 5 (1991), pp. 18–25.

13. D. H. Gitomer, "Performance Assessment and Educational Measurement," in *Construction Versus Choice in Cognitive Measurement*, eds. R. E. Bennett and W. C. Ward (Hillsdale, NJ: Erlbaum, 1993), pp. 241–63.

14. Chris Benson, "Good Country Practice: Put the Horse Before the Cart—and Curriculum before Assessment," *Education Week*, January 17, 1996, p. 32; Debra Viadero, "Researchers Debate Impact of Tests," *Education Week*, February 5, 2003, pp. 1, 12.

15. For a related issue, see Michael W. Apple, "The Text and Cultural Politics," *Educational Researcher* 21, no. 7 (1992), pp. 4–11, 19, regarding concerns about educational content determined by textbook publishers (some of whom are also test publishers) and by large whole-state adoption states, such as Texas, whose draconian testing system under Governor George W. Bush served as the model for NCLB, particularly the work of Walter Haney, "The Myth of the Texas Miracle in Education," *Education Policy Analysis Archives* 8, no. 41 (2000).

16. Linda Mabry, Jane Poole, Linda Redmond, and Angelia Schultz, "Local Impact of State-Mandated Testing," *Education Policy Analysis Archives* 11, no. 22 (2003).

17. Jeffrey K. Smith, "Reconsidering Reliability in Classroom Assessment and Grading," *Educational Measurement: Issues and Practice* 22, no. 4 (2003), pp. 26–33.

18. M. Kane, "Validating the Performance Standards Associated with Passing Scores," *Review of Educational Research* 64, no. 3 (1994), pp. 425–561.

19. Dan S. Stufflebeam, "Both Sides Now: Perspectives of Evaluators and Stakeholders in Educational Evaluations." Paper presented at the annual meeting of the American Educational Research Association, New Orleans, April 2000.

20. E. H. Haertel, "Technical Considerations in the Use of NAEP to Confirm States' Achievement Gains." Paper presentation to the annual meeting of the American Educational Research Association, New Orleans, LA, April, 2002.

21. Richard Elmore and Susan Fuhrman, "Opportunity-to-Learn Standards and the State Role in Education," *Teachers College Record* 96, no. 3 (1995), pp. 432–57; Andrew Porter, "The Uses and Misuses of Opportunity-to-Learn Standards," *Educational Researcher* 24, no. 1 (1995), pp. 21–27.

22. K. D. Beach, J. P. Gee, J. G. Greeno, E. H. Haertel, C. D. Lee, H. B. Mehan, R. J. Mislevy, P. A. Moss, and D. C. Pullin, "Opportunity to Learn and Assessment: Psychometric and Sociocultural Perspectives." Presentation to the American Educational Research Association, Chicago, April, 2003.

23. Susan Ohanian, *One Size Fits Few: The Folly of Educational Standards* (Portsmouth, NH: Heinemann, 1999).

24. June Kronholz, "If You Have Brains You Might Decide to Skip This Test," *Wall Street Journal*, March 26, 1997, p. A1.

25. Gregory H. Cizek, *Cheating on Tests: How to Do It, Detect It, and Prevent It* (Mahwah, NJ: Erlbaum, 1999).

26. Among those who think standards-based reform is working is the Fordham Foundation; see http://www.edexcellence.net/foundation/topic/topic.cfm?topic=Testing%20%26%20Accountability.

27. National Research Council, *Understanding Dropouts: Statistics, Strategies, and High-Stakes Testing* (Washington, DC: National Academy Press, 2001).

28. Smith.

29. Ibid., p. 31. K. Smith came close to making that heretical statement.

30. Harold Berlak, Fred H. Newmann, Elizabeth Adams, Doug A. Archbald, Tyrell Burgess, John Raven, and Thomas A. Romberg, *Toward a New Science of Educational Testing and Assessment* (Albany: State University of New York Press, 1992).

31. See Smith for additional difficulties related to psychometric understandings of reliability.

32. J. J. Cannell, "Nationally Normed Elementary Achievement Testing in America's Public Schools: How All 50 States Are above the National Average," *Educational Measurement: Issues and Practice* 7, no. 2 (1987), pp. 5–9.

33. Gerald W. Bracey, *Put to the Test: An Educator's and Consumer's Guide to Standardized Testing* (Bloomington, IN: Phi Delta Kappa, 1998).

34. Harvey Goldstein, "Group Differences and Bias in Assessment," in *Assessment: Problems, Developments and Statistical Issues*, eds. Harvey Goldstein and Toby Lewis (New York: John Wiley & Sons, 1996), pp. 85–93; P. Rosser, *Sex Bias in College Admissions Tests: Why Women Lose Out*, 2nd ed. (Cambridge, MA: National Center for Fair and Open Testing, 1987).

35. For professional standards relevant to this issue, see American Educational Research Association, American Psychological Association, and National Council on Measurement in Education, *Standards for Educational and Psychological Testing* (Washington, DC: AERA, 1999).

36. Lorrie A. Shepard, "Building Bridges between Classroom and Large-Scale Assessments." Paper presented at the annual meeting of the American Educational Research Association, New Orleans, April 2002.

37. S. M. Brookhart, "Developing Measurement Theory for Classroom Assessment Purposes and Uses," *Educational Measurement: Issues and Practice* 22, no. 4 (2003), pp. 5–12; P. A. Moss, "Reconceptualizing Validity for Classroom Assessment," *Educational Measurement: Issues and Practice* 22, no. 4 (2003), pp. 13–25.

38. Robert L. Linn, "Assessments and Accountability," *Educational Researcher* 29, no. 2 (2000), pp. 4–16.

39. T. M. Haladyna, S. B. Nolen, and N. S. Haas, "Raising Standardized Achievement Test Scores and the Origins of Test Score Pollution," *Educational Researcher* 20, no. 5 (1991), pp. 2–7.

40. L. Mabry, K. Daytner, and J. Aldarondo, *Local Administration of State-Mandated Performance Assessments*; Mary Lee Smith, "Put to the Test: The Effects of External Testing on Teachers," *Educational Researcher* 20, no. 5 (1991), pp. 8–11.

41. George F. Madaus, "The Effects of Important Tests on Students," *Phi Delta Kappan* 73, no. 3 (1991), pp. 226–31; Mary Lee Smith and C. Rottenberg, "Unintended Consequences of External Testing in Elementary Schools," *Educational Measurement: Issues and Practice* 10, no. 4 (1991), pp. 7–11.

42. Linda Darling-Hammond, "National Standards and Assessments: Will They Improve Education?" *American Journal of Education* 102, no. 4 (1994), pp. 478–510.

43. Smith.

44. W. James Popham, *The Truth About Testing: An Educator's Call to Action* (Alexandria, VA: Association for Supervision and Curriculum Development, 2001); S. S. Yeh, "Tests Worth Teaching To: Constructing State-Mandated Tests That Emphasize Critical Thinking," *Educational Researcher* 30, no. 9 (2001), pp. 12–17.

45. Michael Fullan, *The New Meaning of Educational Change* (New York: Teachers College Press, 1991); G. B. Rossman, H. D. Corbett, and J. A. Dawson, "Intentions and Impacts: A Comparison of Sources of Influences on Local School Systems," *Urban Education* 21, no. 1 (1984), pp. 86–106; David Tyack and W. Tobin, "The 'Grammar' of Schooling: Why Has It Been So Hard to Change?" *American Educational Research Journal* 31 (1994), pp. 453–79.

46. E. L. Baker, R. L. Linn, J. L. Herman, and D. Koretz, "Standards for Educational Accountability Systems," *CRESST Line* (Winter 2002), pp. 1–4.

47. Linda Darling-Hammond, "National Standards and Assessments"; W. A. Profriedt, "Other People's Children: The Persistence of Disparities in School Funding," *Education Week*, November 22, 2002, p. 44.

48. L. Abrams, "Multi-State Analysis of the Effects of State-Mandated Testing Programs on Teaching and Learning: Results of the National Survey of Teachers." Paper presentation to the annual meeting of the American Educational Research Association, New Orleans, LA, April 2002.

49. Kathryn Ryan, "Shaping Educational Accountability Systems," *American Journal of Evaluation* 23, no. 4 (2002), pp. 453–68.

50. Ernest R. House, "A Framework for Appraising Educational Reforms," *Educational Researcher* 25, no. 7 (1996), pp. 6–14.

51. Michele Foucault, *The Order of Things: An Archaeology of the Human Sciences* (New York: Vintage Books, 1973).

52. A. Hargreaves, L. Earl, and M. Schmidt, "Perspectives on Alternative Assessment Reform," *American Educational Research Journal* 39, no. 1 (2002), pp. 69–95.

CHAPTER 6

1. R. S. Kaplan and D. P. Norton, "The Balanced Scorecard—Measures That Drive Performance," *Harvard Business Review*, January/February 1992, pp. 71–79.

2. National Forum on Assessment, *Principles and Indicators for Student Assessment Systems* (Boston: FairTest, 1993), http://www.fairtest.org/k-12.htm.

3. L. A. Shepard, "The Role of Assessment in a Learning Culture," *Educational Researcher* 29, no. 7 (2000), pp. 4–14.

4. D. Smith and L. Miller, *Comprehensive Local Assessment Systems (CLASs) Primer: A Guide to Assessment System Design and Use* (Gorham, ME: Southern Maine Partnership, University of Southern Maine, 2003), http://www.usm.maine.edu/ smp/tools/primer.htm; Nebraska School-based, Teacher-led Assessment Reporting System (STARS), http://www.nde.state.ne.us/stars/index.html.

5. R. J. Stiggins, *Student-Centered Classroom Assessment* (Columbus, OH: Merrill, 1997).

6. P. Black, C. Harrison, C. Lee, B. Marshall, and D. Wiliam, *Working inside the Black Box: Assessment for Learning in the Classroom* (London: Department of Education & Professional Studies, King's College 2002).

7. T. J. Crooks, "Design and Implementation of a National Assessment Programme: New Zealand's National Education Monitoring Project (NEMP)." Paper presented at Annual conference of the Canadian Society for the study of education (CSSE), 2002.

8. J. Oakes, *Education Inadequacy, Inequality, and Failed State Policy: A Synthesis of Expert Reports* (prepared for *Williams v. State of California*, 2003), http:// www.decentschools.org/experts.php.

9. J. Oakes, "What Educational Indicators? The Case for Assessing the School Contex," *Educational Evaluation and Policy Analysis* 11, no. 2 (1989), pp. 181–99.

10. L. Darling-Hammond, *Standards of Practice for Learning Centered Schools* (New York: National Center for Restructuring Education, Schools, and Teaching, 1992).

11. A. Urbanski, *Teacher Professionalism and Teacher Accountability: Toward a More Genuine Teaching Profession* (unpublished manuscript).

12. J. Ancess, *Outside/Inside, Inside/Outside: Developing and Implementing the School Quality Review* (New York: National Center for Restructuring Education, Schools, and Teaching, 1996); New Zealand Education Review Office, *Frameworks for Reviews in Schools*, http://www.ero.govt.nz/EdRevInfo/Schedrevs/ SchoolFramework.htm; D. R. Smith and D. J. Ruff, "Building a Culture of Inquiry: The School Quality Review Initiative," in *Assessing Student Learning: From Grading to Understanding*, ed. D. Allen (New York: Teachers College Press, 1998).

13. D. Tyack, *The One Best System* (Cambridge, MA: Harvard University Press, 1974).

14. K. Jones and B. L. Whitford, "Kentucky's Conflicting Reform Principles: High-Stakes Accountability and Student Performance Assessment," *Phi Delta Kappan* 79, no. 4 (1997), pp. 276–81.

15. A. Wheelock, D. Bebell, and W. Haney, *What Can Student Drawings Tell Us about High-Stakes Testing in Massachusetts?*, http://www.csteep.bc.edu/drawoned/mcas/mcaspaper.html; also a study of college student responses about the TAAS, http://comppile.tamucc.edu/TAAS/.

16. K. Mediratte, N. Fruchter, and A. C. Lewis, *Organizing for School Reform: How Communities Are Finding Their Voice and Reclaiming Their Public Schools* (New York: Institute for Education and Social Policy, Steinhardt School of Education, New York University, 2002).

17. P. Schlechty, *Systemic Change and the Revitalization of Public Education*, (San Francisco: Jossey-Bass, in press).

18. F. M. Newmann, M. B. King, and M. Rigdon, "Accountability and School Performance: Implications from Restructuring Schools," *Harvard Educational Review* 67, no. 1 (Spring 1997), p. 47.

19. J. W. Little, "Teachers' Professional Development in a Climate of Educational Reform," *Educational Evaluation and Policy Analysis* 15, no. 2 (1993), p. 133.

20. R. M. Ingersoll, *Who Controls Teachers' Work? Power and Accountability in America's Schools* (Cambridge, MA: Harvard University Press, 2003).

21. C. Abelman and R. Elmore, with J. Even, S. Kenyon, and J. Marshall, *When Accountability Knocks, Will Anyone Answer?* (Philadelphia: Consortium for Policy Research in Education, CPRE Research Report Series RR-42, University of Pennsylvania, 1999).

CHAPTER 7

1. This dialogue is constructed from our conversations with seven school district evaluators, only one of whom is personally acquainted with either author, who represent large and small districts from as many states. Evaluator #1 and #2 are composites created to illustrate the interpretive lens we suspect characterizes many school district evaluators and, indeed, many stakeholders in the discussions of state-mandated testing in schools.

2. These standards are a collaborative effort between the American Educational Research Association (AERA), National Council for Measurement in Education (NCME), and the American Psychological Association (APA). The *Standards* are written for the professional and for the educated layperson, and address professional and technical issues of test development and use in education, psychology, and employment.

3. These standards are sponsored by sixteen professional associations representing evaluators, school administrators, teachers, psychometricians, school boards, and educational researchers, and focus on attributes of good evaluation including utility, feasibility, propriety, and accuracy.

4. These principles were adopted by the American Evaluation Association in 1994 and define the work of evaluators in terms of (a) systematic inquiry, (b) competence, (c) integrity and honesty, (d) respect for people, and (e) responsibilities for the general and public welfare.

5. The complete American Evaluation Association position statement on high-stakes testing can be found online at http://www.eval.org/hst3.htm.

CHAPTER 8

1. This research is supported by the National Science Foundation (Grant no. ESI-9911868). The findings and opinions expressed herein do not necessarily reflect the position or priorities of the sponsoring agency.

2. M. B. Katz, *Class, Bureaucracy, and Schools: The Illusion of Educational Change in America* (New York: Praeger, 1971), p. 131.

3. P. J. Kannapel, P. Coe, L. Aagaard, B. D. Moore, and C. A. Reeves, "Teacher Responses to Rewards and Sanctions: Effects of and Reactions to Kentucky's High-Stakes Accountability Program," in *Accountability, Assessment, and Teacher Commitment: Lessons from Kentucky's Reform Efforts*, ed. Betty Lou Whitford and Ken Jones (Albany, NY: SUNY Press, 2000).

4. See James Popham's chapter in this volume for more on how state curriculum standards are created and teachers' roles in that process.

5. Linda M. McNeil, *Contradictions of School Reform: Educational Costs of Standardized Testing* (New York: Routledge, 2000), p.192.

6. Ibid.

7. Susan Ohanian, *One Size Fits Few* (New York: Heinemann, 1999).

8. See William Cala's chapter in this volume for a more extended discussion of educators' resistance or lack of resistance to state testing.

9. Kevin D. Vinson, Rich Gibson, and E. Wayne Ross, "High-Stakes Testing and Standardization: The Threat to Authenticity," *Monographs of the John Dewey Project on Progressive Education* 3, no. 2 (2000).

CHAPTER 9

1. This research is supported by the National Science Foundation (Grant no. ESI-9911868). The findings and opinions expressed herein do not necessarily reflect the position or priorities of the sponsoring agency. Pseudonyms are used for districts and parents.

2. For a history and impact of school choice in one community, see L. Miller-Kahn and M. L. Smith, "School Choice Policies in the Political Spectacle," *Education Policy Analysis Archives* 9, no. 50 (November 30, 2001), http://epaa.asu.edu/epaa/v9n50.html.

3. B. DeMott, *The Imperial Middle: Why Americans Can't Think Straight about Class* (New Haven, CT: Yale University Press, 1990).

4. S. Goldman and R. McDermott, "The Culture of Competition in American Schools," in G. Spindler, ed., *Education and Cultural Process: Anthropological Approaches*, 2nd ed. (Prospect Heights, IL: Waveland Press, 1987), pp. 282–300.

5. A. Kohn, "Only for My Kid: How Privileged Parents Undermine School Reform," *Phi Delta Kappan* 79, no. 8 (1998), pp. 569–77.

6. For a look at the impact of standards-based reform and testing on the disadvantaged, see Sandra Mathison's "The Accumulation of Disadvantage" in this volume.

CHAPTER 10

1. C. R. Sunstein, *After the Rights Revolution: Reconceiving the Regulatory State* (Cambridge, MA: Harvard University Press, 1990).

2. L. F. Rothstein, *Special Education Law* (White Plains, NY: Longman, 1990).

3. L. McDonnell, M. J. McLaughlin, and P. Morison, eds., *Educating One and All: Students with Disabilities and Standards-Based Reform* (Washington, DC: National Academy Press, 1997); B. Stecher, L. Hamilton, and G. Gonzalez, *White Paper: Working Smarter to Leave No Child Behind: Practical Insights for School Leaders* (Santa Monica, CA: RAND, 2003).

4. M. S. Donovan and C. T. Cross, eds., *Minority Students in Special and Gifted Education* (Washington, DC: National Academy of Sciences, 2002).

5. U.S. Department of Education, *Twenty-fourth Annual Report to Congress on the Implementation of the Individuals with Disabilities Education Act* (Washington DC: U.S. Government Printing Office, 2002), http://www.ed.gov/about/offices/list/osers/osep/research.html.

6. Ibid.

7. J. L. Hosp and D. J. Reschly, "Disproportionate Representation of Minority Students in Special Education: Academic, Demographic, and Economic Predictors," *Exceptional Children* 70, no. 2 (2004), pp. 185–99; D. J. Reschly, "The Present and Future Status of School Psychology in the United States," *School Psychology Review* 29, no. 4 (2000), pp. 507–22.

8. J. J. Zettel and J. Ballard, "The Education for All Handicapped Children Act of 1975 (P.L. 94-142): Its History, Origins, and Concepts," in *Special Education in America: Its Legal and Governmental Foundations*, ed. J. Ballard, B. A. Ramirez, and F. J. Weintraub (Reston, VA: Council for Exceptional Children, 1977); E. L. Levine and E. M Wexler, *PL 94-142: An Act of Congress* (New York: Macmillan, 1981).

9. *Board of Education of Hendrick Hudson Central School District v. Rowley,* 458 US 176, (1982).

10. McDonnell, McLaughlin, and Morison; S. W. Smith and M. T. Brownell, "Individualized Education Program: Considering the Broad Context of Reform," *Focus on Exceptional Children* 28, no. 1 (1995), pp. 1–10.

11. M. J. McLaughlin and M. Thurlow, "Educational Accountability and Students with Disabilities: Issues and Challenges," *Journal of Educational Policy* 17, no. 4 (2003), pp. 431–51.

12. The Education Trust, *The ABC's of "AYP": Raising Achievement for All Students* (Washington, DC: Author, 2003).

13. J. C. Gagnon and M. J. McLaughlin, "School-level Curriculum, Assessment and Accountability Policies in Day Treatment and Residential Schools for Students with EBD," *Exceptional Children* 70, No. 3 (2004), pp 263–83.

14. National Research Council, *Minority Students in Special and Gifted Education* (Washington, DC: National Academy Press, 2002).

15. D. Carnine, "Why Educational Experts Resist Effective Practices," *Report of the Thomas B. Fordham Foundation* (Washington, DC: Thomas B Fordham Foundation, 2000), http://www.edexcellence.net/foundation/publication/index.cfm;

J. S. Chall, *The Academic Achievement Gap* (New York: Guilford, 2000); National Research Council.

16. S. H. Fuhrman, *Redesigning Accountability Systems for Education* (Philadelphia: University of Pennsylvania, Consortium for Policy Research in Education, 2003).

17. S. Thompson, M. Thurlow, and M. Moore, *Putting It All Together: Including Students with Disabilities in Assessment and Accountability Systems*, Policy Directions no. 16 (Minneapolis: University of Minnesota, National Center on Educational Outcomes, 2003), http://education.umn.edu/NCEO/OnlinePubs/Policy16.htm.

18. Ibid.

19. S. G. Sireci, S. Li, and S. Scarpati, *The Effects of Test Accommodation on Test Performance: A Review of the Literature*, Research Report no. 485 (Washington, DC: Board on Testing and Assessment, National Academy of Sciences, 2003).

20. Thompson, Thrulow, and Moore.

21. McLaughlin and Thurlow, "Educational Accountability and Students With Disabilities"; M. Thurlow and D. Wiener, *Non-Approved Accommodations: Recommendations for Use and Reporting*, Policy Directions no. 11 (Minneapolis: University of Minnesota, National Center on Educational Outcomes, 2000).

22. Sireci, Li, and Scarpati.

23. Rhode Island Department of Education, Rhode Island Assessment Accommodation Study: Research Summary (Minneapolis: University of Minnesota, National Center on Educational Outcomes, 2003).

24. J. G. Shriner, L. Danielson, and M. Rouse, "National Assessment and Special Education in the United States and England and Wales: Towards a Common System for All?" in *Educational Reform in the United States and Britain*, ed. M J. McLaughlin and M. Rouse (London: Routledge, 2000).

25. Quality Counts 2004: "Count Me In: Special Education in An Era of Standards," *Education Week* 23, no. 7 (2004).

26. R. L. Linn, E. L. Baker, and D. W. Betebenner, "Accountability Systems: Implications of Requirements of the No Child Left Behind Act of 2001 (CSE Technical Report, Center for the Study of Evaluation, CREST, 2002), http://www.cse.ucla.edu/products/reports_set.htm.

27. Council of Chief State School Officers (CCSSO), *Making Valid and Reliable Decisions in Determining Adequate Yearly Progress: A Paper in the Series: Implementing the State Accountability System Requirements under the No Child Left Behind Act of 2001* (Washington, DC: Author, 2002).

28. D. Figlio, "Aggregation and Accountability," in *No Child Left Behind: What Will It Take?* (Washington, DC: Thomas B. Fordham Foundation, 2002).

29. T. J. Kane and D. O. Staiger, "Validity in School Test Scores: Implications for Test-Based Accountability Scores," in *Brookings Papers on Education Policy*, ed. Diane Ravitch (Washington, DC: Brookings Institution, 2002).

30. Figlio.

31. Council of Chief State School Officers; Figlio.

32. Kane and Staiger, "Validity in School Test Scores."

33. G. W. Bracey, *Thinking about Tests and Testing: A Short Primer in "Assessment Literacy"* (Washington, DC: American Youth Policy Forum, 2000); J. Ysseldyke

and J. Bielinski, "Effect of Different Methods of Reporting and Reclassification on Trends in Test Scores for Students with Disabilities," *Exceptional Children* 68, no. 2 (2002), pp. 189–200.

34. Ysseldyke and Bielinski.

35. K. M. Nagle, *Topical Review 4: Emerging State-Level Themes: Strengths and Stressors in Educational Accountability Reform* (College Park: University of Maryland, Educational Policy Reform Research Institute, 2004), http://www.eprri.org; K. M. Nagle and J. Crawford, *Issue Brief 6: Opportunities and Challenges: Reflections on NCLB by Special Education Directors from Selected Urban School Districts* (College Park: University of Maryland, Educational Policy Reform Research Institute, 2004), http://www.eprri.org.

36. Quality Counts 2004: "Count Me In," http://www.edweek.org/sreports/qc04/article.cfm?slug=17exec.h23).

CHAPTER 11

1. An early version of this paper was published in *Workplace: A Journal of Academic Labor*, http://www.workplace-gsc.com/.

2. V. E. Lee and D. T. Burkham, *Inequality at the Starting Gate* (Washington, DC: Economic Policy Institute, 2002).

3. S. F. Reardon and C. Galindo, "Do High Stakes Tests Affect Students' Decision to Drop Out of School? Evidence from NELS." Paper presented at the annual meeting of the American Educational Research Association, New Orleans, April 2002.

4. Quality Counts 2001, *Education Week*, http://www.edweek.org/sreports/qc01/ 2001.

5. Sherman Dorn, "High-Stakes Testing and the History of Graduation," *Education Policy Analysis Archives* 11, no. 1 (2003), http://epaa.asu.edu/epaa/v11n1.

6. Audrey L. Amrein and David C. Berliner, "High-Stakes Testing, Uncertainty, and Student Learning," *Education Policy Analysis Archives* 10, no.18 (2002), http://epaa.asu.edu/epaa/v10n18.

7. Reardon and Galindo.

8. Walt Haney, "The Myth of the Texas Miracle in Education," *Education Analysis Policy Archive*, 8, no. 41 (2000), http://epaa.asu.edu/epaa/v8n41/.

9. Peter Sacks, *Standardized Minds: The High Price of America's Testing and What We Can Do to Change It* (Cambridge, MA: Perseus, 2000).

10. Ibid., p. 264.

11. FairTest Letter to Governor Jeb Bush, http://fairtest.org/pr/Bright_Futures_lttr.html.

12. D. E. Heller and P. Marin, eds., *Who Should We Help? The Negative Social Consequences of Merit Aid Scholarships* Cambridge, MA: Harvard Civil Rights Project, 2002), http://www.civilrightsproject.harvard.edu/research/meritaid/fullreport.php.

13. B. Dawson, "Performance on the National Board of Medical Examiners Part I: Examination by Men and Women of Different Race and Ethnicity," *Journal of the American Medical Association* 272, no. 9 (1994), pp. 674–79.

14. K. J. Mitchell, D. Z. Robinson, B. S. Plake, and K. T. Knowles, eds., *Testing Teaching Candidates: The Role of Licensure Tests in Improving Teacher Quality* (Committee on Assessment and Teacher Quality, Center for Education, Board on Testing and Assessment, National Research Council, 2001), http://www.nap.edu/books/0309074207/html/).

15. See http://www.eval.org/hstlinks.htm for a list of organizations with such statements.

16. See http://www.eval.org/hstlinks.htm for a list of grassroots organizations, many of which are regional or state-based, but some are national in scope, such as The Rouge Forum or the fledgling ACT NOW (Advocates for Children and Teachers National Organizing Workshop).

CHAPTER 12

1. Thanks are due to Dorothy Shipps, who helped develop many of the ideas on multiple accountability, and my colleagues on the study of state assessment in New Jersey.

2. W. A. Firestone, R. Y. Schorr, and L. Monfils, *The Ambiguity of Teaching to the Test* (Mahwah, NJ: Lawrence Erlbaum and Associates, 2004).

3. J. E. Adams and M. W. Kirst, "New Demands and Concepts for Educational Accountability: Striving for Results in an Era of Excellence," in *Handbook of Research on Educational Administration*, 2nd ed., ed. J. Murphy and K. S. Louis (San Francisco: Jossey-Bass, 1999), pp. 463–90.

4. J. Fairman and W. A. Firestone, "The District Role in State Assessment Policy: An Exploratory Study," in *From the Capitol to the Classroom: Standards-Based Reform in the States*, ed. S. H. Fuhrman (Chicago, IL: University of Chicago Press, 2001), pp. 124–47; A. Peshkin, *Growing Up American: Schooling and the Survival of Community* (Chicago: University of Chicago Press, 1978).

5. National Council of Teachers of Mathematics, *Curriculum and Evaluation Standards for School Mathematics* (Reston, VA: NCTM, 1999).

6. Interstate School Leaders Licensure Consortium, *Standards for School Leaders* (Washington, DC: Council of Chief State School Officers, 1996).

7. National Council of Teachers of Mathematics, p. 5.

8. J. P. Becker and B. Jacob, "The Politics Of California School Mathematics: The Anti-Reform of 1997-99," *Phi Delta* Kappan 81, no. 8 (2000), pp. 529–37.

9. L. M. McNeil, *Contradictions of School Reform: Educational Costs of Standardized Testing* (New York: Routledge, 2000); M. L. Smith, "Put to the Test: The Effects of External Testing on Students," *Educational Researcher* 20, no. 5 (1996), pp. 8–12.

10. Fairman and Firestone.

11. J. P. Spillane, R. Halvorson, and J. B. Diamond, "Investigating School Leadership Practice: A Distributed Perspective," *Educational Researcher* 30, no. 3 (2001), pp. 23–28.

12. Firestone, Schorr, and Monfils.

13. J. A. Marsh, "How Districts Relate to States, Schools, and Communities," in *School Districts and Instructional Renewal*, ed. A. Hightower, M. S. Knapp, J. A. Marsh, and M. W. McLaughlin (New York: Teachers College Press, 2002), pp. 25–40.

14. J. P. Spillane, "State Policy and the Non-Monolithic Nature of the Local School District: Organizational and Professional Considerations," *American Educational Research Journal* 35, no. 1 (1998), pp. 33–63.

15. M. S. Knapp, M. A. Copland, B. Ford, A. Markholt, M. W. McLaughlin, M. Milliken, and J. E. Talbert, *Leading for Learning Sourcebook: Concepts and Examples* (Seattle: Center for Teaching Policy, 2003).

16. A. Hightower, M. S. Knapp, J. A. Marsh, and M. W. McLaughlin, *School Districts and Institutional Renewal* (New York: Teachers College Press, 2002).

17. F. M. Newmann, M. B. King, and M. Rigdon, "Accountability and School Performance: Implications from Restructuring Schools," *Harvard Education Review* 61, no. 1 (1997), pp. 48.

18. F. M. Newmann & Associates, eds., *Authentic Achievement: Restructuring Schools for Intellectual Quality* (San Francisco: Jossey-Bass, 1996).

19. M. Carnoy, R. F. Elmore, and L. S. Siskin, *The New Accountability: High Schools and High-Stakes Testing* (New York: RoutledgeFalmer, 2003).

20. Ibld.

21. Ibid.; Newmann, King, and Rigdon.

22. Carnoy, Elmore, and Siskin.

23. Hightower, et al.

24. J. K. Rice and B. Malen, "The Human Costs of Education Reform: The Case of School Reconstitution," *Educational Administration Quarterly* 34, no. 5 (2003), pp. 635–66.

CHAPTER 13

1. New York State Education Department, "The New York State School Report Card For School Year 2001-2002," http://www.emsc.nysed.gov/repcrd2003.

2. Betsy Gotbaum, Public Advocate for the City of New York, "Pushing Out At-Risk Students: An Analysis of High School Discharge Figures," http://www.advocatesforchildren.org/pubs/pushout-11-20-02.doc.

3. Jay P. Greene and Greg Forster, "Public High School Graduation and College Readiness Rates in the United States," Manhattan Institute for Policy Research *Education Working Paper*, no. 3 (September 2003).

4. New York State Education Department.

5. National Center for Education Statistics, U.S. Department of Education, "Dropout rates in the United States: 2000," http://nces.ed.gov/pubs2002/droppub_2001/.

6. David H. Monk, "Adoption and Adaptation: New York State School Districts' Response to State-Imposed High School Graduation Requirements: An Eight-Year Retrospective," 2001; Dianna L. Newman and Dean T. Spaulding (principal investigators), "New York State's General Equivalency Diploma Program: Perceptions of Young Adults," Evaluation Consortium, University at Albany, NY, 2001.

7. Steven L. Strauss, "An Open Letter to Reid Lyon," *Educational Researcher* (June–July 2001), pp. 26–33.

8. D. Riley, *The Depressed Child—A Parent's Guide for Rescuing Kids* (Dallas, TX: Taylor Publishing, 2001), pp. 85–86.

9. Monk.

10. Michael Gormley, "Records Reveal Teachers Cheated," http://www.timesunion.com.

11. Ibid.

12. Diana Jean Schemo and Ford Fessenden, "Gains in Houston Schools: How Real Are They?" *New York Times*, December 3, 2003, http://www.nytimes.com.

13. Andrea Jones, "Elementary School Principal Found Dead at School," *Atlanta Journal-Constitution*, April 11, 2002, http://www.azstandards.org/news.htm.

14. Bill Blass, "The Man Who Shocked the World," http://www.psychologytoday.com/htdocs/prod/ptoarticle/pto-20020301-000037.asp.

15. Stanley Milgram.com, http://www.stanleymilgram.com/quotes.html.

16. Colleagues are people who do research, speak out, and resist when needed. Unfortunately, few educators meet this standard. I have found several parents to be my most trusted and supportive colleagues in the fight against high-stakes tests.

17. D. Andrich, "A Hyperbolic Cosine Latent Trait Model for Unfolding Polytomous Responses: Reconciling Thurstone and Likert methodologies," *British Journal of Mathematical and Statistical Psychology* 49 (1996), pp. 347–65.

18. To read the full story of the physics scandal in New York, go to http://free.freespeech.org/ccse/.

19. For additional information on these schools, see http://www.urbanacademy.org/default.htm and http://www.beaconschool.org/FLH/.

20. Information on the perils of James Hope and George Schmidt was gathered by personal phone contact and e-mail communications between the author, James Hope, and George Schmidt.

Index

About the Editors

SANDRA MATHISON is Professor and Head of the Department of Educational and Counseling Psychology and Special Education, University of British Columbia, Vancouver. Her research is in educational evaluation and her work has focused especially on the potential and limits of evaluation to support democratic ideals and promote justice. She is currently doing research on the effects of state-mandated testing on teaching and learning in elementary and middle schools in upstate New York, research that is funded by a five-year grant from the National Science Foundation. She is editor of the *Encyclopedia of Evaluation*.

E. WAYNE ROSS is Professor in the Department of Curriculum Studies at the University of British Columbia, Vancouver. He is a former secondary social studies and day care teacher in North Carolina and Georgia and has held faculty appointments at the University of Louisville and the State University of New York campuses at Albany and Binghamton. Ross is the author of numerous articles and reviews on issues of curriculum theory and practice, teacher education, and the politics of education. His books include *Image and Education* (with Kevin D. Vinson), *The Social Studies Curriculum*, and *Democratic Social Education* (with David W. Hursh). He is the cofounder of The Rouge Forum, a group of educators, parents, and students working for more democratic schools and society, and the general editor of *Defending Public Schools*.

About the Contributors

GERALD W. BRACEY is an Associate Professor in the Graduate School of Education at George Mason University, Fairfax, Virginia, and an associate of the High/Scope Educational Research Foundation, Ypsilanti, Michigan. For the last twenty years, he has written a "Research" column for the educational monthly *Phi Delta Kappan*, summarizing research that might be of interest to practitioners. His most recent books are *On the Death of Childhood and the Destruction of Public Schools: The Folly of Current Educational Policy* (Heinemann, September 2003) and *Setting the Record Straight: Responses to Misconceptions about American Public Education* (Heinemann, summer 2004). He was chosen as "Educator of the Year" by the Horace Mann Association in 2002, awarded the Interpretive Scholarship Award by the American Educational Research Association in 2003, and awarded the John Dewey Award from the Vermont Association for the Study of Education in 2003.

WILLIAM C. CALA, Ed.D., was born and raised in the inner city of Rochester, New York, eleventh poorest city in the country. He taught Spanish in the Williamsville Schools outside of Buffalo and has been an administrator in Fredonia, Williamsville, Royalton-Hartland, and Superintendent in Pembroke, Shoreham-Wading River (Long Island) and of the Fairport Schools for the past six years. Dr. Cala has dedicated the last ten years to unlocking the mystery, motivation, and untoward intentions surrounding high-stakes testing in New York and the country. He has been published in numerous national professional journals, been a guest essayist in major papers across the country, and has spoken from coast to coast on testing and learning. He is the author and designer of the National Coalition Diploma, a diploma that offers multiple pathways to success for children of different abilities and intelligences. In 2004, he was honored with Phi Delta Kappa International's Presidential Award for Exceptional Educator Leadership and received the George Eastman Award for Courage and Leadership in Public Policy from the New York based non-profit Center for Governmental Research.

WILLIAM A. FIRESTONE is Professor of Educational Policy at the Rutgers Graduate School of Education in New Brunswick, New Jersey, where he is also Principle Investigator of the New Jersey Math Science Partnership and Director of the Center for Educational Policy Analysis. His interests include policy and program implementation, qualitative research methods, and educational leadership. His most recent book, *The Ambiguity of Teaching to the Test*, is available from Lawrence Erlbaum and Associates.

MELISSA FREEMAN is project manager of an interpretive study exploring the impact of high-stakes testing on teaching and learning in several New York State school districts. Her work emphasizes critical and cultural ethnographic research methodologies, and the theoretical and empirical relationships between culture, ideology, discourse, power, and knowledge. Her present work explores class issues in the discourse/practice of parental involvement.

KEN JONES is the director of Teacher Education at the University of Southern Maine. He has also been a middle school teacher, the director of a university-school professional development collaborative, a district mathematics specialist, and an assistant professor of elementary education. Previous publications include *Accountability, Assessment, and Teacher Commitment: Lessons from Kentucky's Reform Efforts* (SUNY Press), "Equity for Alaska Natives: Can High-Stakes Testing Breach the Chasm between Ideals and Realities" (*Phi Delta Kappan*), and "Let Them Eat Tests: High-Stakes Testing and Educational Equity" (*Journal of Thought*).

ALFIE KOHN is the author of nine books on education and human behavior, including *Punished by Rewards* (1993), *Beyond Discipline: From Compliance to Community* (1996), *The Schools Our Children Deserve* (1999), and, most recently, *What Does It Mean to Be Well Educated?: And More Essays on Standards, Grading, and Other Follies* (2004). *Time* magazine has described him as "perhaps the country's most outspoken critic of education's fixation on grades [and] test scores." A former teacher, Kohn now works with educators across the country and speaks regularly at national conferences. He lives (actually) in Belmont, Massachusetts, and (virtually) at www.alfiekohn.org.

LINDA MABRY is a Professor of Education at Washington State University. Her research focuses on state and national assessment systems and teacher-developed assessments. Current projects include a follow-along study of NCLB in two states and development of a public statement on educational accountability for the American Evaluation Association. Her publications in assessment include *Portfolios Plus: A Critical Guide to Alternative Assessment* (Corwin, 1999) and articles on the implications and impacts of state assessment in Washington, Indiana, Michigan, Oregon, and Pennsylvania. She is a member of Board of Trustees of the National Center for the Improvement of Educational Assessment and of the Performance Assessment Review Board of the New York Performance Standards Consortium.

SANDRA MATHISON is Professor of Education at the University of British Columbia. She is editor of the *Encyclopedia of Evaluation* (2004) and author of numerous publications on evaluation and accountability. She chaired the American Evaluation Association's High Stakes Testing Task Force that created a public statement on testing in K–12 schools (www.eval.org/hst3.htm). Her current research, funded by the National Science Foundation, examines the impact of state-mandated testing on teaching, learning, and school structure in several upstate New York elementary and middle schools.

MARGARET J. MCLAUGHLIN has been involved in special education all of her professional career, beginning as a teacher of students with serious emotional and behavior disorders. Currently she is the associate director of the Institute for the Study of Exceptional Children, University of Maryland. She directs several national projects investigating educational reform and students with disabilities. These include the national Educational Policy Reform Research Institute (EPRRI), a consortium involving the University Maryland, The National Center on Educational Outcomes (NCEO), and the Urban Special Education Collaborative. Dr. McLaughlin has worked in Bosnia, Nicaragua, and Guatemala in developing programs for students with developmental disabilities. Dr. McLaughlin cochaired the National Academy of Sciences Committee on Goals 2000 and Students with Disabilities, which resulted in the report *Educating One and All*.

MARCO A. MUÑOZ, Ph.D. is an evaluation specialist with the Jefferson County Public Schools and an adjunct faculty at the University of Louisville. His principal research interests are program and personnel evaluation in education. Dr. Munoz has published multiple articles dealing with a wide range of theoretical and practical issues in the field of public school research and evaluation. Recent publications appeared in juried journals, such as the *Journal of School Leadership*, *Journal of Personnel Evaluation in Education*, and the *American School Board Journal*. He received the prestigious American Evaluation Association Marcia Guttentag Award for his school-related evaluation research.

KATHERINE M. NAGLE is a Research Associate in the Department of Special Education and Institute for the Study of Exceptional Children and Youth, University of Maryland. Dr. Nagle has been involved in education in the United Kingdom, Kenya, and the United States, first as a regular education teacher and then as a special education teacher for students with visual impairments. She is project director for the Educational Policy Reform Research Institute (EPRRI), a national project investigating educational reform and students with disabilities with emphasis on the impact of high-stakes accountability on students with disabilities.

W. JAMES POPHAM, Professor Emeritus, UCLA Graduate School of Education and Information Studies, has spent the bulk of his educational career as a teacher. His first teaching assignment was in a small eastern Oregon high school where he taught English and social studies while serving as yearbook advisor, class sponsor, and unpaid tennis coach. His most recently published books are *Classroom Assessment: What Teachers Need to Know*, 3rd ed. (2002); *Modern Educational Measurement: Practical Guidelines for Educational Leaders*, 3rd ed. (2000); *Testing! Testing! What Every Parent Should Know about School Tests* (2000), all published by Allyn & Bacon; plus *The Truth about Testing: An Educator's Call to Action* (2001) and *Test Better, Teach Better: The Instructional Role of Assessment* (2003), both published by ASCD. In 1968, Dr. Popham established IOX Assessment Associates, an R&D group that formerly created statewide student achievement tests for a dozen states. In 2002, the National Council on Measurement in Education presented him with its Award for Career Contributions to Educational Measurement.